THE LOST REFORM

This volume is published as part of a long-standing cooperative program between Harvard University Press and the Commonwealth Fund, a philanthropic foundation, to encourage the publication of significant scholarly books in medicine and health.

THE LOST REFORM

The Campaign for Compulsory Health Insurance in the United States from 1932 to 1943

Daniel S. Hirshfield

A Commonwealth Fund Book

Harvard University Press

CAMBRIDGE, MASSACHUSETTS

1970

Distributed in Great Britain by Oxford University Press, London
Library of Congress Catalog Card Number 71-115187
SBN 674-53917-6
Printed in the United States of America

This work is dedicated
to the memory of my father

VICTOR HIRSHFIELD

CONTENTS

PREFACE

The crisis in medical care that the United States is experiencing in the 1970's and that will continue into the 1980's is parallel in many ways to the earlier crisis of the 1930's. First, the problem of medical manpower and its distribution initially became acute during the 1930's; today, it has produced a serious crisis in both the core city and the country. Second, suggestions for organizing medical care services in rational rather than traditional ways became controversial in the 1930's and are today contributing to the continuing debate over rising medical costs. And third, the whole issue of group prepayment for medical care, whether through private, voluntary nonprofit, or governmental action, was first widely raised in the 1930's and is today perhaps the key issue in the entire field of medical economics.

The solutions that were proposed for these problems in the 1930's and the 1960's are also strikingly similar. This is not surprising since many of the men, ideas, and programs of the thirties are still shaping policy today. What is intriguing is that so few new ideas have emerged in this area since the 1930's, that the terms in which the problems are perceived and solutions proposed are essentially so similar. For example, voluntary health insurance, which had its significant beginnings in the 1930's, was originally seen as a way of spreading the financial risks of illness among a large, regularly employed, and mainly middle-income group. It succeeded remarkably well in meeting this objective, but has been totally unable to provide protection for the poor, the aged, and the chronically ill. Even today, with over 170 million Americans participating in some form of voluntary medical insurance, millions of citizens in these categories are not covered. This had, and has, two important results: the uninsured minority are unable to muster support for reform from the largely contented and insured majority, and the minority are forced to rely on their own resources or uneven and often inadequate governmental health programs. Although the decades are quite different in many ways, the role and impact of voluntary insurance has thus remained basically the same.

The ideas of the proper role for government in the area of medical care have not changed in most ways since the 1930's either. In that decade the idea of state-centered legislation requiring citizens' membership in approved health insurance plans was the dominant approach of most reformers. Today, New York, New Jersey, California, and Rhode Island have such laws on their books. Massachusetts and New York are considering extending this idea even further by upgrading the requirements for the approval of plans by the state and by enrolling the indigent as regular subscribers. Medicaid (Title XIX of the Social Security Act) also utilizes this state by state approach and permits the states wide latitude in administering their own programs.

The one new idea of the years since the 1930's is, of course, a system of national compulsory health insurance, similar in operation to Old Age, Survivors, Disability, and Health Insurance (OASDHI). Although a few reformers did advocate this system in the 1930's, most did not become committed to this idea until the 1940's and the struggles over the Wagner-Murray-Dingell bills. Public sentiment, partially impaired by the success of the voluntary insurance plans, was slow to crystalize and did not become decisive until the 1960's. In that decade Medicare, a limited application of the national compulsory insurance idea, was finally enacted and made operational. Its successes and the increasing failure of voluntary insurance to absorb climbing medical costs for the rest of the population opened the way for a new battle for national compulsory medical insurance. Walter Reuther and his compulsory health insurance Committee of One Hundred is only one in a growing cluster of groups advocating and indeed demanding this reform.

With these parallels and developments in mind, I have attempted to do two things in this study. First, I have tried to describe and explain the historical origins of certain parts of the present system of medical care in the United States. Second, and more importantly, I have tried to comprehend and relate the ideas and attitudes of those who engaged in the struggles of these early years. Given the relevance and continuing importance of these earlier problems and attitudes, my hope is to make the rhetoric, passion, plans, and behavior of today's medical care experts more understandable.

I wish, at this point, to express my profound appreciation to those persons and institutions who have made this effort possible: Frank Freidel, who saw the manuscript through its various stages and provided astute advice and warm encouragement; Oscar Handlin, who read the manuscript and made valuable criticisms; Arthur Altmeyer, Nelson Cruickshank, Michael M. Davis, Martha M. Eliot, I. S. Falk, Morris Fishbein, Gordon Fortney, Louis Reed, and C. Rufus Rorem, who generously extended their time and hospitality when I interviewed them; the helpful and courteous staffs of the National Archives, the Roosevelt Library at Hyde Park, and Widener Library; and the Woodrow Wilson Foundation and the Boston College Department of History, who provided financial support and assistance. Finally, I wish to thank my wife, Susan, who knows how much her help has meant.

THE LOST REFORM

Introduction

During 1933 one in twenty Americans was admitted to a general hospital, the total cost of medical care to the nation was two and a third billion dollars, and fewer than 6 percent of the population had any kind of insurance to pay its medical bills. Individual insecurity resulting from illness was the rule during the 1930's, not the exception.[1] This situation had not appeared suddenly, and illness was not the only area of personal risk in the citizen's life. With the beginning of the industrial revolution and the drive toward an urban, cash-oriented economy, the potential disasters of illness, unemployment, old age, and industrial injury had gradually become large dangers in the lives of workers and their families. And now, with a depression blighting the land, these threats had become critical.

Even before 1933 many Americans had felt that society as a whole should do something to lessen these terrible dangers to personal security and thereby help preserve the life, decency, and freedom of the individual. As early as the 1830's certain reformers had been concerned with the rising risks of industrialization and urbanization for the individual worker and city dweller. This interest grew throughout the nineteenth century but only became a major trend with the arrival of the 1890's. During that decade the first modern analyses of human problems in the United States were made, and the first realistic solutions were put forward. From an environment seething with depression, strikes, crowded ghettos of unskilled immigrants, farmers' revolts, and growing corporate power, the leadership of what was to become the social welfare movement emerged.[2]

With the support of their political allies and an increasing segment of the public, reform leaders began to re-examine certain assumptions of the existing American creed in the light of the transformed conditions. The human misery which accompanied the dramatic expansion of mass production, gigantic private corporations, the wage system, tenement living, and political corruption meant to most of these leaders that some parts of the national ideology were becoming dysfunctional. Traditional beliefs were being either ignored or rendered obsolete; a crusade was needed to revitalize or replace them.

Some reformers of the period before World War I worked for a return of the traditional beliefs whereby individual effort and ability, unhindered by governmental or private intervention, would produce its own rewards. Others believed that such a return was impossible under contemporary conditions and worked instead to redefine the concept and role of the individual in a mass society. But the efforts of both groups of reformers in this prewar progressive period were focused on the use of government to help solve the problems confronted by the mass of individual citizens in the new industrialized and urbanized America.

The results of these early efforts were only the beginning steps of an ongoing crusade for social and economic reforms. The reformers defined and studied the various problems in American society, evolved organizational and political methods to pressure for and achieve reform, and produced a more or less coherent system of ideas to explain the need for and justice of their particular programs. Despite the continuing strength of traditional individualistic beliefs, by the end of this prewar period, the reformers and their ideas were by and large considered respectable by the public and its leaders, even though some of the more radical reforms were seen as unwise. The nation had accepted, or so it seemed, the idea that government intervention in individual lives was at times both necessary and useful for the solution of some modern social problems.

American participation in the First World War and the prosperity and disillusionment which followed it seemed to weaken and then negate this acceptance. The reformers still saw massive social problems plaguing the United States and still called for governmental action to solve them. But most politicians and most of the public had lost their ardor for activist reform and had returned to the rhetoric and policies of traditional individualism. The problems brought by industrialization and urbanization did not disappear and in many instances grew more serious; but in the era of Normalcy and business-as-usual, the nation seemed to want little or no governmental action in their solution. The reformers, stripped of their political and popular following, were reduced to a powerless and often ignored remnant.

Despite their weakness and isolation, the reformers continued their often lonely battle. In some instances they clung to their original ideas and programs in the face of an uninterested and mocking audience; in other instances they compromised on their demands and tried to implement them within the limited ideology and institutions of the day. But whatever tactic they chose, they were able to keep alive and to improve their ideas, organizations, and solutions, pending the time when the public and the politicians would be ready to listen. The 1920's were frustrating for the reformers, but they served, nonetheless, as a "seedtime of reform." [3]

With the coming of the Great Crash of 1929 and the deepening of the economic depression in the 1930's, the ideas and programs of the reformers once again found a wide audience. In the harsh glare of economic collapse, the problems which the reformers had been defining and discussing for decades suddenly seemed very relevant. Now, as in the progressive period, the public was concerned and became increasingly willing to adopt many of the reformers' programs.

With the emergence of the New Deal, and especially with the acceptance in 1935 of the Social Security system, final victory for the reformers appeared sure. The politicians and the public seemed to accept the reformers' ideas on individual security and social responsibility, and to adopt their programs and solutions. Old age assistance and insurance, unemployment insurance, and aid to the blind and dependent children were passed with strong public endorsement.

But while the reformers and their programs seemed to triumph in most areas during the early New Deal, one important reform was defeated. Government insurance against sickness (health insurance) was not achieved despite the best and most determined efforts of the reformers. Health insurance, together with the other reforms, had been an early interest of the reformers in the progressive period; it had been supported by various reformers and reform associations in the 1920's and had been included among the proposals considered by those who helped shape the Social Security Act. But although it was proposed and advocated in the same ways as the other, successful reforms, the political climate and the particular conditions found in the system of medical care in the United States helped to exclude health insurance from the 1935 legislation.

After their defeat in 1935, the reformers favoring federal health insurance regrouped their forces, sought new allies, and launched a new effort to round out the Social Security Act with a system of health insurance. They again used the same basic ideas and tactics which had proven successful in 1935 with other reforms. But in 1939 they were once again defeated and their forces scattered. By 1941 the last vestiges of the campaign had died.

Beginning in 1941 a new kind of health insurance campaign supported by a new set of ideas and tactics emerged. Spurred by their earlier defeats, the nature of their opposition, and the political and medical realities of the nation, the health insurance reformers endorsed an essentially different method of insuring individual security against illness and the costs of medical care. Where the earlier reform efforts had envisioned a *federalized,* permissive, and uncomprehensive type of legislation, the new program was based on a truly *national* system of comprehensive health insurance; where the earlier reform campaigns had used basic tactics which had evolved in the pre-World War I era, the new effort used a newer political strategy which had matured in the New Deal.

Thus, the year 1941 marks a crucial watershed in the reform crusade for health insurance. Before that year the old ideas and techniques were tried and exhausted; after that year new ones were devised and implemented. Compulsory health insurance, which before 1941 had remained a lost reform under the old approach, now slowly gained political strength and viability. After another generation of effort and struggle, it would find partial triumph and wide public acceptance.

1

Background Developments 1900–1932

The forces of industrialization, urbanization, and technological advance had had profound effects on the United States by the early decades of the twentieth century. From 1860 to 1910, the population in the cities jumped from 19 percent to 45 percent of the total population, the nonagricultural work force increased from 42 percent to 69 percent of the nation's total labor pool, the percentage of the national wealth produced by industries rather than by farms rose from 58 percent to 78 percent, and the economic productivity of the average American climbed over 50 percent.[1] But life was changing in ways not so easily measured by statistics and not so immediately related to economic trends. These changes were social ones that had to do with the evaluations, interpretations, and expectations Americans were placing on themselves and their society. The populace, caught up in changes then barely understood, was trying to explain the direction and nature of its civilization and to deduce from contemporary trends some comprehensible theory.

1900–1920

Beginning around 1900 and continuing for most of the next two decades, evaluations of social changes were colored by a growing surge of reform sentiment. The public, and especially that segment which thought of itself as middle class, became increasingly worried by what it conceived as a developing social crisis. People feared that the uncontrolled effects of industrial progress and urban growth were rapidly producing two new classes: the extremely wealthy plutocrats and the extremely poor wage slaves.

Since neither was seen as part of the democratic tradition, the public began to fear that in these groups' selfishness or desperation were the seeds of a future upheaval. Only through institutional change and reform could they be controlled, made democratic, or eliminated. Only by reform of the hitherto largely uncontrolled economic and political organs of society could the seeds of disaster be destroyed.

The willingness of the public to undertake or support such reforms was based on its interpretation of how this situation had arisen. Most people believed that the basic values of their society had been and were now sound. They felt that technological progress had been and was still a beneficial force. But, because of individualistic abuse of power by the rich and powerful and because of unfortunate circumstances or subnormal abilities on the part of the very poor, grave imbalances were now arising in the system and threatening the public with disaster. These had to be corrected by specific social action if American democracy was to survive. In the case of the selfish rich, the power to ignore or override the public good had to be checked. In the case of the poor, a system of minimum guarantees of human dignity had to be provided, even if it be in an admittedly paternalistic way.

The results of the increased public concern were, therefore, twofold. First, the influence of the rich and powerful was attacked with economic and political reforms. Consumer protection laws, public regulatory commissions, and devices such as the initiative and referendum were enacted across the United States. Second, the urban population began to deal with the problems of the city's poor in fundamentally social ways more than in any previous period in history. In most cities, the poor were researched and reported on; and in many of these same cities, the structure of relief for the poor was amended, even though not fundamentally altered.[2]

The two responses were the primary reactions of middle-class America. Challenged on the one side by the "malefactors of great wealth" and on the other side by the "sullen masses," tormented by the vision of these two classes cementing an alliance against the helpless middle class, desperately afraid that the technological progress of the previous decade would help bring down the structure of democracy, many Americans joined the reform movement to maintain what they felt was their birthright. For only by acting and acting quickly could the expectations of progress and tranquillity in the nation be realistically preserved.[3]

Many of the middle-class progressives who were concerned with these problems saw a possible solution in social insurance. Defined as "the policy of organized society to furnish that protection to one part of the population which some other part may need less, or needing is able to purchase voluntarily,"[4] social insurance required contributions from all of society through taxes and from the beneficiaries through payroll deductions. Social insurance would not only maintain the all important and traditional American sense of self-reliance on the part of the laborer, it would also use the resources of all classes of society to help solve some of the major economic security problems of the lower classes. The imbalance in the system would be righted, the poor would not be driven down in despair, and the traditional shape of American life would be preserved.

The middle-class reformers tried to justify their support for social insurance in traditional terms. Their beliefs, which were derived from Protestant theology and secular philosophy, held that a man's material fortunes were dependent on his character traits and morality. Earlier reform movements, placing their emphasis on this point, had called upon the individual to reform himself and thereby achieve material success or spiritual salvation or both. If a man did not listen and consequently failed, he was weak, undisciplined, or sinful. He therefore deserved to fail and should not be pitied: he should only be helped by individual charity or the harsh, begrudging relief of the Poor Laws.[5]

The stark and simplistic view of individual free choice which this theory implied seemed increasingly unrealistic to the progressives in the early 1900's. Was a man genuinely free to choose whether or not he contracted tuberculosis in his tenement or lost a hand in an unsafe milling machine? Once disabled by participating in the new technological system, was he free to cure himself and return to the race for success? These working-class citizens were casualties in the industrial army and now millions of them were being treated as if they had never been recruited and had only themselves to blame for their injuries and failures.

The theory of individual responsibility could not rationally explain why now so many workingmen were failing or suffering ill health or injuries. But few Americans ceased to believe either in this theory or in the biological determinism of Social Darwinism and racial theory; even the middle-class progressives who strongly supported social insurance justified it as a better way of preserving individualistic freedoms. But however obtusely, they were in fact advocating a break with individualism and urging social limits on personal freedoms in return for material security.[6]

Although many middle-class progressives avoided or denied it, this central point entailed a new and different concept of freedom and responsibility. The public health laws, for example, which denied certain freedoms to all for the ultimate benefit of all, were within the traditional view of individualistic freedom and the police power of the state. Social insurance that used compulsion to transfer material resources from one social group to another was not. Social insurance forced the poor worker and the middle-class taxpayer into a larger comprehensive system and removed responsibility for individual failure from the individual to the social whole. In the name of providing a minimum economic level from which all Americans could enjoy their rights of citizenship, social insurance called for a real sacrifice of individualistic freedom and responsibility on the part of all participating citizens.

While many middle-class progressives increasingly came to believe that the new type of freedom that social insurance would provide was the only way of preserving the essence of national life, many other Americans did not. Despite the efforts of the reformers and the deepening crisis in conditions among the poor, most people were never really convinced that it was necessary to implement the new concept of freedom. They did not understand why the older system of individual freedom and responsibility in a largely uncontrolled marketplace would not meet most of the newer problems of an urban, industrialized society.[7] Was it really necessary, they asked, to destroy the very value system which seemed to have brought most Americans such progress and wealth?

Because the nation was divided in its evaluation of the social crisis and in its willingness to accept social insurance as a solution, the pre-World War I reform movement for social insurance was almost totally unsuccessful except for the passage of Workmen's Compensation. Only when the social fabric and public experience of America had changed so that the new concept of freedom was tolerable could this reform succeed. Until that time, private interest groups, professional associations, and public apathy could and did block this reform.

One of the specific areas in which many Americans felt government action and social insurance was needed was health and medical care. The impact of technology on factory workers, the problems of living in huge, crowded cities, and the dramatic advances in scientific medicine made the existing health laws and medical care system seem inadequate and obsolete. The original, local public health codes, the pesthouses for the sick poor, and the poorly trained and inefficient family doctor seemed totally unable to cope with the disease-filled slums, interstate health threats, and the multiplying number of industrial accidents. A modernization of public health laws and a reform of the medical care system in the cities was needed, and soon the urban middle class was demanding such action.

The movement for revision and extension of federal, state, and local public health laws reached its full strength shortly after 1900. The revelations of Jacob Riis and Upton Sinclair, the new awareness that the endemic diseases of the slums could spread and infect others who lived in the same city, and the dramatic improvements in medical science which the family doctor did not understand or employ all contributed to the strengthening of this movement. By 1908 the federal government had enacted the Pure Food and Drug Act and the Meat Inspection Act; the states and localities had begun to revise their public health, housing, and factory codes; and the medical profession had started an agonizing process of self-reform.[8]

Although these developments were encouraging and useful, many concerned reformers felt that they did not go far enough to meet the problem of ill health among the urban poor. They realized that while public health measures were an asset, the developing crisis in medical care in the cities would pose an ever more serious threat to large segments of society. In particular, they feared that untreated illness and injury among the urban working classes would tend to make those classes into a social, political, and economic liability on the rest of society. The infirm lower classes, unable to buy medical care, would become dehumanized and might eventually form separate physical castes. They would become more prone to demagoguery which promised better health conditions for the poor; and, if their diseases or injuries were left untreated and if they consequently developed permanent disabilities, they and their families would become financial burdens on the government.[9]

In simple terms, members of the middle class were afraid that unless they did something significant to correct economically caused health problems among the poor, their own security and social position would be threatened. The middle class could buy decent medical care through private purchases; the poor could not. Therefore, some social mechanism for helping the poor solve their personal medical problems was needed—a way which would correct the new imbalance in the medical care system but which would not destroy traditional individualistic values. Social insurance for illness appeared to be a way in which this problem could be solved.

Many of the progressives who saw compulsory health insurance as the solution to medical care problems among the urban poor joined together to form the American Association for Labor Legislation (AALL). Founded in 1906 as an educational and pressure group devoted to health reforms in industry, the AALL was made up of people who had faith in science, progress, and scientific economics. They had become involved in the struggle for industrial reform not only because of their humanitarian concern for their fellow citizens, but also because they felt that reason, intelligence, and scientific method could produce workable remedies for some of the worst by-products of industrial capitalism.[10]

Many of the leaders and members of the AALL had either studied in Europe or read of European experiments with social insurance. They were impressed with these foreign programs and used them in drafting plans for implementation in the United States. While they were careful to adapt their ideas and strategies to the political and social realities of the American scene, the imprint of the European models remained quite clear.

During its early years the AALL concentrated its efforts on a highly successful campaign to have the several states adopt Workmen's Compensation laws. These laws, which changed the common law concept of liability of workers and employers, were the first examples of successful social insurance in the nation. The ease with which public support was recruited, the compensation laws passed, and the problem of industrial accidents brought under control encouraged the adherents of the AALL and shaped their thinking on later reform efforts. Here, as in the case of the European antecedents, the reformers learned valuable lessons.

By 1912 the American Association for Labor Legislation had grown to include a large number of progressive politicians and university professors. These included Henry Seager, John B. Andrews, Louis Brandeis, Richard Ely, Woodrow Wilson, Miles Dawson, Roscoe Pound, Henry Stimson, and Alice Hamilton, Jane Addams, and Samuel Gompers. The efficient John B. Andrews was the AALL's executive secretary and driving spirit.[11]

Many of these influential members naturally rallied to the Progressive Party when it was formed in 1912. They wanted legislation which would use "the rational approach to the problems of health in the industrial worker," and they helped insert the social insurance plank into the Progressive Party platform of 1912.[12] They worked hard for the election of Roosevelt in the belief that his New Nationalism would bring their ideas to realization most quickly. Although the Progressive Party and Roosevelt were defeated in 1912, progressivism continued to grow. By 1913 leaders of the AALL were planning a state by state crusade for compulsory health insurance for industrial workers. Because of the public's support for progressivism and the association's success with its earlier campaign for Workmen's Compensation, these leaders expected victory after only a moderate struggle.[13]

The predominantly middle-class leadership of the AALL based its strategy on several assumptions which were typical of progressive thought during these years. First, this "energetic and largely self-appointed group" planned action in the state governments rather than in the federal government. The states were primarily responsible for health measures and therefore state laws would more likely prove constitutional than federal statutes. The states had been the vehicles for the passage of the earlier Workmen's Compensation laws, and it would be easier and more democratic for the smaller state governments to establish the kind of insurance programs which would effectively involve the individual worker. Such programs would be closer to the traditions and circumstances of medical care with which he was familiar and would not make him the apathetic recipient of government handouts.[14]

The second assumption made by these reformers was that the long-range economic logic of health insurance would convince all groups that it was in their own interest to lend support. Compulsory health insurance, like Workmen's Compensation, would obviously benefit the worker and the state, both of whom could effectively limit their medical costs to their obligations under the plan. The employers would also benefit: better employee health would tend to stabilize labor relations and raise productivity, and, since all employers would be experience-rated on their employees' health records, a direct competitive advantage would accrue to those employers who encouraged preventive and curative health measures among their workers.[15]

This reasoning reveals the third and most basic assumption: health insurance would provide enough economic incentives to achieve the same material ends as the already established public health program, but it would do so more efficiently and effectively. By creating a mechanism of self-interest oriented toward desirable social goals, the terrible health conditions would be more quickly eliminated. Also, personal identification of both worker and employer with the health insurance program not only would preserve individual values and self-respect but would also eliminate some of the most obvious problems of urbanization and industrialization.[16]

The American Association for Labor Legislation, or rather, the activist executive staff which in effect ran the organization, began their efforts for health insurance in late 1912. They appointed a staff of experts to prepare a preliminary study and define standards which could be used in drafting a model bill and in measuring the quality of various health insurance proposals before the state legislatures. The experts finished their work by 1914 and entitled their report "Nine Standards for Compulsory Health Insurance" (see appendix B). This document was based on many of the assumptions of the association's supporters and is therefore worth examining in some detail. First, the plan envisioned by the "Nine Standards" was largely drawn from German and British models and reflected the European orientation of many of the leaders of the reform movement. For example, like the German system, the health insurance proposal was to be limited to the lowest paid and most needy industrial workers, and like the British system, was to pay both cash and service benefits to the temporarily disabled beneficiary. Second, for the sake of administrative simplicity and efficiency, many categories of needy workers were to be excluded from the plan. Compulsory health insurance was not designed, the reformers believed, for agricultural or domestic workers; it would meet only the problems of the industrial workers who, after all, were the primary concern of the association. Third, in keeping with concern for the social by-products of industrialism, the envisioned plan was designed both as an anti-unemployment measure and as an anti-illness device. Therefore it excluded the worker's dependents from medical coverage (because in normal circumstances they were not employed), and it paid the temporarily incapacitated worker cash benefits in the form of sick pay.[17]

With the work of the experts completed, the AALL was almost ready to proceed with its campaign for legislative enactment of compulsory health insurance in the states. A Model Bill for compulsory health insurance was drafted by the association and endorsed by various professional and reform organizations, politicians were recruited for the campaign, and a propaganda effort to educate the public and legislators was started. The association also produced a long and cleverly written "Brief for Health Insurance" which, through the use of quotations from eminent individuals and groups and simple, logical arguments, tried to give the impression that a great majority of the population was convinced of the merits of compulsory health insurance.[18]

The program of the association, as portrayed in the Model Bill, now included: statewide systems of compulsory health insurance for industrial workers organized in pyramid fashion around a series of local and regional insurance funds and advisory councils, cash and service benefits for the worker, experience-rating of employers, voluntary participation of unincluded workers, and medical care for workers' families (this last proposal was a change from the earlier ideas but was only included as a public health measure). The program also contained provisions to preserve the quality of medical care and professional practice and funeral and maternity benefits for covered workers.[19]

The leadership of the AALL was now ready to start its drive for enactment in earnest. First, a nationwide educational campaign aimed at the public, the workers, and the state legislators would be launched. This would produce enough pressure to bring about the creation of a series of State Health Insurance Investigating Commissions during 1917. These commissions would in turn be "educated" by the AALL and bring in favorable reports. The first enactment of compulsory health insurance legislation was expected to occur shortly thereafter, namely in 1918.[20]

Although the publication of their ambitious campaign plan gave the impression that the AALL leadership was united, in reality it was divided in several ways. First, it was split over the ultimate purpose of the enactment of health insurance legislation. Some saw health insurance primarily as an educational and public health measure, while others argued that it was an economic device to precipitate a needed reorganization of medical practice. Second, the leaders were divided over the economic efforts of compulsory health insurance. Some saw it as a device to save money for all concerned, while others felt sure that it would increase expenditures significantly.[21]

While these and other divisions were ultimately to undermine the health insurance campaign of the AALL, they were well hidden at the initial stages of the educational crusade. And all the leaders agreed, at least in principle, that compulsion was a necessary part of any health insurance program both in order to protect the most needy workers and to avoid the problems which had plagued the voluntary European systems both before and after they had been taken over by the state. It would therefore be far better for America to skip the voluntary step entirely and create a practical and economical compulsory program designed to meet her own needs.[22]

As the AALL's campaign for compulsory health insurance got underway, the leadership believed that the timetable they had drawn up in 1916 was indeed an accurate forecast of coming events. Despite the hidden divisions and strains within the AALL leadership, individuals and organizations began to endorse the Model Bill. By 1917 the federal and several state governments had taken an interest in health insurance legislation. Congress had held hearings on a resolution to establish a Social

Insurance Commission, and two specialists from the Public Health Service, Drs. B. S. Warren and Edgar Sydenstricker, had convinced their agency to support compulsory health insurance along the lines of the Model Bill and to act as a national clearing house for information and statistics on that reform. The Model Bill had been introduced in fifteen state legislatures, and health insurance commissions had been established by ten states. The association had also established the National Conference of Health Insurance Commissioners to coordinate the studies being undertaken and provide an effective organization for education of commission personnel.[23]

The leaders of the AALL compulsory health insurance campaign had another reason to feel encouraged; the attitude of their most powerful potential allies, the state, local, and national medical societies, seemed to be increasingly sympathetic. Many of the reform leaders now felt that support by the nation's organized doctors through the American Medical Association (AMA) and its affiliates would prove conclusive in winning enactment of health insurance legislation by the states.

The American Medical Association, the primary spokesman for the organized medical profession in the United States, was by 1917 in a position to lend powerful support to the health insurance movement. It had recently been reinvigorated by constitutional and leadership changes and was fighting a winning battle to upgrade medical education, medical practice, and professional ethics. It also was receiving a large amount of support from many individual physicians in the nation because they, like many other groups during this period, were slowly realizing the necessity for organization in order to obtain and defend those things they considered essential. The reforms wanted by most doctors, whether a system of uniform licensing laws or a federal Department of Health, required effective political organization, and it was this need which led to the support for revitalization of the AMA. The effectiveness of the AMA leadership in fulfilling these needs was in turn responsible for the association's growing position of power within as well as without the profession.[24]

But while the AMA had compiled a reasonably progressive

record in the previous decade, and while its potential and real political power seemed to be expanding, its leadership and membership had been largely ignorant of or apathetic to compulsory health insurance in the years before 1912. This was the result partly of the AMA's preoccupation with internal reorganization of the medical profession and partly of its members' traditional conception of medicine as a strictly individualistic, curative profession. But apathy began to disappear as the internal reform campaign neared fruition; public health services were dramatically expanded, and doctors were forced to recognize that rapid advances in medical sciences were putting high quality medical care beyond the financial reach of a whole class of industrial employees.

The leaders of the AMA became increasingly concerned with the problem of escalating costs, and some of them began to consider social insurance as a possible remedy. The most important factor in their decision to support or oppose a particular compulsory health insurance measure was their estimation of whether or not the proposal conformed to the ethical standards they were fighting to establish and was in the best professional, economic, and political interests of the profession. And the leaders of the AALL had purposely drafted their Model Bill with this consideration in mind.[25] Their Model Bill was designed to permit and even encourage high quality medical care and adequate remuneration of doctors and should, therefore, gain the support of the medical associations. They had helped establish joint AALL-AMA committees on industrial disease and public health which had already served to open lines of communication between the two groups, and by 1915 the AALL was openly encouraging positive action on health insurance by the AMA.[26]

By 1915 the AMA leadership had responded and was taking an active interest in compulsory health insurance. The AMA created its own Social Insurance Committee in close collaboration with the AALL, and various agencies within the AMA reported favorably on their studies of compulsory health insurance. In 1916, largely as a result of the prodding of its Social Insurance Committee and the pro-insurance AMA *Journal*, the

AMA began to move toward open acceptance of compulsory health insurance. Finally, in June of 1917, the AMA's policy-making body, the House of Delegates, officially endorsed the prerequisites for acceptable health insurance plans presented by the Social Insurance Committee. Their resolution went on to note that blind opposition to the "rising tide of social development" would only "leave the profession in a position of helplessness." [27]

These actions by the House of Delegates were cause for celebration among AALL leaders. They meant that the AMA had openly and unequivocally endorsed a form of compulsory health insurance which was not at all incompatible with that described in the AALL's Model Bill. In retrospect to many of the AMA's later leaders, this decision was the association's "single greatest mistake," but to the contemporary leaders of the AALL and other supporters of compulsory health insurance, it was an enlightened policy that would precipitate the needed state legislative action.[28] This belief was reinforced when state and specialist medical societies began to endorse the AMA position in their own right. The medical societies of Wisconsin and New York, the American Academy of Medicine, and the New York Academy of Medicine all endorsed compulsory health insurance at their annual conventions. The medical societies of Ohio and California saw compulsory health insurance as almost inevitable and urged professional cooperation with legislators in the framing of acceptable statewide plans.[29]

Support for the Model Bill was forthcoming from lay organizations as well. A number of state and local Federations of Labor and International Unions began to endorse the Model Bill, and a few national leaders, including William Green of the United Mine Workers, personally lent their support. The Committee on Industrial Betterment of the National Association of Manufacturers (NAM) saw compulsory health insurance as the least objectionable form of state action in the field of health care, and although the NAM itself did not officially support this position, many individual employers did endorse the Model Bill.[30]

The leadership of the AALL now felt that compulsory health

insurance would be quickly enacted. To some individual leaders it seemed as if the campaign was repeating the stages of the earlier effort for Workmen's Compensation, but at a much faster pace. Dr. Rubinow felt that many phases were now occurring simultaneously rather than successively, and that the widespread concern for minute details of the proposed system indicated the closeness of final action.[31]

The apparent strength of the reform campaign seemed to blind most AALL leaders to the speed with which opposition to their compulsory health insurance proposal was growing. At first anti-insurance opinion had been largely passive and fragmented, but in response to the association's intensifying campaign, it quickly gained strength and organization. By 1917 it was a powerful and effective alliance of groups which could easily challenge the timetable of the reformers and delay, if not prevent, the ultimate enactment of the reform.

One significant group in this alliance consisted of some of America's most important labor leaders. These men, led by Samuel Gompers and his coterie, feared that the enactment of social insurance measures would weaken the nation's labor unions. They felt that if compulsory health insurance were passed there would be less need for workers to join and support unions and less reason for employers to be willing to raise workers' wages.[32] This attitude had been a potentially divisive factor within the AALL since its inception, and now, with many states considering enactment of compulsory health insurance laws, an open and public split on this issue was indeed serious. Gompers opposed the establishment of a federal Social Insurance Commission, and his testimony to that effect before Congress helped kill that proposal over the AALL's objections.[33] Other labor leaders testified against compulsory health insurance in hearings before the Illinois State Health Insurance Commission and were partially responsible for its adverse final report.[34]

Allied with labor leaders in opposition to compulsory health insurance were many of labor's supposedly natural enemies, the employers. Their principal reason for opposition was the belief that they would be called upon to pay an unfair portion of the total contributions, thus setting unfavorable precedents for future social insurance legislation. They urged that "more general efforts of society" be used to supply needed health services to the workers instead of health insurance, although it is doubtful that they would have supported the higher rate of taxation which this suggestion implied. Another unmentioned factor in their thinking was probably the fear that local health insurance societies and funds would serve as nuclei around which workers could organize unions.[35]

A third important group in the anti-insurance alliance were the commercial insurance companies that saw compulsory health insurance as a direct threat to their business. Led by Frederick L. Hoffman, an employee of the Prudential Company and a former member of the AALL's Social Insurance Committee, these companies protested against the inclusion in the Model Bill of a death benefit, which would effectively have eliminated the demand for their own industrial insurance policies. They believed that if compulsory health insurance were permitted to include death benefits, other forms of social insurance which would compete with their regular life insurance business would soon be enacted. Life insurance was their primary source of income, and they therefore actively opposed the enactment of health insurance and death benefits as a first line of defense. In 1917 they formed the Insurance Economics Society of America—ostensibly to study social insurance, but in reality to wage a war of propaganda against compulsory health insurance.[36]

The work of "public education" of the Insurance Economics Society was centered in its Educational Committee, whose leaders shrewdly perceived that if the policy of the medical societies favoring compulsory health insurance could be reversed, great and immediate damage could be done to the pro-insurance cause. There was even an excellent chance that the entire health insurance campaign might be thwarted. The efforts of the Educational Committee therefore were quickly concentrated on the medical profession. With a barrage of material, drawn largely from colored and inaccurate accounts of European conditions, the committee effectively presented the point that the doctors' status and income would fall under compulsory health insurance.[37]

Despite the somewhat doubtful nature of the Educational Committee's materials and the protests of the reformers, the results desired by the insurance companies began to appear. The anti-insurance literature vocalized the dormant fears of some doctors, mobilized already opposing doctors into unified action, and frightened other doctors who had given cautious support to the Model Bill. It was as if the Educational Committee's campaign was triggering an already unstable situation into motion: an avalanche of adverse medical opinion suddenly was becoming evident.[38]

By late 1917 the members of many state medical societies were in open revolt against those leaders who had been gradually moving towards support of compulsory health insurance. Doctors in Ohio, Pennsylvania, and Michigan were recognized as being overwhelmingly opposed to compulsory health insurance, and other state medical societies seemed to be swinging to the same position. By early 1918 even the leadership of the AALL was forced to acknowledge the changed climate of medical opinion concerning their reform. Desperately trying to retain the medical profession's support, the AALL redoubled its efforts to educate the medical profession to its point of view, but their best efforts were unable to reverse the movement by doctors away from health insurance.[39]

While the AALL faced this serious erosion of medical support, another factor was deflecting public interest from compulsory health insurance. America's entrance into World War I meant that public concern for the war effort would override all else. The general public grew concerned with war production, total mobilization, and legislation which would protect the worker and soldier during the immediate crisis; it had no time for health insurance.[40]

The leaders of the AALL, along with most other reformers, believed that wartime emotions were temporary and that the reform movements would revive after the war was over. Aside from a few pessimistic prophets, progressives did not realize the magnitude and multiplicity of changes in social attitudes that the war was creating. Wartime pressures and frustrations, based on internal social hostilities and directed by zealous, if sometimes unscrupulous, men, were producing a distinctly unprogressive America. After 1918 the people of the United States became largely prosperous, cynical, and outwardly self-contented. If some of them felt a malaise or guilt reminiscent of the prewar period, they were hardly noticed by the mass of pursuers of "the illusion of normalcy." They avowed that if the do-gooders were kept out of the government and the government were kept out of business, those few imperfections in the free American system which so bothered the reformers would soon work themselves out. In the Golden Twenties their bywords were traditional freedom and individual responsibility. Progressivism, with its newer concept of freedom, was dormant as a dynamic national force.[41]

The leaders of the AALL gradually became aware of this change in the climate of public opinion after the Armistice. In response they moderated the tone of their health insurance appeals when these were resumed in 1919. They also diversified their program to include several less controversial issues. They even went so far as to accept the possibility of voluntarism in all forms of social insurance, although they clung to their earlier belief that social insurance programs would ultimately have to become compulsory.[42]

But despite these modifications in association policy, the changes which had occurred in American society and politics made it almost impossible for their reform campaign to achieve success. In the climate of Red Scare and xenophobia, state legislatures unanimously ignored or defeated the Model Bill and other health insurance proposals. This antireform sentiment which prevailed in much of the nation was exemplified in the Model Bill's history in the New York state legislature in 1919. There the bill passed the Senate, but Assembly Speaker Thaddeus C. Sweet, the leader of the Republican Assembly Caucus, refused to allow the bill to reach the Assembly floor. He claimed that all forms of social insurance were Bolshevistic, and, with the support of powerful manufacturers, he succeeded in having the health insurance bill killed.[43]

Thus, by 1919 all that remained to insure the total defeat of the AALL's health insurance campaign was the formal reversal of the policy of the medical societies—a reversal which had been taking place in fact for over a year. The initial negative reaction to compulsory health insurance among some doctors, precipitated in part by the efforts of the Insurance Economics Society's Educational Committee, had by 1919 been reinforced by several factors. First, many doctors had had unfortunate experiences with government medicine in the armed services and felt that in terms of medical care for the public, the less governmental intervention, the better for all concerned. Second, many doctors felt that a compulsory health insurance system would lessen their professional prestige and freedom as well as hinder their chances of personal financial success. And third, the leadership of the AMA had changed to such an extent since 1917 that its continued support of compulsory health insurance was highly unlikely.[44]

The first signs of change came in mid-1917 when the *Journal of the American Medical Association* became critical of compulsory health insurance plans and began to publicize anti-insurance comments which were being received at the association's Chicago headquarters. Then, during the absence on war duty of the five members of the pro-insurance Council on Public Health and Instruction, the AMA weakened and reorganized its Social Insurance Committee. Next, Dr. Alexander Lambert, the leader of the pro-insurance forces within the AMA, was elected to the largely honorary office of president in 1918 and by tradition was removed from effective participation in policy debates.[45]

Also, as the AMA membership's pressure against health insurance continued to build throughout 1919, the administrative machinery gradually responded until by the next year it was ready to endorse a formal reversal of policy by the House of Delegates. The New York delegation, supported by those from Michigan and Illinois, presented petitions condemning all forms of state health insurance to the House. A fever of anti-insurance feeling seemed to sweep the House as the Reference Committee on Hygiene and Public Health presented a report on April 17th which concluded with this statement: "Resolved: That the American Medical Association declares its opposition to the institution of any plan embodying the system of compulsory insurance which provides for medical service to be rendered contributors or their dependents, provided, controlled or regulated by any state or the Federal government." [46] The resolution was adopted by the House of Delegates and became the official policy of the AMA from that date until after the Second World War.

Thus, by the early 1920's the forces which had fought for compulsory health insurance legislation lay shattered and friendless. Faced by a hostile medical profession and a largely apathetic, if not unfriendly, public, they could do nothing but withdraw from the battle. Their defeat was so complete that in 1923 the *American Labor Legislation Review* did not run a single article on health insurance. Compulsory health insurance legislation as a vital political issue was dead, and most reformers began to turn their efforts towards other projects.[47]

1920–1932

The shape of life in the United States changed during the twenties as significantly as it had during the previous two decades. The forces that had transformed America from a rural agricultural society to a modern industrial state by 1920 continued to work with hypnotic speed. People streamed to the nation's cities and factories, leaving the farms with a shrinking proportion of the country's population. Millions of Americans became entwined, for the first time, in the complexities and pressures of city living and a wage income.

The technological advances of this decade were a major force in accelerating change. Although usually less spectacular than advances of earlier years, they made an impact on human lives which was scarcely less significant. The universal use of automobiles and the changes this brought in economic patterns and social mores, the use of efficiency experts in mass production industries, the extension of electricity to homes, and the perfection of radio and motion pictures all changed the quality of life in America.

But if technological advance held major implications for the outline of society, most Americans were not overly concerned. The middle classes, who once had feared that the initial effects of industrialization and urbanization would create class warfare and destroy the republic, now seemed confident that this would not occur. The lower classes of industrial workers and city residents no longer were the desperate victims of the new industrial machine; instead they appeared to be sharing in the progress and prosperity which all America was enjoying. The fabulously rich no longer were eager to increase their standing and power by manipulating the poor and subverting the national good; instead they seemed to restrain themselves and work with all segments of society to build a stable and progress-filled community. Government, social classes, and economic units appeared to be united at last in the common purpose of moving toward a brave new tomorrow.[48]

Most who bothered to think about why this had happened agreed that a change in the social atmosphere had occurred. The mood of strife, conflicting class interest, and bickering among interest groups had given way. The progressive movement, which had seen these conflicts as a permanent feature of society and had tried to reorganize, regulate, and ultimately control their effects, had apparently proved itself wrong. America was seen as a classless society after all—one in which opportunity was open to all and in which individualistic freedoms and the laws of the free market place would assure the swiftest national progress.[49] At the same time as competition and the profit system acted as the tireless dynamo of progress, the natural decency and basic goodwill of the people would prevent exploitation and discord from gaining supremacy. Individuals, whether rich or poor, powerful or weak, would voluntarily act towards each other in ways that guaranteed that everyone would benefit. Government intervention would only obstruct or unbalance this process, and those who insisted that social interests had to conflict with each other were troublemakers or un-American.

The Americans who believed in this view of their society held that the way to resolve any minor conflict or imbalance in the system was through the cooperation of all concerned parties. If industrial or urban changes had produced a problem, the government did not need to intervene. Instead, the people who were involved in the problem would voluntarily get together, discuss, and resolve the issue themselves. Since the social and economic systems would benefit everyone if they were allowed to operate properly, all sides in the issue would merely have to agree where the proper course lay, take action, and the problem would *ipso facto* be solved.[50] Such action was not seen as a compromise between two or more conflicting interests, nor as a radical solution imposed from without. It was rather an uncovering of the truth of the situation, the application of intelligence and reason, and the initiation of cooperative, voluntary, and socially responsible actions. Cooperation rather than regulated or institutionalized conflict was the American way.

Since the theory of cooperation left little room for government intervention to compel the individual to protect himself from economic insecurity, middle- and lower-class families could turn for help in crises of unemployment, sickness, and old age only to the traditional ideas of freedom and responsibility. Each man or family should prepare to face such uncertainties through individual action or, at best, voluntary association with others. Private saving, insurance, or fraternal pooling of resources were the ways that these problems were to be solved, and those who failed to make such provisions had only themselves to blame. Voluntary cooperation could provide programs for individual participation, but if these proved inadequate or inoperative, the citizen had few places left to go. Charity, help from family and friends, and the begrudged and degrading alms provided by the state were his only alternatives.[51]

Thus, in the 1920's the individual was still held primarily responsible for his own failures, even while new and impersonal forces in society were making it almost impossible for millions of such individuals to avoid such failures. The theory of cooperation could not meet the challenges these forces posed and could not prevent a plethora of individual disasters. The technologically advanced environment of the 1920's, the industrial and urban life, with cash wages, business cycles, dangerous health conditions in cities, and demographic changes had made the hazards of life different from what they had been. Although many persons believed that cooperation and individualistic answers could reduce these hazards, they did not, in fact, do so.

The origins of the problems which plagued American medical care in the 1920's lay in the technological and economic advances made since the late nineteenth century. The scientific achievements which had done so much to reshape society were particularly startling in the field of medicine. New drugs and treatments were constantly being discovered and introduced, and medical care became for the first time in history more than a questionable benefit. Patients who previously had little hope were now dramatically helped by medical science. The medical advances greatly enhanced the value of modern medical care in the public mind. The doctor, who heretofore had generally been called in as a desperate last resort, now became the supplier of effective and critical services. All segments of the population now began to clamor for his professional attention and care.[52]

Expansion of demand for modern medical care created pressing problems of two related types. The economic, geographic, and social distribution of desired medical services became increasingly unsatisfactory as medical science improved. Also, the increased professional skills required of all doctors tended to make it more difficult for the citizen to locate and obtain modern medical treatment. The first series of problems, those dealing with the distribution of desirable services, were basically economic in origin. Medical care was getting better, but also more expensive. Hospitalization, surgery, laboratory tests, new medical techniques, and consultations with specialists greatly improved the quality of medical care, but also increased the average cost per illness. Doctors' fees and expenses rose and were passed on to the patient. Soon the middle classes, which had traditionally paid for medical care through individual budgeting, were feeling the financial squeeze. The lower classes, which had had even less satisfactory service than the middle classes, were even more adversely affected: they were forced either to forego medical care entirely or to rely on such charity care as they could obtain from public or private sources.[53]

The distribution of medical services was adversely affected by economic pressures in other ways. People living in poor or sparsely settled areas found it increasingly difficult to support the expensive facilities which well-trained modern doctors demanded. As a consequence, younger doctors and specialists tended to congregate in rich and urbanized areas. A geographic and demographic imbalance in available medical service was thus created, which, when superimposed on the problem of supplying adequate medical care to specific population groups such as children and veterans, brought about a nationwide social crisis of increasing proportions.[54]

The second series of problems plaguing American medical care in the 1920's was the result of scientific advances and consequent changes within the medical profession rather than of purely economic forces. The American medical profession, which prior to 1900 had been inundated with poorly trained or incompetent men, began to reform itself in the early twentieth century. By using the increasing public demand for competent medical care as a lever, the medical societies gradually raised the legal and educational standards of the profession. Substandard medical schools were closed, quacks and cultists were attacked, and the quality of American medicine began to rise.

These reforms, together with the new tendency of physicians to specialize or enter research, reduced the number of competent doctors in general practice to the public. And this occurred, it should be remembered, at the very time that public demand for physicians' services was increasing.[55]

Thus, by the mid-1920's American medical care was wracked with a multitude of problems which were beginning to affect the middle as well as the lower classes. Increasing numbers of reformers, doctors, and ordinary citizens became concerned with these issues and eager to work out solutions. In the contemporary spirit of cooperative voluntary action, they began to grope toward new practices and approaches.[56]

In the 1920's the reformers, many of whom had taken part in the AALL health insurance campaign, found it necessary to change their tactics.[57] Previously they had sought as much cooperation and support as possible from all elements of the community, but the atmosphere of the progressive period had encouraged them to visualize their efforts as part of a recognizable and ongoing struggle among various interest groups in the community.

Now both political fact and popular ideology dictated that they cooperate with their opponents more closely and undertake only those projects which would not cause open disagreement and strife. In order for this policy to work in practice, the cooperating groups could act only on those programs which were already underway or were widely demanded by the public. Thus, they could try either to expand and modify existing programs in order to meet some of the newer problems of medical care, or to use public opinion to force the opposition into a more cooperative attitude. The reformers who had been in favor of compulsory health insurance during the prewar period, together with their new sympathizers, tried both approaches during the 1920's, but in practice neither was particularly successful. The first type of approach included the expansion of existing health facilities, hospitals, and clinics. With the support of both reformers and most medical societies, governments increased public health expenditures and built new public health units in rural and poverty-stricken areas.[58] The second, which relied on widespread public demand, focused on new government programs for veterans and children, which were seen as efforts to make medical care more readily available to certain portions of the population which otherwise might find it difficult to obtain. These programs culminated in the passage of a revised veterans' medical program in 1924 and a maternal and infant hygiene program in 1921.[59]

A third kind of cooperative effort was also undertaken during these years by reformers and cooperating physicians. It consisted of experimental voluntary programs which made certain types of medical care more available to persons with moderate incomes. While they neither expanded existing programs nor relied on widespread public support for their establishment, they were as much a part of the cooperative movement as the programs described above.

These private plans were based on the assumption that if average rates were set for given medical services, middle-class patients voluntarily would be able to pay a higher percentage of their medical bills than they would under the existing sliding scale system of individual charges. Medical costs would thus become predictable and budgetable, and both doctor and patient would benefit.[60]

While the cooperating groups undertook these three types of programs in order to try to solve the most pressing medical care problems facing America in the 1920's, they seemed to sense that the programs were at best a series of limited and uneven solutions. To meet the long-term crisis, both the reformers and their opponents undertook a fourth kind of cooperative approach; a series of joint reformer-medical profession studies of projected, comprehensive programs.

The two major efforts in this area during the 1920's were undertaken by the American Dental Association and the Committee on the Costs of Medical Care (CCMC). The Dental Association report, entitled *The Way of Health Insurance,* was an ambiguous document which satisfied neither the organized medical profession nor the health insurance reformers and was soon shelved. On the other hand the work of the Committee on the Costs of Medical Care showed all of the qualities which seemed so important to the believers in the scientific cooperative approach to the solution of contemporary problems. But despite these assets and the number of objective studies produced by the committee's staff, its final report and the recommendations of the committee also produced only dissension, controversy, and conflict.[61]

The Committee on the Costs of Medical Care consisted of eminent men in the medical, public health, and economic disciplines; it had a large staff of trained technical experts; and it was funded for five years of work by eight philanthropic foundations. The final report of the Committee on Costs of Medical Care—or rather the final reports, since there were several dissenting reports filed—came to be the focus of this disagreement. The Majority Report, an essentially weak and conciliatory document, proposed that voluntary health insurance experiments be tried and stated that: "The costs of medical care should be distributed over groups of people and over periods of time, through the use of insurance, taxation, or both." [62]

The Minority Report, the product of a group of committee members with strong ties to the medical societies, bitterly criticized the majority recommendations on health insurance. It condemned both voluntary and compulsory insurance and warned of the dangers of group practice and professional reorganization. The Minority Report also criticized and called for an end to the limited governmental programs that had been started in the 1920's to help veterans and children and called for the restoration of the general practitioner "to the central place in medical practice." [63]

The friction between the two groups within the committee continued to grow in the months preceeding public release of the reports. This antagonism flared into open warfare when, with the consent of the AMA trustees, Morris Fishbein, editor of the AMA *Journal,* published a slashing attack on the Majority Report and its signers. Dr. Fishbein wrote: "These two reports represent . . . the difference between incitement to revolution and a desire for gradual evolution based on analysis and study . . . The alignment is clear—on one side the forces representing the great foundations, public health officialdom, social theory—even socialism and communism—inciting to revolution; on the other side, the organized medical profession of this country urging an orderly evolution guided by controlled experimentation which will observe the principles which have been found through the centuries to be necessary to the sound practice of medicine." [64]

The reformers who read this editorial were so shocked that some of them felt forced to reply in print. They felt that the *Journal* editorial had confirmed their suspicions that "short of surrender by all forward-looking practitioners and lay experts, there was no compromise between the progressive and reactionary forces." [65] They blamed the *Journal's* attacks for having frightened away foundation support for a projected permanent research committee on medical care. And, not without some justification, they accused Dr. Fishbein of having beclouded the entire issue of medical care reform with his emotionalism and name-calling.[66]

The well-known *Journal* editorial on the CCMC was only the last step in the deterioration of the reformer-medical society cooperative effort of the 1920's. The process of decay had started almost as soon as the effort was launched; in the middle years of the decade, the issues of medical programs for veterans and children had brought out the first sign of friction between the two groups. Medical societies and individual doctors had attacked the veterans' medical program and the maternal and infant hygiene programs with increasing bitterness and, over the objections of the reformers, had been partially successful in limiting the programs' effectiveness.[67]

While a significant fraction of the nation's doctors concentrated their attacks on the veterans' and children's programs, they also criticized the voluntary, nongovernmental experiments in new methods of distributing medical care. Few doctors opposed the construction of new voluntary hospitals or even the expansion of public health facilities, but many of them did suspect the middle-rate plans at Massachusetts General Hospital and the University of Chicago Hospital of being against the best interests of the profession. These programs limited the traditional doctor-patient relationship by removing the fee-setting function from the doctor and placing it in the hands of a third party. Some doctors and local medical societies saw these plans as potential threats to the freedom of the participating physician and of the entire medical profession and therefore opposed them.[68]

Thus, the way was open for medical society opposition to the governmental and private programs to be supplemented by the controversy over *The Way of Health Insurance* and the reports of the Committee on the Costs of Medical Care. During the 1920's the antagonists had been driven further and further apart by disagreements on particular issues; by 1932 they were deeply divided over both policy and personality.

One of the most important reasons that these cooperative efforts were doomed to failure was the underlying antagonism between the ideas and values of the health insurance reformers and those of the medical societies and their members. While economic motivation no doubt played a major role in leading the doctors to oppose the cooperative reform proposals of the reformers, it must be remembered that the growing opposition of the organized medical profession was also based, in significant part, on the doctors' beliefs and fears concerning their profession. These beliefs and fears were firmly based on the traditional concepts of American individualism and freedom and were communicated through and enforced by the doctors' own professional organizations: the American Medical Association and its constituent societies.[69]

Most doctors who opposed the cooperative reforms genuinely believed in the traditional ideals of individualism and freedom for the doctor and patient. Despite the scientific, professional, and economic changes which had swept over the medical profession since 1900, these men were committed to the idealized and emotionalized image of the rural general practitioner as the true representative of medical practice. Just as many industrialists of these years tended to deny real conditions and look upon themselves as benevolent partners with their employees in society's productive processes, many doctors identified themselves with the self-sacrificing and largely mythical GP of earlier decades. Somehow he, despite the fact that he carried almost all his tools in his little black bag and kept his accounts in his head, supplied the best type of medical care to his patients. And it was he who, by fulfilling his role of family doctor, by preserving the doctor-patient relationship, and by caring for the poor and unfortunate without payment or complaint, upheld the finest traditions of professional service.[70]

By the 1920's it had become apparent to much of the public and the medical profession that few doctors of this sort still existed. But despite this fact, a significant segment of the nation's doctors continued to accept this image as their ideal. They felt that somehow the vast social forces which had produced group practice, contract practice, pay clinics, research centers, and public health programs had also contributed to a moral decline among contemporary doctors and a consequent deterioration in the quality of medical practice. The doctors themselves had yielded to selfishness and greed and were, therefore, largely responsible for the uncomfortable new methods of medical practice. To these men fighting against the reformers was not enough; the doctors must reform themselves as a profession and have their individual practitioners become more like their traditional ideal.

The primary vehicle which these doctors used to accomplish both of these goals was their system of local, state, and national medical societies. The AMA and its constituent organizations were called upon both to oppose such external threats as the Veterans' Act and the Maternal and Infant Hygiene Act and to facilitate the internal reform of the profession. The first of these tasks was to be accomplished through the standard methods of political pressure groups, while the second was to be achieved through a codification and enforcement of a system of professional ethics. Once such codification had occurred, new programs would be judged in ethical terms by the organized medical profession itself. The full weight of the medical organization could then be turned against such of the new programs which proved to be unethical, and toward internal reform of the profession.[71] Contemporary changes in AMA personnel and organizational structure tended to strengthen the organization's position within the profession. By 1926 these new men and structures had made the AMA into an organization both willing and able to defend what its leaders and members considered to be the welfare of the medical profession.[72]

Antireform sentiment in the medical societies was a gradually rising force in the 1920's, but with the crash of 1929 and the ensuing depression, the medical societies' opposition to the reformers' ideas became almost intransigent. This rapid deterioration and disintegration occurred in two related, but significantly different ways. First, the depression greatly aggravated those problems in medical care which were at issue between the reformers and the medical societies. Both sides now admitted that some form of immediate action was needed, but they could not agree on what that action was to be. Second, the depression replaced the relatively relaxed approach which both sides had held in the 1920's with anxiety regarding the future. The medical societies, while demanding a return to traditional medical care as a solution to the crisis, became afraid that they would lose everything they had fought for in a depression-caused fever of reform. As a result they hardened their position. Conversely, the reformers felt that drastic action was immediately needed to preserve if not improve the nation's health. They thought the medical society proposals were unrealistic and obstructionistic and consequently they hardened their position.

As the depression deepened each side began to absorb more of the emotionalism of men like Morris Fishbein and John Kingsbury at the expense of more rational approaches.[73] By 1934 the AMA had officially endorsed the conservative Minority Report of the CCMC, and the reformers had almost unanimously condemned the AMA. Cooperative efforts were dead, and seemingly both sides were where they had been in 1920. The reformers, many of whom had participated in the pre-World War I health insurance crusade and many of whom had hoped to use the 1920's to refine their proposals, win allies, and educate the public, were frustrated and powerless. The medical societies, which had drifted from hostility to impatient tolerance to renewed hostility toward the reformers, were frightened and almost desperate. There seemed little hope that compulsory health insurance in any shape or form could be achieved with the cooperation, good will and voluntary participation of the doctors.

In attempting to explain the complex reasons for the failure of health insurance in the years from 1900 to 1932, various authors emphasize such forces as the weakening of progressivism by World War I and the Red Scare, the inherent weakness of popular support for compulsory health insurance, the costly efforts of the private insurance companies, the political amateurishness and ineffectiveness of the reformers, the inadequacy of the theory of cooperation, and the economic motivations of the medical profession. While there is some truth in each of these theories, all ignore a critical reason for the failure to adopt compulsory health insurance: the *desires* and *fears* of the reformers, their opponents, and the general public.

It is safe to say that by 1913 most of the members of the AALL and of the progressive movement as a whole believed that the political freedom of the individual depended upon his being assured of a minimum of economic security: only if the citizen were guaranteed his physical well-being by society would he be able to enjoy the privileges of his citizenship. The increasing complexities of urban and industrial society were seen as threatening to the individual's economic security and therefore to his potential ability to enjoy and make use of his citizenship. Progressives believed that the state, in order to correct this deficiency, should abandon its laissez faire policies and interpose itself between the individual and the impersonal social and economic system.[74]

It is also fair to say that a significant fraction of the leadership of the medical profession and organized labor were progressives in the sense that they shared these beliefs and had faith in the power of education to teach their respective followings the merits of the social insurance solution. Calm examinations of the facts, they felt, would expose the problems and reveal the obvious solutions.[75]

But the rank and file membership of the medical profession and labor unions were not at all convinced that such solutions were necessary. They, together with the general public, clung to the more traditional views of their positions within society and feared any fundamental changes in them. They did not understand why the older system of individual responsibility, of higher wages or higher professional fees would not adequately meet all the newer problems. More fundamentally, they did not see the necessity of sacrificing part of an individual's freedom, opportunity, and social status in return for a measure of economic security. Why limit the dream of individual success, they asked—a dream which they felt was possible only in a well-balanced, policed, but largely uncontrolled economic system? This was the concept of freedom which these individuals held despite the educational efforts of the reformers, and this was concept of freedom which played a critical role in the defeat of the pre-World War I compulsory health insurance campaign.[76]

When the prosperity of the 1920's seemed to confirm the validity of the older beliefs, even the facade of progressive ideas disappeared from the minds of a majority of the American public. The middle-class fear of the rich and powerful upper class on the one hand, and the poor, industrial working class on the other, seemed no longer relevant to the reality of the early 1920's. The New Era seemed to promise that the strife-filled years of social adjustment to an industrial society were over. All forces and classes in society could now cooperate in assuring progress for everyone; no one would be shut out from prosperity, and at the same time no one would have to surrender his own freedom. The inherent strength of these traditional values had pulled the United States through the crisis, and they were therefore to be enshrined and respected as permanent features of the social system.

As the 1920's wore on and as experiments in cooperation ended in disruption and disaster, it became clearer that there was a force besides public apathy that was preventing the enactment of medical care reforms, namely the opposition of the organized medical profession. Though some theories attribute medical opposition to economic greed or reactionary leadership, it seems clear that a basic explanation is to be found in the doctor's ideas of his profession and himself.

Most doctors of this period probably saw themselves as engaged in the most difficult profession in the world. They were daily called upon by society to take human life in their hands and pit their skill against illness and death. In return, society accorded them high social status. Individual doctors took satisfaction in their work and its social prestige: this was the ideal reward of the medical profession; incidental financial success was not.[77]

By 1910 this ideal of individual self-sacrifice and achievement had little relationship to real conditions. Economic, technical, and demographic changes had made it almost impossible for doctors to subordinate economics to the ideal of service for its own sake. The doctor was now a member of an urbanized, industrialized society in which his status and well-being were intimately connected with his competence and income. The practitioner could no longer be only the spiritual and temporal adviser and friend of his patients; he had to become also a professional student and businessman.[78]

But despite these de facto changes in medical practice, the doctor refused to abandon an idealized concept of his profession. To him the very nature of the profession depended on the individual responsibility of patient and doctor and on freedom from outside interference. Surely the changes in medical practice were not so great that such ideals had to be forgotten.

Disparity between ideal and reality disturbed and frightened the individual doctor who tried to judge the kaleidoscopic changes then taking place in medical care. Reform was needed, but what type? A reorganization of the entire system as proposed by lay reformers, or something less drastic and closer to the tradition of what must once have been?

Faced with the alternatives, the doctor most often chose tradition. The reformers' proposals appeared to subordinate the ideals of the medical profession to an attempt to provide more efficient service for great numbers of patients. The doctors felt that such a policy would destroy the very essence of good medical care. On the other hand, the medical societies proposed reforms which would preserve and strengthen traditional ideals and at the same time promised to alleviate the very real problems caused by social and professional change.

The doctors' structure of belief and desire was the underlying force behind the behavior of the organized medical profession during the decade. In continuing to cling to their belief in individual responsibility and freedom, physicians often acted *against* long-term economic and political self-interest. They felt that they and their elected leaders were acting on principle and once again were sacrificing individual well-being in order to protect their profession and their patients from interference.

The reformers, needless to say, did not agree. Their concept of individual freedom was, they felt, more realistic than that of the doctors or medical societies. They recognized that the social and economic forces which were changing American civilization required equally drastic changes in the organization of medical care. The doctors who refused to recognize this simple truth were reactionaries, and their efforts to arrest progress were considered obstructions of inevitable reform.

The feelings of the public on this issue were harder to interpret. In the 1920's most Americans no doubt felt that voluntary cooperation was better than government interference. But what form of cooperation was most desirable and what type of reform most needed? All that can be said is that the public knew that medical bills were rising, that good doctors were harder to find, and that something should be done. With the coming of the Great Depression these problems grew constantly worse, until millions began to feel that regardless of the debates over tradition and freedom, something extensive and immediate had to be done.[79]

Compulsory health insurance, like all other forms of social insurance that assume a somewhat stable and identifiable working population, could only approach legislative passage when large segments of the public accepted the progressive view of individual freedom. As long as the public clung to the older view of liberty and individual responsibility, compulsory social insurance could go only so far. And despite the problems of industrial America and the efforts of the progressives and reformers of the 1920's, the public was never really convinced of the validity of the new concept of freedom during these decades. The reforms that were passed, even those which, like Workmen's Compensation, immediately affected individuals, were efforts to *recreate* the possibility of the old freedom rather than to usher in the age of the new.

The fate of compulsory health insurance in these decades suggests that the spread of a new social concept from its original propounders to the public at large is intimately tied to the complex of social, economic, and political conditions of the society. A new idea with implications for the structure of life in a community is not advanced solely by education or by economic necessity. Rather the fabric of social existence must gradually change so that the new idea becomes part of the pattern. Ideas, unless and until they become acceptable to the common ideology, can have no life of their own. And in these decades the new ideas of freedom and security had not as yet become a part of the popular ideology.

2

Washington: The First Battle
1933–1935

As the United States sank deeper into the economic paralysis of the early 1930's, the signs of impending disaster multiplied. Measured on a 1929 scale, by 1932 the gross national product had fallen 44 percent, and farm income 52 percent.[1] Unemployment soared toward twelve million, and thousands of economic refugees began to travel the highways and to gather in and around the cities. The nation was no longer filled with happy, successful people and a minority of failures: it now abounded with failures who only a few years before had shared in the dream or substance of prosperity.

Most Americans initially believed that little could be done to alleviate or end the depression. Business cycles were a familiar and necessary part of life and people had to suffer through them as best they could. The important thing was that the system itself was basically sound, and once the economy "bottomed out" things would get back to normal. In the meantime voluntary groups or local government should supply aid to the most needy in order to prevent anyone from starving.[2]

But as years went by and the depression grew constantly worse, many people began to feel that somehow things were different this time. Business leaders were discredited, millions of hard-working, honest laborers were thrown out of work, and even the middle classes began to fall victim to the creeping paralysis. Relief rolls were hopelessly overburdened, and the economy seemed to get worse rather than better.

Despite outward signs of disaster, the public refused to believe that American society had really failed. The depression was caused, they believed, by specific imbalances and abuses which had gone unchecked for years. Once these anomalies were eliminated through careful reform, prosperity would return and another serious depression would be preventable.

Permanent federal reforms of the economic and political life of the nation were to be as limited as possible. Sectors in which abuses had occurred, thereby contributing to the depression, needed serious action; others that were basically sound did not. Even in the areas where the need for reform was widely recognized, its shape had to conform as much as possible to the traditional views of individualism, freedom, and responsibility. Thus, if a less drastic or nongovernmental solution would suffice in meeting a specific problem, any proposals calling for more radical action would probably gain little public or political support and would therefore be defeated.

This was the fate of compulsory health insurance during the early years of the New Deal. Many reformers who had been active in the 1920's and the days before World War I expected to achieve their reform during the New Deal. They believed that the reform was needed, that Roosevelt was sympathetic, and that the public was ready to accept reform in this area. Using their old political techniques and new governmental allies, they set out to enact compulsory health insurance as part of the proposed new federal social security legislation.

The plans of the health insurance reformers were to be defeated by a combination of interlocking factors. First, the public was uninformed, unorganized, and largely apathetic concerning government reform of the medical care system. The people were not sure that this area of society needed massive governmental reform and did not rally to the support of the reformers. Second, the Roosevelt administration, which sensed public disinterest and had its own priorities for reforms, was unwilling to push health insurance at the risk of losing its other proposals. And third, the organized medical profession, which for its own reasons rejected the reformers' assumptions and proposals, and which also sensed the public apathy toward compulsory health insurance, was able to frighten the administration and frustrate the reformers' plans. Compulsory health insurance in the early New Deal was defeated simply because to most Americans it seemed either a strange, unneeded device or an overly radical and precipitous one.

In the early days of the New Deal the compulsory health insurance reformers felt that they had reasons to rejoice. President Roosevelt and his close advisers on social welfare had shown a distinctly progressive attitude during his governorship in New York, and he now promised significant federal action to bring recovery, relief, and reform to the United States. Although the President seemed to be delaying reform of the social welfare system in favor of economic and agricultural recovery, his priorities seemed valid and his underlying commitments to reform sincere. He would eventually get to the needed reforms, and when he did, they would be enacted.[3]

As the months went by and no social welfare reform program materialized, the reformers became more insistent. By 1934 Roosevelt's recovery program was having only limited success, the temporary federal relief program was uneven in its effects, and demagogic national political movements were beginning to appear. Quick action was needed, and at last Roosevelt began to respond.[4] He decided to act on social welfare reform after meeting with his Cabinet in June 1934. Turning to his natural allies, the social insurance reformers, the President established a cabinet-level Committee on Economic Security (CES) to "study problems related to the economic security of individuals."[5] The committee would use both the reformers and other groups to prepare a series of expert reports on the needs of reform in social welfare, and Roosevelt would send these reports to Congress as a set of guidelines for federal legislation. Congress would then create a social security program which would meet the nation's needs and more or less conform to the ideas of the reformers.[6]

The CES was to consist of five cabinet members under the

chairmanship of Frances Perkins. It would delegate most of the work to a technical staff and specialist committees and would have a civilian advisory board to review and discuss the expert proposals. An executive director would be placed in charge of this entire expert effort and would look to the cabinet committee only for general policy guidelines.[7]

Since so much of the responsibility for the concrete recommendations was to be delegated to the executive director and the technical staff, it became quite important to choose sympathetic, reform-minded persons to fill these posts. After some delay, Edwin E. Witte, a progressive Wisconsin professor favorable to social insurance, was selected as executive director of the CES. Dr. Edgar Sydenstricker, one of the most eminent health insurance reformers, was chosen to direct the Technical Committee on Medical Care. Such personnel choices seemed to indicate that the committee would come out strongly for compulsory health insurance as part of any program which they might recommend.[8]

Appearances were deceiving, however, and relatively early the policy of the CES began to reveal that the administration had some reluctance about including compulsory health insurance in its proposals. Roosevelt and Perkins were controlling the committee's general policies fairly closely, and by July 1934, they had become worried by potential opposition to health insurance. They held discussions with Witte, who, because of their political hesitance and the short time available to the committee for research and drafting, decided that the committee should not consider health insurance as part of the "immediate program" to be presented to Congress for swift enactment. It should instead be grouped with other of the committee's proposals to the country as part of "a long-time comprehensive program" designed for ultimate enactment. This decision meant that the advocates of health insurance within the committee's staff would initially have to overcome the reluctance of Roosevelt, Perkins, and Witte in order to place their reform on a par with those dealing with old age and unemployment.[9]

Sydenstricker and his staff assistant, I. S. Falk, set out to do just this in the summer of 1934. Almost as soon as they were appointed to the staff of the committee, they began to work on a general preliminary report on health insurance which they could use to win over the cabinet committee, Perkins, and Roosevelt himself. To be effective, this report would have to be a fast but forceful job which could quiet the administration's fears regarding the potential strength of medical society opposition to health insurance and thereby prove its political feasibility. This, of course, assumed that the medical opposition to health insurance would be limited—a theory which would be proven when some support for health insurance proposals was forthcoming from the medical societies.

Sydenstricker and Falk anticipated that this would indeed be the case if certain procedures were followed by the CES. If the committee consulted the medical leaders on an advisory basis from the beginning of their own efforts, other pressures on the doctors would force them to "begin a constructive program" which "a large and substantial fraction of the medical practitioners will endorse." Sydenstricker and Falk therefore urged the creation of a Medical Advisory Committee when they first began their work for the committee.[10]

Action on the creation of the advisory committee was delayed, but in October Witte finally approved it when a barrage of letters, telegrams, and phone calls from doctors began to flood the committee's offices. These letters protested against compulsory health insurance, and more important, against the way in which it was being handled by the cabinet committee. If Sydenstricker and Falk were right, and medical leaders were invited to sit on an advisory committee, then the barrage of letters would subside.[11]

With Witte's approval the formation of a Medical Advisory Committee was publicly announced and the process of selecting its membership started. But the letters and telegrams, many of which were worded identically, kept arriving from members of state and local medical societies who protested either the cabinet committee's bias in choosing its own staff or the make-up of the Medical Advisory Committee. These protests were followed by a host of editorials in state and national medical journals which made the same complaints and often warned against any medical care proposals emanating from the CES.[12]

Sydenstricker and Falk had expected some of this kind of opposition to persist despite their recommendation to form the advisory committee. The medical leaders were not completely united, they believed, but the basic medical sentiment was for real reform in medical care. By co-opting reform-minded and moderate medical leadership, the cabinet committee and its technical staff could greatly strengthen their own chances of having health insurance included in the committee's immediate program and isolate the medical reactionaries. They were therefore not alarmed when the barrage of protest letters from the reactionaries did not subside.

Witte, however, was surprised. He had apparently believed that the formation of the Medical Advisory Committee would pacify *all* medical opposition, and when this did not happen he was somewhat alarmed. Sydenstricker again reassured Witte that the idea behind the advisory committees (the idea had been extended to include other health professions by October) was sound and when the number of protest letters finally did decline in early November, Witte seemed confident that Sydenstricker had been right.[13]

By the end of October it seemed as if Sydenstricker's plan to convince the administration to include health insurance in the immediate program was making progress. The cabinet committee had approved Sydenstricker's general preliminary report on health insurance on the first of the month, and Sydenstricker and Falk had begun to work on a more detailed proposal. Witte now seemed to be convinced that health insurance was at least a political possibility, and was expressing that view within the administration. For example, on October 26, 1934, he wrote to Frances Perkins: "I certainly believe that we cannot dismiss health insurance at this time without being entirely satisfied that it cannot be put into operation on a compulsory basis in the near future." [14]

One way in which the CES hoped to gain a broad base of

support for its recommendations to Congress was by calling the National Conference on Economic Security in November 1934. The committee invited representatives of the public, the government, and interested groups in order to have them discuss the issues and tentative proposals in a series of small Round Table Discussions. The discussions would lead to a consensus, the committee hoped, and would therefore hasten congressional approval. Neither the round tables nor the entire conference were to take formal policy positions, however; they were merely ways to air the problems and proposals and clarify the issues.[15]

One of the round table discussions at the National Conference on Economic Security was devoted to the field of medical care. With their recent experience in the selection of the Medical Advisory Committee still fresh in their minds, Witte, Sydenstricker, and Falk were very careful in selecting the medical members of that panel. Since they believed that the medical profession was not united in opposing health insurance, they felt that in all fairness they could select medical panelists who were both for and against health insurance and have them discuss their differences. They would probably not agree on health insurance but their very disagreement would demonstrate to the public and to the administration that health insurance had some significant support among the nation's doctors.

The medical societies who claimed to speak for the entire profession did not accept this view. They felt that the staff of the CES was trying to magnify a minor difference of opinion among doctors by their arbitrary selection of the panelists. The medical societies had spoken out clearly against health insurance and felt the administration should deal only with the legitimate representatives of the societies' negative position. The committee's tactic of selecting representatives from both sides was therefore unfair, and the medical societies were justified in taking serious remedial action.[16]

The outcome of the conflicting tactics became obvious when the Round Table Discussion on Medical Care convened on November 14th. Henry Luce, the coauthor of a pro-insurance report in Michigan, spoke first. Sydenstricker and Falk expected him to deliver a mildly pro-insurance speech which would later be balanced by an anti-insurance statement. But much to their surprise and shock, Dr. Luce read a speech which merely rephrased the official position of the AMA concerning reforms in medical care. Something seemed very wrong to Sydenstricker and Falk.[17]

The shock of Luce's statement had not worn away before another, equally surprising event occurred. Harvey Cushing, a respected doctor and the father-in-law of one of Roosevelt's sons, broke his heretofore unblemished record of neutrality on health insurance and bitterly attacked the pro-insurance speakers at the round table. Shortly thereafter, in a mood of complete disruption, the round table was adjourned.[18]

To the pro-insurance reformers on the cabinet committee staff, these events seemed like part of a concerted policy by the medical societies to discredit the work of the committee and its efforts for health insurance. The barrage of anti-insurance, anticommittee letters from the doctors had resumed with full intensity, and it appeared that the medical societies were preparing for an all-out, no-holds-barred struggle. Health insurance was clearly in danger from this attack, and both Witte and Perkins felt that there was once again some chance that the opposition could spill over into opposition to the immediate program of the CES.[19]

Although Sydenstricker and Falk did not agree with this view, Witte and Perkins now readopted their earlier belief that health insurance was too controversial to be included in the immediate program. They also feared that the confrontation at the round table conference might produce rash action in the first meeting between the Technical Committee on Medical Care and the Medical Advisory Committee scheduled for the next day, so Witte and Perkins agreed to play for time and hope for reconciliation.

In accordance with this new policy, Secretary Perkins made a conciliatory speech to the meeting of the Medical Advisory Committee on November 15th. She praised the dedication of the nation's doctors and medical societies and explained that because of the volume and seriousness of the cabinet committee's other work, she and the rest of the committee would be willing to grant an extension of several months for the preparation of the report of the Technical Committee on Medical Care.[20] Meanwhile the other recommendations of the CES would be forwarded to the Congress for consideration and enactment. In other words, the strategy of Sydenstricker and Falk was overthrown, and health insurance was once again removed from the category of immediate programs and relegated to an inferior position and priority.[21]

Although the medical societies had won this skirmish by appearing united in the face of the administration, the tactics they had used to achieve unity led to a split within their own leadership. This division seemed to prove to Sydenstricker and Falk that they had been right in their estimate of medical society division over health insurance and to confirm the wisdom of their basic strategy of dividing the doctors for the future. The schism within the medical leadership became obvious during the early meetings of the Medical Advisory Committee when Dr. James Bruce presented what he felt was conclusive evidence of the unfair and distasteful tactics the AMA leadership had been using.[22] Such tactics were totally unacceptable to doctors such as Bruce, J. S. Horsley, and Rexwald Brown. Together with Dr. Cushing, who became much more favorable toward the cabinet committee after a luncheon with Roosevelt, they threatened that unless the AMA ceased such activities, the organized medical profession would be "split wide open." [23]

The leaders of the AMA present at the early meetings did not deny the allegations of Dr. Bruce; indeed, they tacitly admitted to them when they promised that the AMA attitude would change and that the organized medical profession would be "willing to work with the Medical Advisory Committee and the CES" in trying to reach a generally acceptable solution.[24] As a token of their promise they made it clear that the attacks on the personnel and agenda of the CES and the Medical Advisory Committee would be discontinued in medical society publications as long as the cabinet committee's plans for health insurance were under active consideration.

Sydenstricker and Falk saw this promise of cooperation as an admission of defeat by the conservative medical leaders and as an opportunity to push forward their proposals for health insurance. They hoped that the postponement offered by Witte and Secretary Perkins would not prove damaging, and that their proposals would quickly be found acceptable by the various advisory committees. After that, there was a good chance that the proposals would consequently win the support of some of the organized medical profession and of related health professions. Health insurance could then be put back into the immediate program category and transmitted to Congress as an additional part of the imminent Economic Security Bill.[25]

The hope for quick action was soon dashed by developments within the Medical, Dental, and Hospital Advisory Committees. It did not matter that the proposed programs were largely permissive in nature and closely followed the mild "CCMC Majority Recommendations;" the more conservative members of each of these committees requested that they be given the additional time promised by Secretary Perkins to "study" the proposals. After negotiations among Witte, Sydenstricker, and Perkins, these requests were honored, and the date for submission of final recommendations was extended until March 1, 1935.[26]

Postponement of the due date of the final recommendations was of critical importance to both the supporters of health insurance and their opponents. It meant that the proposals made by Sydenstricker and Falk would definitely not be included in the Economic Security Bill to be presented to Congress, and it implied that the best the pro-insurance forces could hope for would be the inclusion of a health insurance amendment at a later date.[27]

Perhaps even more important was the significance of postponement to that segment of the organized medical profession which was completely opposed to health insurance. To these doctors the delay meant that influential members of the administration were worried that the inclusion of health insurance would endanger the passage of the entire Economic Security Bill, and they would therefore be willing to sacrifice health insurance altogether if necessary. If the organized medical profession could use the next few months to enhance the administration's fears on this score, they could conceivably kill the reformers' hopes that health insurance could be included in the cabinet committee's report.

Sydenstricker also understood the implications of the delay. He knew that the White House was soon going to call for firm recommendations from the cabinet committee in order to draft the Economic Security Bill. He also realized that the Technical Committee on Medical Care would, because of Perkins' granting of the delay, be unable to submit specific recommendations in time. Health insurance was in danger of being completely omitted from the CES report, and Sydenstricker knew that if this happened there would be little chance of introducing it later. He therefore convinced the cabinet committee to include a statement on health insurance in their general report of January 1935. This statement said that the committee was still actively considering health recommendations and outlined eleven principles basic to their studies (see appendix B).

The principles were an outgrowth of the proposals Sydenstricker and Falk had originally presented to the advisory committees. They described a nonprofit, comprehensive system of compulsory health insurance which would give considerable administrative power and freedom to the medical profession. Both cash and service benefits would be provided, and these would be paid for through payroll deductions. (In the case of unemployed or indigent workers the premiums would be paid by the relief agency.) The entire structure would be created and administered by the separate states with the federal government limiting itself to a standard-setting and subsidizing role.[28]

The attempt to keep health insurance alive in the cabinet committee infuriated the anti-insurance forces within the AMA. When they discovered Sydenstricker's plan to include this statement, they interpreted it as a violation of the truce arranged in the first meetings of the Medical Advisory Committee. They decided to respond, and in late December they began a general anti-insurance propaganda campaign in the medical journals. At the same time, the medical leaders assured Witte that they did not intend to resume their personal attacks on the cabinet committee or its staff and were planning to respect the truce in this area. In effect they would criticize the work of the committee without using its name or the names of its personnel.[29]

At this point Witte grew even more pessimistic about the chances of including health insurance in the Economic Security Bill in any form. He felt that the only way health insurance could be included in the nation's new social insurance structure would be through a separate bill, introduced *after* the Economic Security Bill had been passed. He saw little hope even for this if the advisory committee were to remain divided in its recommendations.[30]

Witte's apprehensions concerning the political dangers of health insurance left only one avenue of action open to Sydenstricker if he hoped to have health insurance salvaged in the CES; an appeal to President Roosevelt for support. This was at best a doubtful business, for the President himself was not wholeheartedly committed to health insurance. Although Roosevelt was sympathetic to the idea of social insurance and had been made aware of the potential benefits of health insurance through conversations with Harry Hopkins, he was also conscious of the medical society opposition to the inclusion of health insurance in the Economic Security Bill. His contacts with Dr. Cushing and his own physician, Dr. McIntyre, apparently impressed him with the extent and determination of this opposition. At this time he probably shared the fears of Witte, Miss Perkins, and Under Secretary of Labor Altmeyer concerning the political effects of recommending this reform. He felt that old age and unemployment programs were to be given top priority and that a health insurance program should be offered to Congress only if it were noncontroversial.[31]

Given Roosevelt's feelings on health insurance, Sydenstricker and Falk had to be extremely careful in framing their appeal to the White House. They could not ask for open endorsement of a health insurance title on the one hand, and their personal beliefs would not let them let health insurance quietly die on the other. They took a middle ground and in late December urged the President to avoid appearing too weak regarding health insurance in his forthcoming economic security message to Congress lest it "hamper our earnest efforts to get the medical profession to actually sit down and work with us on the problem."[32] If the President appeared uninterested in health insurance, they argued, the rank and file of the organized medical profession would "get the idea that nothing is to be done, then Fishbein and his crowd will say that they were successful in scotching the President's interest in health insurance."[33]

This statement implied that Sydenstricker still hoped that the Medical Advisory Committee might reach some kind of agreement with the Technical Committee in their forthcoming meetings. He therefore wanted to maintain the appearance of administration support for his proposals at least until that time. If things went well and the advisory committee reached agreement, then health insurance could be presented to Congress, either in the form of an amendment to the Economic Security Bill, or as a separate bill.[34]

Sydenstricker's slim hopes on this score were dashed when the Technical Committee on Medical Care met with the Medical Advisory Committee in late January and early February 1935. The intervening period, which was to have been used for study, had not healed the division within the advisory committee over health insurance. The Technical Committee's latest effort, the "Interim Report for the Consideration of the Medical Advisory Board," was a modification of the Preliminary Report and had been prepared with the cooperation of the AMA's employees, Leland and Simons. But it still proved unacceptable to some members of the advisory committee. Sydenstricker soon realized that he could not obtain unanimous support of the advisory committee for the Interim Report,[35] and he therefore decided on a stratagem often used by government officials when dealing with advisory bodies: he let the advisory committee pass on the separate details of the proposed plan and he reserved final decisions on policy to the CES and the President.[36]

The Medical Advisory Committee promptly divided into hostile factions over Sydenstricker's strategy, and it was only Sydenstricker's personal skill which prevented an open and public split. The advisory committee considered the various parts of the Interim Report program for two days and Sydenstricker closed the meetings with a restatement of his policy regarding the role of the Medical Advisory Committee in forming the Technical Committee's final recommendations; namely, that the various points brought out during the meetings would be considered in the drafting of the final report but that the report itself would be a product *solely* of the Technical Staff. The Medical Advisory Committee would "have no responsibility with [sic] it whatsoever." [37]

Both Sydenstricker's tactics in regard to the Medical Advisory Committee and his method of conducting the joint committee meetings disturbed the anti-insurance doctors on the advisory committee. On February 4, 1935, Dr. Bierring, the President of AMA and an advisory committee member, wrote to Witte protesting what he felt was unfair treatment of the medical profession. By a mysterious coincidence, on the same day, Dr. Cushing, who was now eager to win election to the presidency of the AMA and was aligning himself with official policy, also wrote to Witte and to President Roosevelt. In his letter to Witte, Cushing was particularly bitter in his criticism of the Technical Committee on Medical Care and of its leader's conduct in the recently concluded meetings:

> You are probably aware that the deliberations of the Medical Advisory Committee were controlled by a group of persons who have long been committed to a program of compulsory sickness insurance.
>
> The few of us in attendance who felt that such a program would lead to the deterioration of the doctor, the demoralization of his professional code and the placing of the profession under a bureaucracy were not permitted to discuss the advisability of such

legislation but were only allowed to take up the points of the bill laid before us that had been drawn up to provide for it. We therefore found ourselves in the position of advocating legislation, some form of which may perhaps some day be advisable but which the medical profession in general in the country is not yet prepared to accept for the reasons I have given . . .

In thus handing onto you my personal reactions in the matter I do so chiefly because of my apprehension lest I be put in the false position before the medical profession of being an advocate of compulsory sickness insurance from the fact of my having been a member of the Committee.[38]

To Witte, these letters meant that there was no longer any hope at all for unified action in the advisory committee. Witte was now concerned lest the bitter medical society discontent spill over into general opposition to the Economic Security Bill. He wanted to prevent this and to remain on at least superficially good terms with the organized medical profession. Therefore he drafted polite replies to Bierring and Cushing which were not at all vigorous in their defense of Sydenstricker or the Technical Committee on Medical Care.[39]

Dr. Sydenstricker reacted drastically to Witte's mild tone in these letters. The issue, he believed, had grown beyond mere support or opposition to health insurance; the question now openly involved Sydenstricker's personal integrity. Sydenstricker delayed the dispatch of Witte's letters until he could draft a personal reply to Cushing. In a stinging letter to Cushing, dated February 11, Sydenstricker refuted each of Cushing's points and questioned the factual content and underlying interpretations of Cushing's remarks. He summarized the proceedings of the advisory committee, because he felt that misstatements by a man of Cushing's eminence "could not be allowed to stand uncorrected,"[40] and he later told Witte that he was "at a loss to understand how Dr. Cushing had been so utterly mistaken."[41]

This misunderstanding between Witte and Sydenstricker was amicably settled within a week. But its underlying causes illustrate the division of opinion which disunited much of the proreform camp. On the one side, Sydenstricker and his followers felt that the leaders of organized medicine were so afraid of positive action on health insurance that they were behaving desperately. The proper course for the President and the CES to follow, Sydenstricker believed, was to remain strong in support of health insurance and force the doctors to confront the issue honestly. If the CES showed weakness, the leaders of the organized medical profession might "grab at anything that might be interpreted as a difference in the point of view of the Committee's staff" and use it to defeat health insurance.[42] This action by the medical societies would put the administration in the "embarrassing position of having been licked by a group of doctors."[43]

The other group of pro-insurance reformers did not agree with Sydenstricker's interpretation. Witte, and to a lesser extent Secretary Perkins, felt that the issue of health insurance was so politically explosive that the planned publication of the Medical Technical Committee's pro-insurance Final Report on March 1st would in fact threaten the passage of the entire Economic Security Bill. The medical society's opposition was a powerful force which could be turned against unemployment and old age legislation, and they wanted to avoid this contingency at all costs.

In order to protect those programs to which they gave the highest priority, these senior members of the CES evolved a policy which could legitimately delay or ultimately suppress the publication of the pro-insurance Final Report of the Technical Committee on Medical Care. According to this policy, the decision on when and to whom to submit the Final Report was placed in the hands of the cabinet committee itself. This really meant that the fate of the health insurance recommendations would be determined by the cabinet committee and the President, and that the most important considerations in determining that fate would be the administration's political strategy regarding the Economic Security Bill. It seemed that Witte's policies and fears had finally prevailed over Sydenstricker's plans and hopes.[44]

The contents and fate of the Final Report confirm this evaluation. The health insurance proposals of the Technical Committee were filed in March 1935 and were a direct outgrowth of the plans described in the Preliminary and Interim reports of November and January, respectively. Entitled "Risks to Economic Security Arising out of Ill Health," the report called for the creation of a system of state programs which would have both federal supervision and federal subsidization. Each state plan would provide "medical benefits to insured persons and their dependents, in health and in sickness, without waiting period and without payment except through previous contributions."[45] A separate system of cash disability payments similar to the proposed unemployment compensation system was also recommended.[46]

In reality, by the spring of 1935 this program for a nationwide system of medical care was doomed. The cabinet committee had decided that Witte was right and that the report was too controversial to be proposed to Congress or even made public. The committee therefore decided to prevent its immediate publication. Sydenstricker did not give up all hope because of these adverse decisions. At the March 15th meeting of the cabinet committee, he and Falk urged the committee to submit a health insurance plan as an amendment to the Economic Security Bill. Relief Administrator Hopkins, as well as Undersecretary of Agriculture Tugwell and Assistant Secretary of the Treasury Roche, agreed, but Chairman Perkins, Executive Director Witte, and Thomas Eliot of the Technical Board all objected. The latter group felt that health insurance should be delayed until after the passage of the Economic Security Bill so as not to endanger that most important piece of legislation. Witte, who had learned from Dr. McIntyre that the President also wanted the health insurance proposals delayed, urged the committee to retain its earlier policy of consulting the President before making any final recommendations. Roche and Perkins then consulted with Roosevelt and were asked by him to submit a report favorable to health insurance but to leave the final decision as to its use up to him. The cabinet committee agreed "even though every member of the committee understood that it meant that the President did not intend to come out for health insurance so long as the Economic Security Bill was pending" [47] and that FDR "had not made up his mind what he would finally recommend on the subject." [48]

These actions marked the final defeat of Sydenstricker's efforts to have the CES openly support health insurance legislation; both he and Falk were in effect removed from further responsibility for health insurance by the President and the CES. They took several weeks to finish their pro-insurance report, which was submitted to the cabinet committee and approved in early June. It was then sent to the President with a covering letter from Perkins urging that it not be made public until after the passage of the then-pending Social Security (Economic Security) Bill. Nothing more was heard about it for the rest of the summer.[49]

In September, after the Social Security Act had been passed, Miss Perkins met with Roosevelt to discuss publication of the Health Insurance Report. The President explained that he did not want action on health insurance in Congress until after the 1936 elections and asked that the original letter of transmittal which had urged immediate congressional consideration be modified to conform to this decision. Miss Perkins consequently had Assistant Secretary of Labor Altmeyer redraft the letter of transmittal in such a way as to make it less definite.[50]

This long public silence by the cabinet committee and the Roosevelt administration on health insurance during mid and late 1935 disturbed certain pro-insurance reformers outside the government. Men like John Andrews of the AALL and Paul Kellogg of the Survey Associates publicly began to ask why health insurance was not being supported by the administration and to urge that the President immediately throw his strongest support behind a health insurance bill. But the CES, which had started off with much noise about health insurance, now remained ominously silent.[51]

Sydenstricker and Falk might have secretly sympathized with the sentiments of these reformers in March, but by the early summer of 1935, even they had realized that immediate congressional introduction of health insurance legislation might seriously endanger the chances for passage of the Social Security Bill. Sydenstricker wrote to Witte in May that although he felt that the immediate publication of the Health Insurance Report of the cabinet committee would change the minds of many doctors, he did not want the report released until "the present Economic Security Bill is out of the way because it might gum up the works a bit." [52] And in fact the Social Security Bill without health insurance had encountered unexpected difficulty in Congress.[53]

Such difficulties seem to confirm the wisdom of the Administration's policy of pigeonholing the Health Insurance Report of the Committee on Economic Security. Indeed, the strength of anti-insurance feeling in Congress is illustrated by the action taken by the House Ways and Means Committee to delete the words *health insurance* from the list of topics on which the bill authorized the Social Security Board to conduct research.[54]

Signs of the strength of anti-insurance sentiment in Congress continued to grow and apparently convinced the President that the whole issue was too politically explosive to keep in open view. Roosevelt therefore retreated further and withdrew his consent to the revised plan of having the Cabinet Committee's Health Insurance Report released after the passage of the Social Security Act. Instead he took a wait-and-see attitude and effectively removed health insurance from the public arena by secretly referring the Health Insurance Report and its revised Letter of Transmittal to the Social Security Board for further research.[55]

A large and perhaps crucial part in the defeat of compulsory health insurance in the CES was played by the nation's medical societies. Indeed, the AMA, the national leader of these professional groups, might be singled out as probably the most important force in the anti-insurance faction. Using its power both inside and outside the medical profession, it first upset the reformers at the round table discussion and then delayed and defeated their plans in the Medical Advisory Committee and the Committee on Economic Security as a whole.

To interpret these actions as symptoms of a purely negative policy toward all reform, however, would be misleading. The AMA and its constituent societies were indeed deathly afraid of government health insurance and opposed it in every way they could. But the more powerful medical leaders realized that a permanent hostility to all reforms would probably alienate the public and make governmental health insurance inevitable. They therefore used the period during which the CES was considering health insurance to begin moving AMA policy toward what they called moderate medical care reform.[56]

Most of the leaders of the AMA House of Delegates and Board of Trustees seemed to realize that the crisis in medical care which faced the nation in the early 1930's called for some sort of large-scale action. They wanted only such action as would be ethical and supervised, if not controlled, by the medical profession. The cabinet committee's plans, like those of the CCMC majority's report before it, did not meet these requirements and therefore had to be opposed. At the same time the real need for reform required that some acceptable medical society alternatives had to be introduced.[57] Whether as the result of economic pressures, public demand, or a political decision to "steal the thunder" of the compulsory health insurance advocates, these leaders introduced one such alternative plan to the 1934 AMA House of Delegates. This program, which soon passed the House and became known as the "AMA Ten Principles" (see appendix B) was intended to induce and guide local medical society experiments in new forms of medical care distribution.

The program demanded that any medical service plan be "under the control of the medical profession," and that the medical profession be solely responsible for the character of the medical service thus provided. Free choice of doctor by patients and preservation of the traditional, confidential doctor-patient relationship were insisted upon as fundamental. The medical profession was also to control all medical phases of institutional care, and all qualified doctors in an area were to be permitted to participate in these programs. Medical benefits should be separated from cash benefits, and the medically indigent should be defined as only those below the "comfort level" standard of income. The patient was to pay the immediate cost for service at the time it was purchased no matter how he was later reimbursed for these expenses by the medical care plan.[58]

While it is not inconceivable that the health insurance proposals of the AALL in 1916, the CCMC in 1932, and the CES in 1935 could have been made to conform to the "Ten Principles," the entire thrust of these medical society recommendations was in a direction quite different from those proposals. The "Ten Principles," as interpreted by the leaders of the organized medical profession, were guidelines for the establishment of group payment indemnity plans to be controlled in all respects by the local medical societies. Governmental programs and private group practice clinics were both still seen as unacceptable—the former because of necessary lay intervention in the doctor-patient relationship and the setting of standards, and the latter because of the restrictive nature of professional memberships.[59]

The Technical Committee on Medical Care and most other health insurance advocates did not seem to understand how the AMA was interpreting its own "Ten Principles." The pro-insurance reformers' analysis of the "Ten Principles" led them to conclude overoptimistically that certain leaders of the AMA were willing to have government participation in a widespread and permanent health insurance program. This misunderstanding explains why in 1934 and early 1935, Sydenstricker seemed to believe unrealistically that the passage of the "Ten Principles" meant that the AMA would soon actively cooperate with the Medical Advisory Committee in shaping a federal-state health insurance proposal.[60]

In retrospect it is clear that the AMA steadfastly opposed the cabinet committee's plans beginning in August 1934. In that month the association's publicity organs began carrying out a House of Delegates directive that doctors fight "socialized medicine" (that is, the expected committee proposals), and these publications were loudly critical of the formation and proposed agenda of the cabinet committee. The *Journal* warned that the organized medical profession might be ignored in the deliberations and decisions of the cabinet committee and instead urged gradualism under the "Ten Principles." It expressed the hope that the "government would seek the advice of the medical profession," and shortly thereafter the first wave of doctors' protest letters were sent to the cabinet committee and the President.[61]

Perhaps because Sydenstricker believed that the *Journal* was controlled by a reactionary and unrepresentative clique, he tended to discount its role as spokesman for the majority of the profession. His comments to Witte during these weeks (October 1934) indicate that he may have believed that a real split existed between the conservatives within the AMA hierarchy and the bulk of the profession. The continued editorial attacks and the bombardment of anti-insurance and anti-cabinet-committee letters did not disturb him; he probably thought they were only the expressions of a small but vocal group of AMA leaders.[62]

The effectiveness of the November truce of hostile criticism seems to have convinced Sydenstricker that his interpretation of the AMA was right. The *Journal* respected the agreement that the Technical Committee and the Medical Advisory Committee should not be personally attacked, and it treated the topic of government planning for compulsory health insurance in a neutral way. The volume of protest letters also dropped drastically, giving Sydenstricker further seeming proof of his theory.[63]

But while the November truce and the decline in letters were significant, they were not at all symptomatic of the split in medical opinion imagined by Sydenstricker. The agreement, as described above, was only a tactic to retain the loyalty of a few restive members of the Medical Advisory Committee. The decline in letters was the logical result of the truce: the rank and file of the medical societies were relying on the *Journal* for information and interpretation of the cabinet committee's activities, and when it grew silent, so did most potential letter writers.[64]

The interpretation of Sydenstricker and allies notwithstanding, the leadership of the AMA was in fact unanimously opposed to any CES action on compulsory health insurance. When the "Eleven Principles" of health insurance was released by the CES in late January, the AMA leaders reacted sharply. The *Journal* criticized the proposed Economic Security Bill and warned that the submission of the Technical Committee on Medical Care's final report on March 1st would probably signal the beginning of a successful legislative battle for federal health insurance. It pleaded with its readers to present their opinions on this issue to the Medical Advisory Committee, and shortly thereafter the barrage of letters and telegrams resumed.[65]

The AMA's actions seem to indicate that the medical leaders at this time did not know that health insurance had already been effectively eliminated from consideration with the Economic Security Bill by Witte and Miss Perkins. They feared that there was a real possibility of a health insurance amendment to the impending bill. In order to defeat such an action, the AMA Trustees requested the calling of an extraordinary special session of the House of Delegates early in 1935 to consider and restate policy on compulsory health insurance.[66]

This Special Session of the House of Delegates met in Chicago on February 15th and 16th. It immediately established a Special Reference Committee to consider policies concerning state medicine, compulsory health insurance, and group payment for medical care. The report of this select committee was supposed to clarify the opposition of the AMA to the expected recommendations of the CES Technical Committee on Medical Care, and at the same time to advance the AMA's new campaign for professionally controlled experiments in group payment plans. The AMA leaders hoped that these tactics would simultaneously win the loyalty of those few renegade medical societies which had urged cooperation in the shaping of compulsory plans and give the *coup de grâce* to the unacceptable CES health insurance proposals. Thus, it was hoped the medical societies would regain the initiative from the pro-insurance reformers.[67]

The report of the Special Reference Committee conformed to the leadership's expectations. It enumerated current AMA policy in six points:

1. The AMA continues to oppose state medicine except for public health and military medicine.
2. The AMA sees "many inconsistencies and incompatibilities" in the Health Insurance section of the Report of the CES and urges further detailed study before any action is taken.
3. The AMA opposes government subsidies to lay bureaus for purposes of creating and administering medical programs.
4. The AMA opposes the lack of legal provision for inclusion of a medical doctor on the proposed Social Security Board.
5. The AMA opposes the state health insurance plan of the American Association for Social Security.
6. The AMA urges local medical societies to experiment with new plans for the provision of medical care under the policies stated in the "Ten Principles" and with the cooperation of the Bureau of Medical Economics of the AMA. The AMA instructs the Bureau of Medical Economics to prepare model skeleton plans of such programs for submission to the regular session of the House of Delegates in June 1935 and the AMA:
   a. reiterates its belief that no single plan for the provision of medical care can be successfully applied to all localities in the United States and;
   b. states that hospital bills and medical bills must be administratively separate in any acceptable plan.[68]

Late in February, after the special session of the House of Delegates, the AMA *Journal* began a series of editorials which reiterated these criticisms and policy statements. Other AMA agencies soon joined this anti-insurance campaign. The Bureau of Legal Medicine and Legislation actively lobbied against health insurance in Washington and kept in close touch with state and local legislative developments in medical care. The Bureau of Medical Economics prepared for a two-year fight against attempts to have health insurance programs enacted in the various states. Meanwhile, the Committee on Legislative Activities, the chief lobbying agency of the AMA, tried to align the specialty medical societies behind the AMA policy. It also initiated talks with the American Legion and the American Federation of Labor in order to set up a common front against compulsory health insurance legislation.[69] And in the middle of June 1935, the House of Delegates endorsed a two-year program of the Committee on Legislative Activities that was designed to defeat any "trial horse legislation" which the reformers might introduce.[70]

Compulsory health insurance failed in the Committee on Economic Security for two related reasons. The immediate cause was the superiority of the political tactics and strategy of the anti-insurance forces. The more fundamental cause was the lack of any broadly based public feeling that medical care needed a reform as drastic as compulsory health insurance seemed to be.

In the area of immediate strategy there are three ways to measure the political astuteness of any interest group, including those which fought over health insurance. First, interest groups inside and outside the government should know where the centers of political power are and who is able to use them. In simpler terms this means that the interested party should know which men and institutions have the most to say about the ultimate political fate of the proposal. Second, any political alliance should also be realistic in estimating the strengths and weaknesses of its opponents and should be willing and able to act on these estimates. And third, any group should be as united as possible within itself regarding its political and tactical decisions.

On first glance it appears that both the reformers and the organized medical profession knew where political power was and who was able to wield it. Sydenstricker correctly deduced that Witte and Perkins shared the responsibility for final cabinet committee policy with the President, and the leaders of the AMA made a similar discovery at a very early date. Acting on these assumptions Sydenstricker at one time appealed to the President for support over the head of Witte. The AMA similarly directed much of its protest to the cabinet committee and the President.

But on closer inspection it is seen that the AMA leadership had a far more sophisticated understanding of the factors which influenced political decisions on the health insurance issue. For example, they concentrated much of their pressure on the Medical Advisory Committee in order to use its inability to agree as a lever on Witte and Roosevelt. Sydenstricker did little but react to this attack; he did not use a corresponding tactic but merely appealed for the President's support. The AMA was able to finesse neatly these direct appeals to the President by predicting dangerous political repercussions if Roosevelt supported Sydenstricker and ignored the divided Medical Advisory Committee.

Though the effectiveness of this AMA tactic was dependent on the President's desire for unanimity in the cabinet committee proposals, its use also reflects a certain political awareness by the AMA of the immediate power structure. True, if that power structure had been different, perhaps the reformers would have finessed the AMA. But that is not really the issue. The organized medical profession did, in fact, outmaneuver the pro-insurance reformers in this struggle because they had a better understanding of the dynamics of the relevant political power structure.

On examining each group's evaluation of its opponent's strengths and weaknesses, we find that a different situation existed. Both sides apparently misinterpreted the other's weak points and implemented policies based on these miscalculations. The reformers understood the "Ten Principles" to mean that a large segment of the medical profession was willing to cooperate with the administration in the framing of a health insurance bill. They saw the opposition of certain AMA leaders as the obstructionist efforts of a small cabal of reactionary and small-minded men. The leaders of the AMA, on the other hand, saw the "Eleven Principles" of the January 1935 cabinet committee report as the work of a small band of powerful and unscrupulous men who were intent on remaking American medicine even if it meant destroying its greatness. These men, the doctors seemed to believe, had the ear of the administration and were going to use its power to rush health insurance through Congress.

Although both of these interpretations were incorrect, they were quite real to the men who held them and who made policies based upon them. And it is the policies which have to be judged for effectiveness. In this case, despite the fact that they were based on fallacious assumptions, the policies of the organized medical profession were more effective than the reformers' policies. The reformers, in estimating that a large group of doctors would cooperate, were overoptimistic. They were therefore easily thrown off balance when a large segment of the profession did not rally to the cabinet committee and their policy of cooperation proved almost worthless. The AMA leaders were, on the other hand, overpessimistic. They believed that the Technical Committee on Medical Care was more powerful than it actually was, and they shaped a policy to meet the envisioned rather than the real magnitude of its threat. When Witte and Roosevelt proved to be less committed to the Technical Committee than the AMA had believed, the doctors' basic policy was still sound and effective. Instead of being left with an inoperable, overoptimistic policy, the medical societies were in a position to press home their demands with overpowering force.

This mutual misinterpretation of each other's weaknesses points directly to the third attribute required for waging a successful political battle: the necessity for unity within one's own group and for knowledge of any internal division of the enemy. Here, too, the medical societies were much more perceptive than the reformers.

The reformers believed that the AMA was split over compulsory health insurance and unable to prevent local and specialist societies from bolting the conservative leadership. Indeed, prior to December 1934, they seemed to believe that the leadership might itself cooperate under pressure from its own members. The actual situation was quite different. The rank and file of the organized medical profession did not basically disagree with their conservative leadership; they looked to that leadership to protect the profession from disastrous government intervention. Although a few state and specialist societies temporarily diverged from the AMA policy, the vast majority of organized doctors was willing to let the AMA leaders conduct a fight against the health insurance proposals of the CES. Whether through fear of professional sanctions, doubt about economic conditions, or honest ideological conviction, they felt that the AMA should determine policy regarding both the cabinet committee proposals and acceptable medical care plans under the "Ten Principles." Most of them, therefore, did not support the cabinet committee or put pressure on their leaders to modify the AMA's anti-insurance policy.

The leaders of the AMA, on the other hand, correctly understood and exploited the divisions within the reformers' ranks. The Witte-Sydenstricker split of February 1935 was, after all, precipitated by Dr. Cushing's letter and Witte's response. And it should be remembered that the AMA's constant insistence that the entire Social Security Bill might be in danger if it included health insurance did nothing to bring Perkins, Roosevelt, and Witte closer to Sydenstricker and Falk. The reformers were clearly split over health insurance policy, and once the medical societies discovered this split, they did all they could to aggravate it.

While the failure of the health insurance reformers in the CES can thus be traced to their relative lack of political astuteness in comparison to that of the medical society leaders, this phenomenon did not mean that they were ready to surrender after their 1935 defeat. The reformers remained dedicated to their project, and in the following years they tried to correct their political deficiencies vis-à-vis the organized medical profession. When the struggle for compulsory health insurance was renewed a few years later, the medical societies were more evenly matched and a more bitter struggle ensued.

The most fundamental problem of the reformers, that of convincing the public that the problem of medical care demanded the enactment of health insurance, was not so easy to attack. The public would not support a far-reaching reform unless it was convinced that nothing milder could work. In the mid-1930's it was not yet at this point. Although it was increasingly aware of the failures of the existing medical care system, the public, as shall be seen, was willing to experiment with moderate reforms in the hope that these would solve the problems. While it was engaged in such experiments, it would not support the more radical, tradition-breaking device of compulsory health insurance.

The health insurance reformers either misunderstood or underestimated the public's unwillingness to support compulsory health insurance. In the struggle over health insurance in the CES, the reformers largely ignored the public and concentrated their efforts on the medical societies. Later, after their defeat in the cabinet committee, the reformers turned more and more of their efforts towards convincing the public that compulsory health insurance was the only way to solve medical care problems. However, even in these attempts, the reformers misunderstood the public. The reformers' logic, educational efforts, and rhetoric could only go so far. Before the average American would act he would have to feel that a real crisis existed. Until that condition was reached, the forces and interest groups which aligned themselves against compulsory health insurance could continue to win; and, until that time, the reformers could only perfect their ideas, organize themselves and their supporters, establish liaisons with persons in power, and impatiently await their time.

3

Voices from the Hinterland 1932–1943

The American system of medical care underwent a period of prolonged and widespread crisis during the 1930's, since at bottom it was only the system of the 1920's immeasurably exacerbated by the economic chaos of the Great Depression. The same problems of escalating capital needs and training requirements, lopsided distribution of medical facilities and personnel, and inability of many individuals to purchase adequate care privately were at the root of the crises; the unemployment, deflation, and uncertainty of the depression years only accentuated these basic flaws.

The public became increasingly concerned about medical care during this depression decade. To most people it remained a personal not a social problem, which required personal not social remedies. However, public interest, together with the desperate need for effective action, did produce a series of private and public medical care programs. These plans were usually unrelated to one another, but often had certain features in common. First, the proposals and programs were reactions to the immediate medical crisis. Except for a few long-term reforms which were defended as being also applicable to the short-term emergency, all the programs and proposals were seen as solutions to current depression-caused dislocations in medical care. Second, they were usually limited in their intended impact and envisioned scope. Most were created as emergency mobilizations of community or government resources to meet local or regional crises. Third, they were experimental and pragmatic. Based on existing facilities and ideas, these plans usually introduced only one or two new concepts and were constantly changed, amended, or modified to meet problems more effectively. The groups who sponsored or participated in them usually saw them as nothing more than practical ways of remedying existing problems. Consequently, most of these programs were judged mainly on their effectiveness in specific situations.

Programs that solved real problems in medical care distribution and, in addition, were least disruptive to the traditional medical care system won public and professional support and survived. Those which failed to solve problems effectively or which seemed to disrupt the medical care system too radically were rejected and failed. By the end of the 1930's several programs were firmly established and promised to become permanent. More important, they pointed toward a restructuring of medical care which was to alter fundamentally the efficiency and utility of that system.

The growth and evolution of these programs significantly changed the task of the compulsory health insurance reformers. Before the appearance of these programs, they had to educate the public and the medical profession to the viability of *any* proposal. But after these plans became operative, they could be used as examples of how new and more radical proposals might work. The reformers by and large sensed this phenomenon and because they hoped both to make their own task easier and to use these measures to ease some of the nation's pressing medical problems, they usually cooperated with and assisted in the creation and development of these limited plans.

In sum, the collective impact of the experimental, limited programs was exceptionally significant: they helped ease the depression's medical crisis; they reshaped the nation's health care system; and they gave the public and the medical profession knowledge and experience with new ways of delivering medical care. The practical experience thus gained, more than any theoretical argument or educational campaign, affected the developing struggle for enactment of compulsory health insurance. After such experience, millions began to understand that the changes which compulsory health insurance would precipitate did not need to be overly radical. They also began to realize that compulsory health insurance was based on a new concept of individual freedom, which was acceptable to them and their modern industrial society. Slowly and cautiously, the American public started to accept the less radical arguments of the reformers as they applied to limited programs; slowly and cautiously, the reformers were able to reshape their strategy to gain and try to hold this new support.

The reformers, looking for ways to aid the expansion of the limited programs, turned to private foundations, pressure groups, government agencies, and other organizations that had been sympathetic to their cause in earlier years. The private foundations, several of which had supported the work of the Committee on the Costs of Medical Care, were important reform strongholds. For example, in the 1930's the Milbank Memorial Fund (under the direction of Edgar Sydenstricker) sponsored several local and regional plans which reorganized distribution of and payment for medical care. The Twentieth Century Fund made itself available as an adviser to voluntary health insurance plans which were organized so that groups of doctors could provide medical service to groups of consumers at prices which could generally be afforded. The Julius Rosenwald Fund, under the direction of Michael M. Davis, took interest in various cooperative medicine experiments and subsidized research and experimentation in voluntary group hospitalization insurance.[1]

Because their activities were limited and the seriousness of the medical care emergency was publicly recognized, the foundations were able to continue their research efforts and experiments for the most part without more than verbal opposition from the organized medical profession.[2] The foundations' leaders and personnel were thus able to produce and circulate a vast amount of educational material on new forms of medical care. This information, along with the experience and knowledge of the participating reformers, was then available to governmental and private groups interested in establishing medical care programs for various segments of the population. In the early 1930's they cooperated in drafting the medical relief program of New York State's Temporary Emergency Relief Administration, helped the still struggling voluntary hospitalization insurance movement get underway, and supplied advisory personnel to the federal government in the fields of medical relief and health insurance.[3]

Most of the foundations did not actively participate in political lobbying for compulsory health insurance on the state and national levels because they realized that if they were identified with that reform by the organized medical profession their effectiveness in the immediate crisis would be hampered.[4] Although many of them had the support of social workers, social scientists, and public health experts who favored compulsory health insurance, and although many of their staffs were privately committed to the enactment of this reform, they chose not to participate in the kind of public pressure tactics which had been undertaken by the American Association for Labor Legislation before World War I. Instead, they concentrated on the immediate and limited educational campaigns which they hoped would eventually arouse wide public support.[5]

Because the foundations refused to endorse and overtly work for compulsory health insurance, the pro-insurance reformers had to turn for this task to separate pressure groups. The first, the Survey Associates, contained many individuals who were interested in the enactment of social welfare programs. It devoted most of its energy to the investigation of materials touching on this topic, and to the publication of its results in two periodicals, the *Survey Graphic* and the *Survey Mid-Monthly*.[6] Survey Associates Editor Paul Kellogg and the other members of the Associates' staff actively participated with other reformers in shaping and supporting governmental efforts for reform. For example, Mr. Kellogg was elected vice chairman of the Advisory Council of the Committee on Economic Security in 1934, and he played a crucial role in determining and executing that council's policies. He also served on numerous other advisory councils, was a delegate to the National Health Conference of 1938, and, together with his aides, spent considerable time lobbying for the passage of social welfare legislation of all types.[7]

Although many reformers openly supported and worked with the Survey Associates, large numbers were unable to participate openly because of their official positions in foundations or the government. The organization therefore acted to a certain extent as their pseudo-political agent. I. S. Falk, for example, could write an "educational" article on health insurance for the *Survey Graphic* and support Kellogg's activities on behalf of that reform while he could not himself engage in unauthorized open lobbying or propagandizing as an employee of the Social Security Board. Similar situations existed for Josephine Roche, I. M. Rubinow, and Harold Ickes.[8]

The other openly pro-insurance pressure group which some of the health insurance reformers supported during these years was the American Association for Social Security (AASS). Founded in the 1920's by Abraham Epstein as the American Association for Old Age Security, the AASS concentrated almost exclusively on compulsory old age insurance and pensions before the passage of the Social Security Act of 1935.[9] Under the fiery leadership of Epstein, it played a significant role in shaping most aspects of that comprehensive legislation, and then, after 1935, it expanded its attentions to include other reforms such as health insurance.[10]

The AASS was similar in administrative organization and methods of operation to the AALL. Though its membership included I. M. Rubinow, Jane Addams, and many other members of the Survey Associates, for example, these people played a relatively small part in shaping actual policies. Abraham Epstein, the executive secretary and editor of the AASS journal, *Social Security,* was, like John B. Andrews of the AALL, the guiding spirit of his group. In a real sense he *was* the association, for his own opinions and philosophy rather than those of the membership guided his policy decisions. His lobbying activities and his written and spoken statements on behalf of the

AASS were formulated by him alone, and, not infrequently, their content and vehemence irritated some of the more influential AASS members.[11] In 1934 and 1935, for example, the AASS, in consultation with the staff of the Milbank Fund, drafted its Model State Health Insurance Bill. Although I. S. Falk and other experts worked closely with Epstein on the project, Epstein was able to shape the bill according to his own wishes. The bill called for the creation of a health insurance system which was similar to the one in the old 1915 Model Bill of the AALL and which by the 1930's was considered antiquated by experts such as Falk.[12] Epstein rejected this criticism, pressed his own version of the Model Bill, and had it introduced in the Congress and in several state legislatures. There it continually antagonized a large number of doctors and did obvious damage to the cause of compulsory health insurance, but Epstein refused to back down and withdraw or modify it.[13]

Epstein's attitudes led to an unfortunate relationship between him and the majority of the well-known health insurance reformers that continued to disrupt the compulsory health insurance movement until Epstein's death in 1943. Although Epstein no doubt was sincere in his efforts on behalf of the Model Bill, the net effect of his activities was to divide and weaken the movement as a whole. His unfulfilled desire to have a major public role in drafting and administering the Social Security Act and his frustrated dream of being leader of the health insurance crusade in the United States led him to participate in bitter, internecine battles with other health insurance reformers, which helped to expose the entire movement to attacks from opposing forces. "A great propagandizer, but a poor team worker," Epstein became a "sad and lonely person" by the end of the 1930's.[14] Committed to personal triumph and to an outmoded plan for reform, he had failed to grow and develop with the changing currents of the health insurance battle of the 1930's.

The crisis in American medical care, which encouraged the reformers in their use of pressure groups and pro-insurance foundations, also encouraged them to support a series of autonomous health insurance movements within several states. The nationally oriented reformers worked closely with, supported, and often guided the local leaders of pro-insurance pressure groups in Michigan, California, Wisconsin, Massachusetts, and New York. In each campaign the national and local reformers tried to use public concern about the existing medical care crisis as a basis for passing effective statewide health insurance legislation. In responding to requests for advice, the Social Security Board and the pro-insurance foundations helped to coordinate the strategies of the various state health insurance movements.

In most states the local reformers first agitated for appointing a legislative investigating commission. They next presented evidence on the need for health insurance to the commission. Finally, they tried to align legislative support behind the proposed bill. In each case they tried to win the support and cooperation of the organized medical profession of the state, hoping, thus, to avoid the disastrous effects of the mistakes of the AALL campaign. Such cooperation was difficult to get and preserve; yet without it the reform movements were doomed.

Developments in Michigan during this period illustrate some important features of this pattern. In the early 1930's a liberal faction had gained control of the state medical society and had begun to move towards a cautious endorsement of compulsory health insurance. These doctors, led by Henry Luce, consulted with lay experts and sponsored a study of health insurance by Luce and Nathan Sinai. By 1933 they seemed ready to give official support to at least a limited form of compulsory insurance.[15] However, the period of lay-professional cooperation ended before it could lead to legislative action. In 1934 the conservative faction of the state medical society began to regain control, and it immediately called for a postponement of any society policy statements on compulsory health insurance. Simultaneously the AMA began an intensive campaign against the liberal leaders who had sponsored the reform recommendations—a campaign aimed at the intimidation of men such as

Dr. Luce and at the turning of the Michigan society against compulsory health insurance. By 1935 these joint antireform efforts had proven successful: Sinai and the liberal wing of the medical society had been forced to turn their support from compulsory insurance to voluntary plans of indemnity insurance for medical expenses.[16]

The course of the health insurance campaign in California was somewhat different from that in Michigan. Experience with group clinics and unscrupulous private health insurance companies, accentuated by the economic pressures of the depression, had created wide public and legislative interest in compulsory health insurance in the early 1930's. Partly in anticipation of a favorable report on compulsory insurance by a state senate investigating committee, and partly out of a sincere desire to see the development of a mild form of compulsory health insurance, the House of Delegates of the California State Medical Association actually endorsed compulsory health insurance in March of 1935.[17] This apparent victory for the reform forces was limited and ultimately negated by the nature of the medical society endorsement. While the majority of the society's members indicated that they supported compulsory health insurance, they also specified that such insurance was to be restricted to certain population groups and was to be under the control of the medical profession itself. The medical society, by thus limiting the conditions of its endorsement, divided the state's medical profession and antagonized many of the lay reformers. In the confusion which followed, the state medical society emerged as the strongest faction and succeeded in having its conditions written into the bills being presented to the state legislature during the late 1930's. This in turn deepened the antagonism of the opposition and led to the killing of these bills in legislative committee. Within a few years the struggle dissolved as public attention shifted from compulsory insurance to the new experiments in nonprofit hospitalization and medical indemnity insurance organized on a voluntary group basis.[18]

The course of events in Wisconsin and Massachusetts differed from those in both Michigan and California. In Wisconsin the state medical society maintained a steadfast opposition to compulsory health insurance throughout the 1930's. Although the bill which Socialist State Representative Andrew Biemiller had introduced was similar in many ways to the AALL bill which the medical society had endorsed before 1920, the society opposed the new one with an intensive campaign of lobbying and public education. The efforts of organized labor, Milwaukee socialists, and consumer cooperatives to get the bill passed were repeatedly defeated by the state medical society and its allies, and attempts to pass either it or related health bills were abandoned in the late 1930's.[19] In Massachusetts there were also repeated efforts to have the state legislature consider health and temporary disability insurance through floor debate on specific bills or through the establishment of an investigative commission. These attempts consistently met with failure, however, for the anti-insurance forces succeeded in having all such proposals tabled in committee.[20]

Whether because public interest was greater or because state legislators were more determined and persistent, the New York State health insurance campaign came much closer to success than the one in Massachusetts. Assemblyman Robert Wagner, Jr., the son of the U.S. Senator, introduced a bill to establish a state commission on health insurance in 1938. Working with personnel from the Social Security Board, Wagner guided his proposal through the legislature and saw it gain both public and legislative support. In 1938 a Temporary Legislative Commission to Formulate a Long-range State Health Program was created and ordered to report by May 1939.[21] Its report urged continued study of compulsory health insurance and public medical care by an enlarged commission. The following year the expanded agency called for a limited system of state compulsory health insurance, and the issue was placed on the state ballot for a popular referendum. The voters overwhelmingly endorsed it, but the coming of war delayed and ultimately defeated this movement for reform. By 1942 New Yorkers were experimenting with voluntary hospitalization and indemnity insurance and were losing interest in the proposed compulsory system.[22]

The reformers also worked through federal, state, and local governments, which were launching emergency medical programs to meet many of the same immediate problems that pressure groups and foundations were concerned with. The reformers expected that such emergency programs would provide fertile ground for broadly based experiments in new forms of medical care.

The governmental activities fell into two basic groups: programs which provided medical care to the needy as part of a general *direct relief* system; and those which provided medical care to certain population groups as one ramification of a fundamentally different area of concern. The first category of program included those administered by the Federal Emergency Relief Administration (FERA) and the state and local relief authorities, while the second group included those sponsored by the Civil Works Administration (CWA), the Works Progress Administration (WPA), and the Farm Security Administration (FSA). The relief programs which included medical care components were a new device for meeting the health problems of the indigent. The existing structure and philosophy of most American programs for supplying medical care to the needy had been inherited from the English Poor Laws system. From colonial times to the 1930's, the local governments, and later some states, took sole financial and administrative responsibility for the provision of medical care to the indigent. Like more general forms of direct relief, medical services tended to be of uneven quality and were usually surrounded with residence requirements as well as an unpleasant aura of charity. The county or city officials often hired a county or town doctor, or paid the bills for emergency care of the local sick poor from the general tax fund, thus relieving themselves and their constituents of further concern or responsibility.[23]

Gradual public acceptance of the theory that adequate medical care was a right of every citizen and the massive economic and social dislocations caused by the depression had undermined this traditional system of medical relief by the mid-1930's. The existence of millions of "decent" unemployed, falling state and local revenues, and a growing conviction that individual financial status should not affect the quality of care received forced many states and localities to re-examine and change their system of providing medical care to the needy.[24]

New York was one of the first states to undertake reorganization of its medical care program for the needy. With the advice of Frances Perkins and Harry Hopkins, the administration of Governor Franklin Roosevelt established in the early 1930's a system which used the family physicians of relief clients to provide needed medical care. The New York Temporary Emergency Relief Administration supervised and paid for this care, and it negotiated and cooperated with the state medical society in making policy decisions and establishing administrative procedures. By 1933 New York City had established a similar program for its needy residents, and other states were beginning to study the New York system with some interest.[25]

After Roosevelt became President in 1933, the major outlines of this system were adopted by the federal government. The Federal Emergency Relief Administration was designed and created to provide federal funds to the state and local governments for most forms of direct relief. But shortly after the FERA started its programs, Harry Hopkins found that federal contributions to the states for direct relief were not being used to provide adequate medical care to eligible recipients. After consultations with representatives of the AMA and various federal agencies, Hopkins issued on September 10, 1933, FERA "Rules and Regulations No. 7" to remedy the situation.[26]

FERA "Rules and Regulations No. 7 Governing Medical Care Provided in the Homes of the Recipients of Medical Care Relief" established a set of rules for the provision of emergency nursing, dental, and nonhospital medical care. The state relief administration and the state and local medical societies were to agree on uniform policies which would provide the same types of basic services available to private patients. Because of the limited amount of funds available to the relief agencies, these plans were to provide only a "minimum of such services" consistent with good professional judgment.[27]

"Rules and Regulations No. 7" made it clear that each state and local relief agency should have a uniform administrative plan, that responsibility for the establishment and policing of such programs was given to the state emergency relief administrations, and that the programs were to be open to all licensed personnel in the individual states. Each plan was to have maximum limits to care for acute and chronic illnesses and was supposed to "augment and render more adequate facilities already existing in the community" rather than finance existing programs in the absence of adequate state or local funds.[28]

The early confusion and unevenness of the FERA medical relief program were only moderately relieved by the issuance of "Rules and Regulations No. 7." For the two years following the directive problems of all sorts appeared and participating doctors, administrators, and relief recipients accumulated a growing list of grievances.[29] The AMA complained about lay control and sought a larger voice in making medical policy. State, local, and national health officials and administrators demanded that a full-time medical director be appointed. Related professions, such as osteopathy and chiropracty, demanded that they be included in the program, and Negro physicians complained about being excluded from participation in certain southern states. Various state emergency relief administrations began to quarrel with state and local medical societies or with the regional or state representatives of FERA, and the national administrators were called upon to mediate these differences of opinion.[30] The problems were compounded by the administrative chaos which accompanied the attempts of the FERA to help millions in a few months. For example, by April 1934, forty-six states were receiving federal funds for medical care relief, but only fifteen of these had filed copies of their programs in Washington as required by "Rules and Regulations No. 7."[31]

Handicapped by these weaknesses and problems, the FERA

medical care program continued in operation until the Roosevelt administration decided to stop all direct relief grants to the states on November 1, 1935. Many reformers protested that this action would leave welfare clients without adequate funds to purchase medical care and would financially overburden the states, but Harry Hopkins, under orders from an economy-minded president, discontinued the program. The federal government, it was decided, would pay for the medical care of only those groups which it had supported prior to 1933.[32]

During its hectic existence the FERA program achieved both positive and negative results in its attempt to provide medical care to a large fraction of the population. On the positive side, cooperation and mutual understanding between physicians, public health officials, and relief workers were no doubt increased in many areas, as was the public awareness of the scope of the problem of medical care for the needy. Many communities were acquainted with the concept of medical care as a right of every individual for the first time. Large numbers of doctors learned that the government could be trusted to administer medical care programs fairly, and discovered that the profession could preserve its identity and value system under such programs. And, not of least importance, millions of Americans received needed medical care from a local family physician—care which they otherwise might not have received.[33] On the negative side, the quality of medical care provided varied from area to area, as did the soundness of its local administrative units and their economical use of program funds. Hospital and relief administrators, doctors, and relief recipients all complained of arbitrary, wasteful, and unwise administration, spotty quality control, and endless mountains of bureaucratic red tape. Local and professional policies also damaged the program as did the limitation on available funds. Medical services were often not adequately coordinated under the program, and friction between relief administrators and the medical profession crippled the program in several areas.[34]

That the FERA program had a very real impact on American

medical care was made apparent after the program was discontinued in 1935. When the federal relief subsidies were stopped the quality and quantity of medical care provided for the indigent declined. Those few states that tried to continue the program with their own funds found their financing insufficient for more than a few months' operation. In the 1930's it seemed that without federal aid, adequate and effective medical care programs for the needy were impossible.[35]

While the federal government was providing medical care through the direct relief facilities of FERA, other agencies within the government were initiating medical care programs as part of their more general and nondirect relief functions. The Works Progress Administration and the Farm Security Administration were the two principal ones. Although neither saw provision of medical care as its primary goal or openly strove to use its medical care program to lay the groundwork for a compulsory health insurance system, both agencies were willing to experiment and improvise in order to maintain high health standards among those parts of the population they served. The health insurance reformers welcomed these programs because they saw them as providing needed services and as forerunners of a permanent federal health insurance program.

The Works Progress Administration was created in 1935 after the Roosevelt administration decided to provide work relief to the employable indigent and return responsibility for the unemployable indigent to the states. Those on the WPA rolls were considered employees of the federal government and as such received subsistence wages with which they were supposed to purchase all necessities, but they were not entitled to the full benefits of the United States Employees Compensation Act, and they had no right to medical care on the basis of need. If unable to pay for medical care from their wages, they were expected to seek it at the free public clinics maintained by hospitals and state and local governments.[36]

Although limited and restricted in these ways, the WPA indirectly provided valuable medical services for its needy enrollees. WPA workers were instrumental in gathering data for the National Health Survey of 1935–1936, which was directed by the Public Health Service and upon which so much of the National Health Program was ultimately to be based. The program helped provide labor to build and improve many clinics, medical centers, diagnostic laboratories, and hospitals, and it assigned personnel to assist the regular staffs perform their clerical and housekeeping duties.[37] The WPA also participated in locally planned medical projects which had a more immediate and noticeable effect on the life and health of much of the needy population, such as mass innoculations, dental health projects, examinations of school children, and research efforts in the field of medical care and public health.[38]

The WPA health programs continued in existence through 1943, although after 1940 they were primarily oriented towards the national defense effort. They provided some medical facilities and services to millions of Americans and helped acquaint the public, the medical profession, and the state and local governments with some of the possibilities of federal cooperation in the distribution of medical care to certain population groups.[39]

The Farm Security Administration medical care program also helped educate many individuals to the advantages of selective federal participation in medical care programs. Beginning in 1935 the Resettlement Administration tried to meet medical problems first, by attempting to provide adequate medical services to the new resettlement communities through group payment for medical services, and second, by providing loans to its noncommunity clients, part of which could be used for contributions to cooperative medical service plans created and administered by the clients themselves. When the FSA took over and expanded the functions of the Resettlement Administration in 1937, it decided to enlarge the medical care program as rapidly as possible.[40]

The early pattern established by the Resettlement Administration was modified and amended during the early years of the FSA. The resettlement community medical program proved unsatisfactory and was quickly abandoned, but the cooperative medical care program based on loans proved popular and was rapidly expanded with only minor modification. Under these cooperative plans clients in a local area negotiated an agreement with the local medical society with the aid of the FSA staff. In return for an annual payment to the cooperative, the clients were guaranteed needed medical service for the current year. The local medical society agreed to provide this care at a fixed fee scale and to accept pro rata division of funds if the cooperative's resources proved inadequate for that year.[41]

The cooperative plans sponsored by the FSA received a great stimulus for expansion from the drought which hit the middle west in 1936–1937. Hundreds of thousands of farm families were rendered unable to purchase medical care in the traditional way, and many rural doctors were unable to collect fees for the services they were called upon to provide. In the face of this crisis, the program of medical cooperatives mushroomed.[42] Cooperative plans spread from the Dakotas to the south and west. Eventually they existed in eighty-eight different counties in forty-three separate states. In the peak year of 1943, over half a million persons were covered by cooperatives—persons who otherwise would have found it difficult to purchase needed medical care for themselves and their families.[43]

The effects of the FSA cooperative medical care program were widespread and lasting. Although wartime pressures and postwar legislative changes brought the program gradually to an end in 1947, participation in this program was the first experience many rural families, government officials, and rural physicians had had with group prepayment for medical care. Like many of the urban workers who had benefited from the FERA and WPA programs during these years, the participants in FSA programs were quick to realize that the voluntary non-profit medical and hospitalization insurance plans which were gaining popularity during the 1940's were similar to the governmental programs in which they had just been enrolled. For that reason participation in the voluntary plans was considered desirable by these groups, and they joined in large numbers.[44]

While the health insurance reformers were busy with the efforts of the foundations, the pressure groups, and the government agencies, an extremely important series of events in which they were not directly involved was taking place. The private sector of society began to experiment with new forms of medical care to meet the emergency. Programs were started that seemed to solve some of the problems of medical care distribution without surrendering too much of the doctor's or patient's freedom. Because they proved more acceptable than either the traditional system which no longer worked, or the new and often radical solutions proposed by the reformers, they kept gaining public support. Thus, these programs, rather than those of the government supported by the reformers, had the greatest impact on the pattern of American medical care in the postdepression years.

Voluntary private efforts were of three basic types: cooperative medical care plans established and administered by lay groups; plans for budgeting of medical expenses under the control of the organized medical profession and limited to specific income groups; and private nonprofit hospitalization insurance plans covering certain broad groups of the population. Variations of each approach were tried in various sections of the country under differing economic and social conditions, and, not surprisingly, they met with varying degrees of success.

Cooperative medical care plans had first received national attention during the 1920's with the research and recommendations of the CCMC. Under cooperative plans participating members paid annual fees into funds which were controlled by membership-elected boards of directors. The fees were used by the boards to hire physicians and other professional personnel, build or rent medical facilities, and administer the plans. In return for their fee prepayments, the participating members were eligible to receive as much of the specified categories of medical care as they needed from the cooperatives during the current year.[45]

The cooperative plans differed from traditional contract

practice or corporate medicine in several ways. Since the participating physicians were full-time employees, they were not confronted with the same pressure of choosing between contract and private patients which doctors participating in part-time lodge or contract practice often faced. Physicians were protected from the exploitative practices of profit-making corporate medicine because the cooperatives were nonprofit and because the patients had ultimate control over the entire plan. The latter feature also protected the patient from exploitation.[46]

The first significant cooperative medical care plans began to appear in the United States in the mid-1930's in response to the medical care crisis. Dr. Michael Shadid, in cooperation with the Oklahoma Farmers' Union, launched one of the earliest attempts in Elk City, Oklahoma in 1932. The Farmers' Union Cooperative Hospital at first encountered strong opposition from the medical societies and some local politicians, but by 1936 Shadid and his backers managed to establish a successful and expanding cooperative plan.[47]

The Elk City Plan was in many ways a pioneering effort. Its approach and organization were studied and to a certain extent copied by the Resettlement Administration. The success of the Elk City Cooperative was also largely responsible for the formation in 1936 of the Bureau of Cooperative Medicine by the Cooperative League of the United States. Under the directorship of Dr. Kingsley Roberts, the bureau tried to advise groups interested in establishing medical cooperatives and attempted to coordinate the efforts of existing plans in the United States.[48]

Although most medical care cooperatives were meeting with only small local successes during these years, one, the Group Health Association (GHA), was growing fast and becoming the center of a nationwide controversy over cooperative medicine. The GHA had been established in response to the financial problems that many government employees were encountering in paying for medical care, and it rapidly gained members and operating funds during its first years of existence. Fearful that its imminent success might prove dangerous, local and national medical societies undertook a campaign designed to obstruct

GHA's attempts to hire qualified doctors or to use the existing hospital or medical facilities in the Washington area. By 1938 an antitrust conspiracy suit against the AMA and some of its officers was filed. The legal action was won in 1939, and the door was opened for the continued formation and expansion of cooperative plans across the nation.[49]

Cooperative medical plans continued to be formed after 1939, but their public appeal and ability to provide comprehensive medical care to the entire population were severely limited. The general opposition of the medical societies to cooperative plans, even when legal, remained a significant handicap to cooperatives, such as the Health Insurance Plan of Greater New York and the Community Health Association of Detroit. Also, the exclusion of all nongroup individuals and of those unable to pay the annual fees made the cooperative of limited, but important, usefulness.[50]

Another type of private medical care program was started during the 1930's by the organized medical profession. Aware of some of the needs and demands for medical care reform, the medical societies launched a series of programs under their own control. They hoped to provide effective solutions to many of the more pressing problems while preserving the traditions and forms which they believed both patients and physicians held dear. The voluntary medical care programs undertaken in these crisis years by the medical societies were of widely varying types, and for a time they remained of only local or regional significance.[51] The plans fell into several categories: those which permitted patients of small means to budget their individual medical bills *after* they had been incurred, and those which were open to the middle class and incorporated group *prepayment* as an integral part of their organization.

The budget plans, of which the Detroit Medical Service Bureau was a leading example, in effect merely transferred the responsibility for the collection of fees from the individual practitioner to the local medical society. As such, it institutionalized the individual doctor's traditional function of assessing his patients' ability to pay and setting the terms of payment. Although the participating doctors agreed to a moderate fee scale for eligible, low-income patients, the individual was still personally responsible for the total cost of the care he received and subject to an inquiry into his financial status. He could not prepay a fixed sum in return for an insured status with benefits of broad coverage. He therefore had none of the financial protection which group purchase of medical care afforded.[52]

The other type of medical society plan that developed during the depression did not have these liabilities. Medical indemnity insurance plans included prepayment features, free choice of doctor, and broad benefit coverage, and they were potentially capable of meeting most medical care needs of the middle class. Founded in the states of Washington and Oregon in response to economic pressure on doctors and to a public outcry against the abuses of contract practice, prepayment indemnity plans served as models for California Physicians' Service and Michigan Medical Service in the late 1930's. They were later imitated by state and local plans across the nation and ultimately became the constituent parts of the Blue Shield system.[53]

Medical indemnity insurance plans were in effect the middle ground between consumer-controlled medical care cooperatives and completely free private practice. The participating patients were guaranteed a measure of *financial* (not service) protection by the payment of a fixed annual fee, but they had very little control of the organizations to which they paid these funds. The participating physicians remained in private practice, but shaped the plans to conform to their standards of ethical and professional behavior, and used them to guarantee that they would be paid a high percentage of insurance patients' fees. Both doctor and patient thus received some of the benefits of group prepayment insurance while preserving most of the traditions of private medical practice.[54]

The primary weaknesses of indemnity plans were their lack of administrative control of fees and utilization and their failure to cover most of the low-income population. The plans' organizational and financial structures were unable to cope with overutilization of services by patients and maximization of fees by physicians, and when such phenomena began to appear in the 1940's, the amounts of covered services were reduced, membership fees rose, and deductible clauses and income ceilings were introduced. Membership complaints soon appeared, but because of the underlying philosophy and structure of the plans, little could be done to arrest this trend. For the same reason, they were unable to serve the low-income groups as a whole, though several limited experiments in this area were made.[55]

Another major private response to the medical care crisis in the 1930's was voluntary group hospitalization, a movement which proved extremely popular among the middle class it was designed to serve and which rapidly grew into the national Blue Cross system. The enthusiastic reception was the result of several factors. By the late 1920's the public was aware that hospitalization was desirable and beneficial in the treatment of serious disease, and that although the high cost of hospital care was commensurate with the quality of service provided, individual financial responsibility for large hospital bills could disrupt a family's economic situation and endanger the social status of its members. With the advent of the depression this problem became even worse and began to threaten ever larger numbers of families.[56] Therefore most of the population had great interest in the problem of hospitalization costs and was very receptive to the effort to expand group hospitalization as a money-saving device for individual patients.

The first real movement in this campaign was made by the CCMC and by philanthropic foundations such as the Rosenwald Fund. Some supporters of compulsory health insurance encouraged voluntary hospitalization as a first step toward a compulsory system, but organizations such as the American Hospital Association and the American College of Surgeons rejected this argument. They lent their support because they felt that hospitalization insurance was merely a viable and permanent method of solving a critical problem. They hoped that this type of insurance would protect the interests of hospitals and patients, help preserve the financial status and self-respect of the largely middle-class membership of the plans, and forestall hasty and badly drafted compulsory legislation.[57]

Educational efforts by the group hospitalization advocates

began to show results in the early 1930's. The Baylor University Hospital plan, created in 1929 to provide group hospitalization and guarantee the hospital's income, served as an early model for other prepayment plans in the southwest. Other more or less spontaneous hospitalization experiments took place in Newark, New Jersey, Sacramento, California, and St. Paul, Minnesota. The successes of these plans and increasing public interest led to the creation of similar plans in New Orleans, Washington, D.C., and Cleveland by 1934.[58]

The early plans shared common features, but each had its own particular characteristics. All limited enrollment to members of certain groups (such as teachers or government employees); all were organized on a nonprofit basis and employed the principle of periodic group prepayment for covered hospital *service*. Some of the plans included only one hospital, while others included all accredited hospitals in the area. A percentage were launched by loans from the participating hospitals themselves; others received their initial funds from civic groups or philanthropic organizations. Some were controlled by the local medical society and hospital administrators, while others were administered by civic leaders and public representatives in cooperation with these professional groups.[59]

The American Hospital Association made an early attempt to police these mushrooming hospitalization service plans. In 1933 it established a series of guidelines for acceptable plans and on January 1, 1934 appointed C. Rufus Rorem as a special consultant on group hospitalization. Rorem worked with the American Hospital Association Committee on Community Relations and Administrative Practices to give advice to groups which were interested in founding new hospitalization plans and to judge the acceptability of new plans as they were created and submitted.[60] This somewhat makeshift system continued to operate until 1937, when the rapid growth of the hospitalization service plans and the administrative burdens of coordinating and supervising their activities caused the American Hospital Association to create the Hospital Service Plan Commission under C. Rufus Rorem. Financed by the Rosenwald Fund and designed to coordinate the plans on a national basis, the commission created the Blue Cross symbol to signify that a particular plan had met with the Hospital Association requirements and was a cooperating member of the national system.[61] From 1934 to 1939 the enrollment and number of hospitalization plans snowballed. Membership grew from two thousand in 1933 to over a million in late 1937, and to over four million in 1939. Many state governments began to enact enabling legislation permitting the formation of local plans, and although operational experience caused a relatively constant revision of benefits and membership fees, the public continued to join in increasing numbers.[62]

The obvious success of the voluntary hospitalization plans tended to obscure their serious shortcomings in organization and coverage. Families of members often received only partial coverage; low-income families and independently employed individuals found it very difficult to gain membership; and medical services, even when used in the hospital, were seldom included in the benefits. During unemployment or following a change of job, a subscriber often lost eligibility for membership, and because of the organizational structure, the average subscriber had little voice in determining the extent of his coverage or the size of his annual fee.[63]

Many leaders of the voluntary hospitalization insurance movement were aware of these shortcomings, but the federated and localized nature of the constituent Blue Cross plans prevented real national leadership on anything beside a standard-setting and vague policy statement basis. For example, the administrators of the local hospitals and insurance plans during the 1930's were reluctant to include high-risk, low income families or farmers because it would be too difficult and costly.[64] They also avoided the issue of using the plans to pay in-hospital professional bills because the national and local medical societies initially opposed group hospitalization as violating the ethical code of the profession and endangering the doctor-patient relationship. Finally, since the bulk of middle-class members seemed content with the partial coverage provided by the plans and were not interested in expanding them, there was little motive to move ahead in these areas.[65]

The Blue Cross voluntary hospitalization plans, limited as they were in coverage and philosophy, had deep, although uncalculated, effects on the entire structure of American medical care. By 1948 they had over 30 million subscribers and had provided a technique of payment for hospitalization which most patients and physicians found acceptable. But the popularity and effectiveness of the group hospitalization had another result: the progress of medical care reform in other areas was retarded for many years. The vocal and politically powerful middle class was pacified by the partial coverage of the plans, and therefore saw no real need to support more radical measures. The reformers, who were hoping for middle-class support on programs for the poor as well as for the general population, found themselves largely without allies and doomed to failure.[66]

The development of noncompulsory programs in the 1930's was of great and constant concern to the nation's doctors. Most physicians, in trying to understand and take a position on these programs, turned to their medical societies for guidance and leadership. The associations responded with a series of policy statements and administrative actions which effectively combined the ideology of the profession with the administrative machinery of the medical societies to create a powerful and dynamic force.

The democratic and federated structure of organized medicine in the United States was probably the essential factor in the success of this policy. Every member of the AMA belonged to a local society and was free to participate in its proceedings to the extent of his interest. The local societies were federated into state associations, which in turn were represented on the national level by the AMA. Majority rule in theory guaranteed the democratic nature of the entire organization.[67] But democratic procedures in practice produced a subtle form of continuing minority rule. As in so many other voluntary associations, most doctors were only casually interested in their local society and therefore tended to elect those who, for their own political reasons, were willing to serve. A similar process prevailed on the state and national level, with the more successful and conservative doctors usually winning elective office.[68] Delegates to the AMA were usually eminent and popular local doctors with little or no knowledge of the intricacies of current issues facing the profession. A minority were exceptions: they were long-term officeholders or appointees who became experts in their fields and were trusted to make policy recommendations to the annual House of Delegates meetings. The short-term delegates who made up a majority of the House usually accepted this minority's recommendations with only minor amendments. Because of their desire for a public image of unity, they usually did so without open dissent. Thus, in practice, the majority surrendered their policy-making function to the minority.[69]

Yielding of authority was possible because the majority trusted the minority to administer efficiently the AMA bureaucracy and make only those policy recommendations which would prove acceptable to the mass of casual members on the local level. Working behind the scenes in the key reference committees, the minority drafted policy statements which the current delegates could hold up to their constituents proudly. In so doing, the minority guaranteed its continued popularity and tenure through the next annual convention.[70] Such elaborate machinery no doubt tended to stifle open dissent and give the individual member a feeling of political impotence in the face of the powerful minority. But its continued operation would have been impossible without the common ideology which tied together a majority of the leaders and members of the medical societies. In effect, these beliefs were the consensus which permitted decisions to be made, policies to be implemented, and actions to be taken.[71]

The majority of the members of the medical societies during the 1920's and 1930's believed that high quality medical care was intimately tied to the doctor-patient relationship, free competition, individual initiative, and fee-for-service. They admired the family doctor, frowned on specialization and group practice, and feared and despised lay or governmental interference in the professional and financial affairs of individual physicians. Above all, they were individualists who liked to think of themselves as dedicating their lives to the service and welfare of the entire population.[72]

The ideology of the doctors and the machinery of organized medicine that was based on it were used to meet many of the medical issues of the 1920's and 1930's in a variety of ways. The AMA opposed the Children's Bureau in the 1930 White House Conference on Child Health, fought against the majority report of the CCMC, and campaigned against the health insurance proposals of the CES and the Interdepartmental Committee. At the same time it cooperated with the FERA and FSA medical care programs, gradually endorsed voluntary hospitalization insurance, and launched a program of voluntary medical indemnity insurance under medical society supervision. In other words, the organized medical profession was selective in what it chose to accept or reject, based both on its members' ideology and its own ethical code.[73] For example, voluntary hospitalization insurance was endorsed only after it had proved that it did not exploit the medical profession and after the AMA had set rules to which acceptable hospitalization plans had to conform. In another case, voluntary insurance for the costs of doctors' fees was endorsed only upon condition that the medical societies have an important voice in the direction of individual plans. The government's relief programs were accepted only as emergency measures made necessary by the economic and medical crisis of the 1930's.[74]

When the AMA decided that proposed or existing plans did not conform to their members' ideology or code of ethics, both the association and its constituent societies took action against them. Such initiatives could include political lobbying, as in the case of the recommendations of the CES, campaigns of propaganda, such as those launched against unacceptable forms of health insurance, and, most serious of all, disciplinary action against individuals and plans which were ruled unacceptable.

This last form of action could range from professional ostracism of participating physicians to intimidation of hospitals and clinics which cooperated with the plans. One of the more zealous applications of this form of sanction precipitated the antitrust suit against the AMA in the Group Health Association case.[75]

The developments described were, for the most part, reactions to either local or temporary conditions of the 1930's in America. They were *generally* not conceived of as parts of a larger plan for building a comprehensive national medical care system, nor were they established in accordance with any abstract theory of social justice. Although some reformers read other meanings into the developments, these programs were pragmatic reactions within a society that was shaken by the destructive and divisive effects of a major economic depression.

Many of the medical care programs born during this time of social and economic distortion were either poorly conceived or badly executed. Both governmental and private plans were often imperfect, and if they survived at all, they usually underwent a long series of major, internal revisions. But many of them did survive and become essential parts of the postdepression system of medical care. How and why did this selective process work? The answers to these questions lie in the operation of a free and competitive American society.

Given the need and public desire for action, the nature and magnitude of experimental programs was limited only by the consensus of what was acceptable to the parties immediately concerned. Thus, as long as doctors, reformers, and patients agreed that a medical care plan was satisfactory, there was little, if any, opposition to its establishment or operation, whatever its size or stated goals. This held true for private as well as governmental medical care plans, for programs supported by hospitals or medical societies as well as by the FSA or the FERA.

Once plans lost the support of any of the three groups, either because of inefficient operation or because of ideological or economic factors bearing on the nature of the plans themselves, their potential effectiveness was greatly undermined. Since de facto voluntary cooperation among all participating groups was required for successful operation, programs that lost the support of one or more of these groups were usually doomed to early collapse.

The need for voluntary cooperation and support created a real, if unofficial, competition between many of the medical care experiments created during the 1930's. Blue Cross and Blue Shield plans, for example, competed with the cooperatives for public, reformer, and professional support and the ultimate success such support would bring. Later, the Farm Security Administration program would compete with the Blue plans, and still later, commercial health insurance companies would present their own health insurance policies. Each of these attempts was an effort to achieve more success through the presentation of a more desirable consensus position.

This competition for support and consensus was neither totally free nor thoroughly comprehensive. The actions of the medical societies and some of the reformers handicapped some of the plans from the start, and some of the programs filled real needs which were not even touched upon by other proposals. But in broad perspective, the competition for widespread support was the key factor in determining which plans were to achieve success and permanency.

While it may be argued that comprehensive government programs would have been more rational, effective, and economical than the host of private and temporary plans which were put into effect in the 1930's, this viewpoint overlooks the tradition and meaning of free social action in the United States. The very plethora of limited local efforts launched during the 1930's and the wasteful competition among them seem to be an essential feature of the American way of dealing with social problems. Citizens, willing to solve the problems of their own society, have traditionally met the issues by producing a host of small experiments in various regions and among differing population groups. The lessons learned from such pragmatic experiments are then applied to larger and more comprehensive plans—plans under government control or supervision if financial or organizational factors so require.[76] Only then, when the public is comfortable with the reality of the new situation, can the theoretical basis of the new program be accepted.

The limited and problem-ridden experiments of the 1920's and 1930's were only the beginnings of this process as it applied to American medical care. Government proposals for compulsory health insurance made during this period did not have, as yet, the advantage of being able to draw upon voluntary insurance experiences or upon the public awareness which such plans would eventually create. People were still preoccupied with immediate solutions, and the reformers' educational campaigns and limited programs could not convince them to support more extensive proposals and the new type of freedom they implied.

The supporters of compulsory health insurance, eager as they were for legislative action on their proposals, did not seem to understand the slow pace at which the public was moving. They felt that since the contemporary, limited programs were more or less successful, the public was now ready to support compulsory health insurance. The reformers did not understand that only slow and gradual experience, which was only beginning to be gained in a free and competitive context in the 1930's, could make the public aware that their reform proposals were worth supporting.

4

Washington: The Battle Renewed 1936–1939

The economic and social dimensions of the crisis in American medical care were permanently changed by the host of public and private programs initiated in the early 1930's. Government medical programs and private voluntary plans grew profusely, but the basic goal of supplying adequate medical care to all citizens continued to remain a problem. Too many of the unemployed or underemployed were not receiving adequate care; too many farmers were finding doctors and medical facilities harder and harder to locate and pay for; and too many middle-class people were still facing individual financial and social disaster because of serious illness. By the late 1930's private and governmental programs had begun to modify the problems, but the underlying causes remained untouched. All the while, economic and scientific pressures were focused on the modern medical care system and were rapidly changing it. Stopgap measures were limiting some serious dislocations temporarily, but a reformation of the structure of medical care was needed or the entire set of halfway measures and experimental programs would eventually collapse. By 1937 the reformers believed that a fundamental change was imminent because the public, after experience with more limited public and private medical care programs, was at last ready to support compulsory health insurance. More important, the reformers believed that they could bring about progress through the federal government by using traditional political strategy and new governmental tactics. In traditional terms, they would unite the government agencies in which they had power in a pro-insurance alliance, with each agency being promised administrative responsibility for part of a new and sweeping National Health Program that would include compulsory health insurance. Each agency would therefore be loyal to the overall program, and their combined strength would defeat all opposing forces. The reformers' tactics were based on a new view of the government's role in social reform in which the government routinely took responsibility for proposing new programs, supervising legislative enactment, and playing an active and critical role in recruiting and mobilizing public opinion and support.

The leaders of the nation's medical societies did not agree with many of the reformers' ideas. They were firmly committed to the traditional medical system and believed that the new voluntary and limited experiments in time would *permanently* solve the nation's major medical care problems. Fundamental reform was neither desirable nor necessary, and the public would not and should not support the radical changes which the reformers were advocating. The federal government should not interfere in medical care unless and until all interested parties, including the public, demanded it. The government was to remain a broker, or at most an arbiter, between private interest groups: it was wrong and un-American for it to become an advocate of specific proposals publicly, since activism of this sort would lead to totalitarianism. The doctors thus distinguished between the strategy of forming a pro-insurance alliance, which was acceptable, and the attempts to mobilize and use public opinion, which were not.

Disagreement between the reformers and the medical societies was another aspect of the more basic confrontation between the progressive and the traditional concepts of government action, freedom, and security. Should reform be initiated by individual citizens and private groups? And should it come about through the political machinery of the classic liberal state? Or should the government recognize the new realities of the society and assume an active role in recruiting the support of individual citizens for specific reforms? This debate was not resolved in the late 1930's. The individuals who listened to both sides were neither fully committed to the traditional system of medical care nor fully convinced by the reformers' arguments. The tactics of the health insurance advocates hinged on gaining open public support for their National Health Program, but in reality the people were still most interested in the limited government and private medical care experiments. Consequently, the reformers were unable to arouse the public support they anticipated; their tactical interagency alliance collapsed; and the medical societies were once again able to forestall the enactment of compulsory health insurance.

During late 1935 and 1936 the health insurance advocates employed by the federal government were primarily concerned with setting up programs which the Social Security Act had created. Those employed by the Children's Bureau, the United States Public Health Service, and the Social Security Board were engaged in this work full time and were therefore unable to engage in much pro-insurance activity within the federal government.[1]

By 1937 most of the Social Security programs were firmly established, and the reformers were again freed to renew their efforts for federal health insurance legislation. At first, they began to work on the problem individually and in informal groups, slowly reestablishing their contacts with health insurance supporters in private life. Then, in order to gain an effective platform for decision-making and political action, they began to turn their attention to the Interdepartmental Committee for the Coordination of Health and Welfare Activities, which had been created in late 1935 to coordinate the expanded health and welfare activities of various federal agencies.[2] The committee consisted of assistant secretaries of the agencies involved and had a small permanent staff. Josephine Roche, Assistant Secretary of the Treasury for the Public Health Service and a supporter of federal health insurance, was its chairman.[3]

During its first year the Interdepartmental Committee concerned itself with routine matters of interagency coordination and cooperation. Its orientation was changed in late 1936, however, when several of its members suggested that the committee begin to consider other areas which might need federal attention and for which they might take responsibility. At the urging of Miss Roche and Arthur Altmeyer (by then chairman of the Social Security Board), the Interdepartmental Committee decided in early 1937 to turn its attention to a "comprehensive survey of health needs of the nation and the development of a national health program to meet these needs." [4] The committee approached this project by establishing a Technical Committee on Medical Care consisting of staff experts from each of the participating agencies.

The ideas of a national health survey and a list of recommendations gained the President's approval, and in March 1937 the Technical Committee on Medical Care was formally established within the Interdepartmental Committee. Dr. I. S. Falk, a veteran of the CCMC and the CES and now an official in the Social Security Board's Bureau of Research and Statistics, was named to represent the Social Security Board. Martha Eliot, assistant chief of the Children's Bureau and administrative head of the Maternal and Infant Health Program that the Social Security Act had created in that agency, represented the Children's Bureau and was appointed committee chairman. Joseph Mountin, George St. J. Perrott, and Clifford Waller represented the United States Public Health Service and made up the remainder of the Technical Committee.[5]

For the first few months after its creation, the Technical Committee on Medical Care studied various aspects of existing medical care programs in which the federal government participated. Then, on September 28, 1937, it met with the full Interdepartmental Committee to request "further instructions on how it should proceed." The representatives of each of the participating agencies presented their views, and after several hours of debate a general policy was agreed upon. "It was the consensus of the meeting that the Medical Care Committee should continue its work," and "a charge was made to this group to formulate plans for a national medical care program."[6] Thus was born the second major attempt to achieve compulsory health insurance through federal action in the 1930's.

The Technical Committee soon met again and decided to study possible extensions of existing programs, and then, to examine possible next steps for federal action toward a national health program. They agreed on a series of principles which would form the basis for any projected programs—principles which, not surprisingly, were very similar in philosophy to the "Eleven Principles" of the CES report of 1935.[7] The Technical Committee began to compile a statistical base, and after several weeks, Chairman Martha Eliot suggested a new course of action: instead of having the committee as a whole frame all aspects of the projected health program, the representatives of each participating agency would work independently on only those segments which directly concerned them. After the representatives had prepared their specific recommendations, the Technical Committee as a whole would pass on them and submit them to the parent Interdepartmental Committee for approval.[8]

This decision had very serious implications. It meant that each agency would shape its own recommendations and thus have a stake in the overall Interdepartmental Committee program, but it also meant that if and when certain parts of the program encountered public or Congressional apathy or opposition, each agency might try to salvage its own recommendations by withdrawing its support from the other, more objectionable, ones. For example, the Public Health Service might withdraw its support for disability insurance proposals if it might endanger the Service's immediate objective of more extensive public health programs.

The strategy also had particular significance for any projected federal health insurance proposal. The Social Security Board, the newest of the participating agencies and one which still had few congressional allies, was the only member of the Interdepartmental Committee with a primary interest in the insurance components of the anticipated National Health Program.

If these features encountered serious opposition, the Public Health Service and the Children's Bureau might remove their support and concentrate exclusively on their own parts of the program. The fact that the insurance proposals were the most radical part of the projected program and were sure to arouse the most heated conservative opposition in Congress and the nation's medical societies only aggravated this situation. Although it is not entirely clear whether or not the health insurance reformers recognized the inherent weaknesses of their coalition approach, it is obvious that they had little alternative but to go along. For these were the only terms on which they could have compulsory health insurance included in the projected National Health Program.

By December 1937 the Technical Committee finished its study of medical care needs and began work on specific legislative recommendations to meet them. The primary responsibility for proposals concerning compulsory health insurance, tax-supported medical care, and temporary cash disability insurance was given to the staff of the Social Security Board and to its representative on the Technical Committee, Dr. I. S. Falk.[9] The early drafts of the Social Security Board suggestions for health insurance and medical care were largely outgrowths of the earlier recommendations contained in the CES Health Insurance Report of 1935 and the Social Security Board "Memorandum on Health Insurance" of 1936. Provisions for supplying medical care to the needy, for a federal rather than national structure of health insurance, and for limiting the federal government's role to one of subsidizing and standard-setting were all drawn from these earlier works. There were many specific changes in administration and cost estimates, but the essential nature of the National Health Program was identical to the programs developed several years before.[10]

When these tentative proposals, as well as those of the other agencies represented on the Technical Committee, were ready for consideration by the whole Technical Committee, they included proposals to establish programs for public health, maternal and infant hygiene, aid to crippled and blind children, hospital construction, compulsory health insurance, tax-supported medical care, and temporary disability insurance. Each program was to be administered through the state governments with an agency of the federal government supplying financial and technical aid and establishing standards of quality.[11]

The Technical Committee on Medical Care approved these proposals, but then decided (with ominous implications for health insurance), to establish a system of priorities within the proposals themselves. The public health, maternal and infant hygiene, and hospital construction programs were considered most important, while the compulsory health insurance, tax-supported medical care, and temporary disability insurance were relegated to a secondary position. A majority of the Technical Committee members already anticipated difficulty in the passage of the latter programs and were now adjusting their report accordingly.[12]

The policy of placing compulsory health insurance in the category of a lesser, more expendable part of the National Health Program was confirmed when the Interdepartmental Committee asked for certain changes in the proposals before it approved them. The most important of these requests was one for a liberal definition of medical indigency. Congress, the Interdepartmental Committee probably believed, would be more amenable to an extensive program of medical relief than to more radical proposals such as health insurance. The Interdepartmental Committee's decision further deterred the supporters of compulsory health insurance because they could no longer claim that their reform was the primary remedy for the medical care problems of the medically indigent in the National Health Program.[13]

Compulsory health insurance was also segregated from other, high priority parts of the National Health Program in the financial section of the amended report of December 1937. Having revised the proposed program in accord with the Interdepartmental Committee's wishes, the Technical Committee now estimated that it would cost the federal government $600,000,000 per year at the end of a five year period of gradually increasing expenditures. This figure would be supplemented by state funds, but would *not* include the costs of compulsory health insurance, general medical care, or temporary disability insurance programs. The omissions could have been made because of the variable nature of these programs' costs, the expectation that health insurance would be self-financing, or the massive amounts of money involved. Whatever the cause, however, omitting cost estimates had the effect of further lowering the priority of the health insurance proposals.[14]

While the Technical Committee was redrafting the National Health Program, the members of the parent Interdepartmental Committee were beginning to align administration support. On December 23, Surgeon General Parran urged the President to include a reference to the forthcoming National Health Program in his annual message to Congress. Simultaneously other members of the Interdepartmental Committee conferred with senior cabinet members and administration advisers to recruit their support.[15] The discussions may have convinced the Interdepartmental Committee that a further revision and limitation of the National Health Program was needed, because when it met in late December, members suggested that the Technical Committee again revise the program for medical care for the needy and further separate it from the proposals for health insurance or general medical care. They in fact wanted the National Health Program to include "something in the nature of a medical assistance recommendation independent of the broader recommendation for grants-in-aid to permit the states to develop straightforward insurance programs."[16] Congress would probably more willingly accept such a medical relief program if it were not tied to compulsory health insurance.

Compulsory health insurance was thus seriously enfeebled by the time the Technical Committee finished its final report in February 1938. It had been segregated and insulated from the other recommendations of the National Health Program, assigned the lowest priority, and couched in the least specific terms. The efforts and hopes of the pro-insurance reformers were to no avail; the administration was apparently once again willing to sacrifice this reform on the grounds of political expediency.

Once the National Health Program (NHP) had been drafted and approved, the next step was to mobilize public support for its enactment. This meant convening a national conference to discuss the NHP before all types of public leaders. With President Roosevelt's consent, Altmeyer, Roche, and other members of the Interdepartmental Committee's staff began to plan for such a conference to meet in July 1938. The date would fall during the congressional recess and would allow several months for the reformers to recruit public support.[17]

After months of intense work and preparation by the committee's staff, all was ready. On the morning of July 18, 1938, over 150 delegates gathered at Washington's Mayflower Hotel to open the first session of the National Health Conference. Representatives of labor, farmers, business, health professions, and government were present.[18] After an opening speech by the chairman of the Interdepartmental Committee, Josephine Roche, the delegates, in a series of short addresses, discussed the "tremendous public opinion" which was "represented" at the National Health Conference and supported with greater or lesser enthusiasm the Technical Committee's statements on the need for a national health program. Each delegate concentrated on the most pressing health problem of the group he represented and spoke only generally of the other parts of the report on needs.[19]

The fragmented interest in the various aspects of the National Health Program exposed the divided nature of the delegates' interests. Most groups represented at the conference were deeply committed only to those parts of the program which immediately affected their constituencies. Although their statements were parochial, the effect of their disconnected and self-interested speeches was to create a feeling among delegates that a program of national scope was needed. By the end of the first session consensus was clearly evident. Immediately before the conference recessed, Paul Kellogg, editor of the *Survey Graphic* and president of the National Conference of Social Work, asked if anyone wished to challenge the Technical Committee's report on the need for a National Health Program. The chairman put the question formally before the conference. When not a single delegate rose to challenge any part of the report, most were convinced that a *national* program would be supported by the conference.[20]

Having thus achieved unanimity on the question of the need for a national health program, the Interdepartmental and Technical Committees now turned to the specific recommendations which the Technical Committee had prepared. The five recommendations, which were to be described to the conference at its second session, restated the recommendations contained in the Technical Committee report of February 1938 and incorporated all of the revisions which had been made up to and including that date. The report recommended the expansion of the existing public health and Maternal and Child Health programs and added a ten-year program to expand hospital facilities with special emphasis on geographically remote areas. It also called for a state-federal grant-in-aid program to establish a system of medical care for the indigent and those able to support themselves but unable to afford medical care, the medically indigent. It recommended the "consideration of a comprehensive program designed to increase and improve medical services for the entire population" to be financed by general or special taxation or insurance contributions. Last, it stated that systems of temporary and permanent disability insurance "can perhaps be established."[21]

The recommendations, in accordance with the policy decisions of the Interdepartmental Committee, separated programs for medical care for the needy from those for general medical care and compulsory health insurance. Their wording also hinted at the system of priorities which had been adopted by the Interdepartmental Committee, but in order that there be no possibility of confusion concerning this decision, the report included the following statement:

> The Committee does not suggest that it is practicable to put into effect immediately the maximum recommendations. It contemplates a gradual expansion along well-planned lines with a view to achieving operation on a full scale within ten years. Except insofar as they overlap and include portions of the first three recommendations, Recommendations IV and V [health and disability insurance] involve chiefly a revision of present methods of making expenditures rather than an increase in these expenditures . . .
>
> The Committee calls attention to the fact that in some important respects, the five recommendations present alternative choices. However, the Committee is of the opinion that Recommendations I and II [public health and hospital increases] should be given special emphasis and priority in any consideration of a national health program more limited in scope than that which is outlined in the entire series of recommendations.[22]

This decision to de-emphasize health insurance, disability payments, and, to a lesser extent, aid to the medically indigent (Recommendation III), was also reflected in the official cost estimates prepared by the Technical Committee. While the total costs to federal, state, and local governments of the public health, hospital, and medical indigency programs were presented as $850,000,000 per year in the last year of a ten-year program of increasing expenditures, no cost estimates at all were officially presented for health insurance or disability payments. The Interdepartmental Committee explained this absence by claiming that the funds were already being spent in the private sectors of medical care, and the adoption of these programs would, therefore, involve no new expense to society. But the very fact that even a vague estimate of the total cash outlay was omitted indicates how weak the Interdepartmental Committee's official support for these controversial measures before the conference really was.[23]

Although this policy was cautious certain members of the Technical and Interdepartmental Committees hoped that the compulsory health insurance recommendation would rise in priority and become a more integral part of the National Health Program. If presented to the National Health Conference in an exciting and simple way, they believed there was a chance that the public and the delegates would support it. The President, they reasoned, would be more likely to back it openly in Congress if it had such public support, and it might very well become law.[24]

In accordance with this strategy for winning public and delegate support, I. S. Falk presented a detailed defense of the health insurance and disability payments recommendations on July 19th, during the conference's second session. He delivered a long and impassioned plea for support, in which he repeated almost every argument that had been used by health insurance supporters during the previous thirty years: the great need for expanding medical care; the advantages of distributing medical costs over groups of people and periods of time; the economies possible in a rationalized system; the stabilizing and elevating influence health insurance would have on most professional incomes; the possibility of preserving individualism and initiative under compulsory health insurance; the wide latitude left to the states and localities in deciding what form their medical system should take; the preservation of the individual's dignity by his contributions to his own medical expenses; and the increased efficiency of these programs' use of funds that were already being spent for private purchase of medical care.[25]

Falk then went beyond the formal recommendations of the Technical Committee and discussed projected costs. By his estimates, a national system of health insurance and medical care would require from one to three billion dollars per year, including part of the costs of the public health proposals and all of the expenses of hospital, medical indigency, and health insurance proposals. He explained that this enormous figure was not as formidable as one might at first assume, since the total bill for medical care in the United States in 1929 had been $3,700,000,000 and since the cost of the program would only rise gradually over a ten year period from $260,000,000 to $2,600,000,000. At the end of the ten years, Falk believed, all Americans would be receiving adequate medical care at a significantly lower total expense to the public and private sectors than had prevailed in the inadequate system of 1929.[26]

After Falk's presentation, the conference heard speeches from a series of delegates who had special interests in the entire proposed National Health Program. These general statements varied from cautious conservatism on the part of several doctors to outspoken radicalism on the part of some labor leaders and health insurance supporters from outside the government. Intermixed with these speakers were delegates who followed the patterns of the first session and addressed themselves to those parts of the program which most interested their constituents. The overall effect was disorderly; little continuity obtained from one speech to the next, and little discussion of the National Health Program as a whole occurred.[27] The Interdepartmental Committee had expected and was prepared for this phenomenon. The diversified statements gave the appearance of a significant amount of support for each of the recommendations. The agencies had counted on such segmented interest in these proposals when they originally entered the coalition in 1937; now they hoped to weld it into a large enough public force to push most or all of the National Health Program through Congress.[28]

The strategy of the Interdepartmental Committee seemed to be working so well at the conference that Olin West, the secretary and general manager of the AMA, felt obliged to counterattack at the close of the second session. He reiterated the traditional AMA policies concerning medical care reform, even though he professed to be "quite satisfied that my views may be of little interest to this audience." He argued against lay interference in medical care, claiming that a free and untrammeled medical profession was the only agency capable of rendering the quality of service desired and deserved by the American public. He warned that the National Health Program was visionary and based upon distorted statistical evidence and that a compulsory health insurance system would ultimately fall under political control and produce worse evils than those it might eliminate. He said, "I know you don't believe that, but that is what I believe."[29]

These strong and bitter statements seemed to set the tone for the conference's final session on the following day. At this meeting, Robert Osgood, a leader of a reform group of physicians, broke with the policy of the AMA and supported the National Health Program. Then William J. Kerr responded by reiterating Dr. West's statements of the preceding day. Kingsley Roberts, a supporter of lay-controlled medical cooperatives, joined the debate by criticizing the organized medical profession for its reactionary position and tactics and warned that such policies would merely slow, rather than stop, the progress of the reform campaign.[30]

Dr. Fishbein, the loquacious and provocative editor of the AMA *Journal,* spoke next. His statement was crowded with overt and implied criticisms of the National Health Program and of the people who had drawn it up. Sincerely interested people, he argued, should not take drastic action but rather should begin a campaign to educate the public to use existing medical facilities intelligently; local action should correct local problems and deficiencies. He identified the National Health Program with a type of state medicine which he described as wasteful of money and effort; it was unscientific from both the medical and the economic viewpoints and was un-American. The medical profession, Fishbein concluded, was invited to the National Health Conference "merely to endorse" a plan which had already been drawn up exclusively by laymen.[31]

Several others followed Dr. Fishbein on the conference program. John P. Koehler, Commissioner of Health of Milwaukee, and Michael M. Davis, chairman of the Committee on Research on Medical Economics, were both critical of the organized medical profession. Edwin Witte, former director of the CES, called for a united front of popular support for the National Health Program. Joseph Slavit, leader of the tiny socialist-oriented American League for Public Medicine, urged a system of state medicine in which all forms of medical care would be provided free by the state.[32]

The final statement to the National Health Conference was made by C. E. A. Winslow, a respected public health expert who had been active in efforts for the reform of medical care for over twenty years. Winslow had originally declined a place on the conference agenda, but he had become so upset with the bitterness of Fishbein's and West's attacks that he asked for and received permission to make a personal statement. Speaking without notes, Winslow reminded the conference of its unanimous agreement on the need for a national health program expressed during the first session. He appealed to the finest traditions of the medical profession and asked that they be applied in the needed reorganization of medical care. He pleaded for local communities to organize themselves in order to provide adequate medical care to their entire populations, and he requested the conference delegates to work for a compulsory health insurance law which would make such community action possible.[33]

The delegates sat in silence during Winslow's impassioned speech, and when it was over they gave him a great ovation. Winslow seemed to have moved the conference delegates on an intimate and personal level, and many of them seemed filled with proreform emotion. Only with some difficulty did the chairman of the conference, acting under the Interdepartmental Committee's decision to refrain from taking formal votes, manage to prevent the conference from unreservedly endorsing the entire National Health Program.[34]

The supporters of health insurance within the Interdepartmental and Technical Committees were greatly elated by this turn of events. Immediately after the conference prorogued, they began planning the next steps in their campaign to achieve congressional passage of the National Health Program. On July 23, 1938, Miss Roche sent a cable to the President reporting "amazing public support" for the National Health Program, and simultaneously, the Technical Committee began "to develop scientific proposals" incorporating the program to be presented to Roosevelt on his return to Washington.[35]

The President at first seemed very impressed by the events of the National Health Conference. When he met Roche and Altmeyer upon his return to the Capitol, he was so enthusiastic about the delegates' response that he thought he might make the National Health Program an issue in the pending off-year congressional elections. Then, without any explanation, he suddenly said that he thought that it would be better if the National Health Program were not made a political issue until the 1940 presidential election, and he asked Altmeyer and Roche to delay any further public action on the National Health Program.[36] The President's decision may have been based on anxiety concerning the difficult congressional campaign then being waged or may have been the result of his concern with the Republican Party's flirtations with a group of medical conservatives. Another very real reason for Roosevelt's timidity might have been the gathering of war clouds in Europe and Asia and the ultimate implications of this for an isolationist, unprepared United States. Whatever the cause, the Interdepartmental Committee was forced to accept his decision to refrain from further public action. They continued their nonpublic activities, however, quietly assigning members of the participating agencies' staffs to rework the National Health Program and draft it in the form of specific amendments to the Social Security Act of 1935. Cost estimates were revised, usually downwards, and the proposals for aid to the indigent and health insurance were reunited in a single title which omitted cost estimates entirely.[37]

Probably in response to a developing AMA opposition to government health insurance, the Interdepartmental Committee and the coalition of agencies supporting the National Health Program began a gradual retreat at this time.[38] It was most obvious in the treatment of those recommendations which were most radical, namely, aid to the indigent, health insurance, and temporary disability insurance. Thus, on the one hand, by November 1938 the Interdepartmental Committee had received and approved the intricate proposals for the implementation of the public health and hospital construction titles put forward by the Public Health Service and the Children's Bureau. On the other hand, up to this time the Interdepartmental Committee had not looked as favorably upon the more radical recommendations put forward by the fledgling Social Security

Board. Its proposals for indigent care, health insurance, and disability payments were in trouble and as yet had not been approved by the Interdepartmental Committee.[39]

The Social Security Board's suggestions had encountered opposition both within and without the government. Under the guidance of I. S. Falk, they were submitted to administrators in other interested agencies who strongly advised Falk against taking too strong a stand. They criticized the Social Security Board's proposals for being too specific in descriptions of acceptable state health programs, and one administrator urged Falk to delete the words *health insurance* from those recommendations altogether. Simultaneously, a rising wave of protests against health insurance from the medical societies was inundating Washington. These letters and telegrams seemed to portend considerable congressional opposition to the health insurance recommendations and frightened several of the members of the Interdepartmental Committee.[40] Given the warnings from the other members of the National Health Program coalition and the protests from the nation's medical societies, it is not surprising that by late 1938 the Social Security Board began to adopt a cautious policy concerning sponsorship of controversial issues such as health insurance. The board now stood nearly alone in its support of more radical programs and apparently felt that retaining its earlier optimism of July would be reckless. The Social Security staff, therefore, began to revise and weaken their proposals to the Interdepartmental Committee.[41]

The wisdom of caution became even more apparent when Roche and Altmeyer discussed the Interdepartmental Committee's work with the President once again in November. Roosevelt told them that he would send the weakened National Health Program to Congress with a message commending the approach taken by the Interdepartmental Committee and advising the Congress of the need for a national health program. But Roosevelt was worried by European developments and apparently felt that even this weakened version of the National Health Program was too controversial for his complete endorsement. He told Roche and Altmeyer that he would only recommend that Congress study the program as submitted and that he "did not want to go further at this time." [42]

While the administration was thus becoming more conservative in its attitude towards the National Health Program, Senator Robert Wagner of New York began to show an independent interest in national health insurance legislation. On November 19th, Philip Levy, secretary to Senator Wagner, visited I. S. Falk and indicated that Wagner might be interested in entering the health field directly. Since neither the President nor the members of the Interdepartmental Committee objected to having the revised National Health Program introduced in Congress as a nonadministration measure, negotiations between Wagner and the leaders of the Interdepartmental Committee were opened. By late December, most of the reformers were certain that the modified National Health Program would be introduced by Senator Wagner and expected that if it did not pass Congress, it would at least be put before the public by extensive congressional hearings.[43]

With the added support of an influential government figure not directly associated with the administration, the Social Security Board apparently felt that it could once again give more open support to its parts of the revised National Health Program. The December 30th Report on Recommended Changes in the Social Security Act stated that "enactment of the National Health Program would not only result in meeting more adequately the needs of those now receiving aid under the Social Security Act, but would also have a material effect in reducing the future cost of public assistance under the Act." [44]

Although there was growing hesitation on the part of the National Health Program coalition members in late 1938, many of the more optimistic supporters of compulsory health insurance were still more or less united in the hope that their reform would pass in the near future. They believed that the National Health Conference had revealed that "representatives of our citizens showed themselves ready and eager to get on with the job," [45] and that public sentiment could overwhelm the reluctance of the administration, Congress, and the medical societies. They believed and hoped that health insurance, whether or not it was included in the National Health Program, should gain quick national approval and enactment.[46]

Although most health insurance reformers privately had similar sentiments to a greater or lesser degree, many were immediately divided by more specific factors. Personality conflicts, policy choices, political evaluations, and bureaucratic loyalty all tended to divide the reformers, while their fundamental belief in medical care reform tended to unite them. The two trends, present in most large groups in which policy is shaped, were perhaps the most important ingredients in their reactions to specific events. Indeed the fate of the National Health Program and the coalition which supported it can only be understood in such terms.[47]

The dangers of factionalism which were inherent in the coalition approach of the Interdepartmental Committee began to materialize in late 1938. The jealousies and fears of the various agencies loomed large as open opposition to various parts of the program began to appear. The Public Health Service (PHS), which had long been friendly to the medical societies and antagonistic towards the Children's Bureau, now suspected the Social Security Board of trying to usurp control of programs which it believed rightly belonged to the PHS. Since its leaders reasoned that medical care should be under the administrative jurisdiction of the PHS, the Public Health officials regarded as undesirable most proposals which either originated outside their agency or gave other agencies predominant administrative control. A reserved coolness often marked dealings with personnel connected with rival agencies, and the PHS let it be known that it had great reservations regarding certain radical parts of the National Health Program.[48]

A feeling of responsibility for the nation's children was the official reason that the Children's Bureau began to withdraw its support from the National Health Program coalition in late 1938. The leaders of the bureau feared that its programs would be damaged if their agency was removed from the Department of Labor, or if its programs were tied too closely to general systems of medical care or health insurance. They reasoned that a future economic crisis might place a comprehensive system in more fiscal danger than a separately financed program limited to mothers and children. They also feared that the Public Health Service, in alliance with the nation's medical societies, would, if given the opportunity, seize control of their agency and severely limit the bureau's programs. When forced to make a choice between its own and a more general medical care program, the bureau had to support its own clients.[49]

The Social Security Board knew that the other members of the coalition had such feelings and special interests, but since it wanted to gain all possible support for its own program, it was forced to participate largely on their terms. The Board compromised and weakened its own recommendations in order to keep even the lukewarm support of the other agencies. Support of this kind was of questionable value but served at least to keep a vague outline of the Social Security Board's proposals in the National Health Program.[50]

In addition to loyalty to one's bureau, which often overrode the private sentiments of individual staff members, reformers were divided by differing personal evaluations of the political realities concerning health insurance. Falk tended to be very optimistic in appraising public support for all aspects of the National Health Program, while Roche and Altmeyer tended to be much more conservative. Witte, now outside of the government but still an active critic and sometime adviser to the Roosevelt administration, took the middle ground. Martha Eliot of the Children's Bureau and Surgeon General Thomas Parran were apparently even more conservative than Altmeyer and Roche, and were very cautious in their estimates of public support.[51] Outside the government, supporters of health insurance were divided just as seriously over the issue of popular interest. Men like James Rorty, Paul Kellogg, and John Kingsbury were very optimistic in their appraisals. Other individuals, like Michael M. Davis, Nathan Sinai, and C. Rufus Rorem tended to be more cautious.[52]

Another issue dividing the reformers was that of personality. Falk and Altmeyer found it difficult to work with men like Abraham Epstein and James Rorty, and Nathan Sinai occasionally frustrated and angered his pro-insurance colleagues. Other individuals also experienced various degrees of difficulty in working together, and these conflicts did not improve the chances for the passage of the National Health Program.[53]

Cooperation with medical society representatives also was a divisive factor. On this issue an interesting phenomenon occurred: reformers who were most optimistic about the possibilities of achieving enactment of the National Health Program were the least eager to seek such cooperation. Falk, a man who had personally felt the effects of AMA opposition in the CCMC and the CES, "tended to be as impatient with the physicians as the physicians were with him." Both he and Altmeyer tended to be "just a bit highhanded in their dealings with the doctors." The result, in the case of these two men, was "more or less of a standoff from the point of view of meaningful negotiations" and a growing mutual suspicion between them and the leaders of organized medicine.[54] On the other hand, the more conservative Dr. Parran and other Public Health Service personnel tended to cultivate their traditionally close relationship with the nation's medical societies throughout the period of interagency coalition. Their responses to many pro-insurance letters from the public were gruff and critical, but they simultaneously were, on the whole, conciliatory and respectful when addressing organizations of physicians.[55]

The split among the supporters of the National Health Program over cooperation with the medical societies was most dangerous, because it gave immediate and direct notice to the doctors that the reformers were at least partially divided. The AMA was seriously concerned by the apparent public support for the National Health Program shown at the National Health Conference, and it was eager to arrest the movement before it gained further momentum. The divisions within the reformers' ranks apparently gave the AMA and its local affiliates hope that a campaign of opposition based on the strategy of divide and conquer might cause the shaky coalition to split apart entirely.

The anti-insurance campaign which the AMA launched in 1938 was an outgrowth and expansion of its efforts against the CES in 1934 and thereafter. After the committee's Report on Health Insurance had been pigeonholed in January 1935, the AMA had relaxed its efforts, but continued to fear that reformers might at any time push for a federal compulsory insurance system. Consequently, they continued a mild version of their anti-insurance campaign throughout 1935, 1936, and 1937 with the hope that they would be ready for the challenge when it came. When the National Health Program of 1938 was finally released, it seemed to the AMA that the threatened government action was indeed at hand. The doctors' campaign, therefore, was immediately expanded and intensified.[56] The official organs of the AMA produced a constant barrage of articles, pamphlets, and speeches attacking compulsory health insurance. Several leaders of the medical societies made public attacks on the organizations and individuals who were prominent in the study or legislative support of health insurance. Appropriate agencies of the AMA kept in close contact with state and national legislative developments and diligently cultivated anti-insurance alliances with professional and lay pressure groups.[57] The fundamental theme of their anti-insurance campaigns was derived from the 1934–1935 struggle, but from 1936 to 1938 it was modified by a host of specific developments and changes. For example, the AMA policy of officially opposing what it called radical innovations created and administered by laymen, had long been an excuse for medical standpattism and de facto opposition to all serious reforms.[58] Now in the late 1930's, the medical societies began to take more constructive action.

The reasons for the change in tactics were complex. By the mid-1930's many citizens had become aware of the acute crisis in medical care, especially for the indigent and medically indigent. The state, local, and federal governments had recognized this problem and undertaken emergency measures to solve it. The organized medical profession had cooperated with government programs for the needy but had found them unsatisfactory in several respects. Doctors, therefore, began to press for and support the development of more acceptable programs which would effectively meet the needs of these indigent groups.[59]

Such programs were adopted in many local areas. The leaders of the AMA from the start saw that the success of these experiments would be an excellent political weapon against permanent government systems of health insurance and care for the needy. The leaders reasoned that if the needy were receiving adequate medical care through the voluntary efforts of the doctors and the communities, there could be no justification for instituting complex and expensive government plans.

In the late 1930's, therefore, the leaders of organized medicine began to urge broad extension of these plans on the basis of the "Ten Principles" of 1934, not only as a means of helping the poor, but also as a political tactic against compulsory health insurance. The AMA Board of Trustees in late 1936 stated:

> Members of the medical profession, locally and in the various states, are ready and willing to consider with other agencies ways and means of meeting the problems of providing medical service and diagnostic laboratory facilities for all requiring such service and not able to meet the full cost thereof . . .
>
> The willingness of the medical profession to adjust its services so as to provide adequate medical care for all the people does not constitute in any sense of the word an endorsement of health insurance, either voluntary or compulsory, as a means of meeting the situation.[60]

The reference to voluntary insurance reflected another liberal change in policy in the late 1930's. The AMA was increasingly concerned with the growing middle-class trend towards voluntary hospitalization insurance as a means of reducing financial risk to the individual family. As has been seen, the mid-1930's had witnessed an amazing expansion of plans which were limited to hospitalization and which were open only to those in the population who could pay the premiums. Medical societies had initially adopted a policy of reserved hostility to these largely lay-administered hospitalization plans. But as it became apparent that they were a permanent, growing segment of American medical care, the AMA decided to liberalize its policy towards them.

After several years of study, the House of Delegates passed a resolution in June 1937 which embodied "Ten Principles for Group Hospitalization" (see appendix B). The leadership hoped that these principles would protect the interests of the public, the hospitals, and the medical profession and guarantee the medical societies a voice in the plans' futures. The "Ten Principles for Group Hospitalization" called for nonprofit hospital service insurance plans under the control of medical societies or hospital organizations. They would include all local reputable hospitals, exclude high-income families and all *medical* services, and be subject to state supervision. Commercial salesmanship or use of funds for recruiting new members was prohibited, as was the use of insurance funds for the relief of financially imperiled hospitals. Also hospitals were called upon to experiment with other plans for relieving medical problems.[61]

The policy liberalization represented by the AMA decisions on medical care for the needy and group hospitalization between 1935 and 1937 was possible because there was no immediate threat of radical federal or state legislation. The profession was able to continue an orderly evolution of policy on a nonemergency basis, meeting each new issue calmly and adjusting its responses to changed medical, economic, and political conditions. Whether the liberalizing policy changes arose out of sincere desire for reform or were a political response to the potential ever-present threat of compulsory health insurance, by 1937 the AMA had undergone a basic, qualitative shift in what it considered to be acceptable and ethical forms of medical service—a shift which was basically progressive and constructive.[62]

When the report of the Interdepartmental Committee's Technical Committee on the health needs of the nation was made public in February 1938, this atmosphere of gradual change and evolution was immediately dispelled. The AMA leadership felt that the as yet unrevealed National Health Program would be a direct threat to their profession's interests. If it included compulsory health insurance and if it were to pass Congress, not only the voluntary reform programs but the entire pattern of American medical practice would be radically changed. Special measures were now needed that would go beyond the usual condemnations and warnings about precipitous and radical reforms that had been the main ingredients of their 1935–1937 campaign.[63]

Several such special measures were taken at the June 1938 session of the AMA House of Delegates. The House reendorsed the "Ten Principles" of 1934 and the 1937 guideposts for group hospitalization insurance. The delegates restated their support of group plans for the payment of professional fees as long as these programs were under the control of the local medical societies and were limited to cash indemnities. They also expressed their confidence in the Board of Trustees and in the editor of the AMA *Journal* and rejected several resolutions which called for the reversal of their policy of encouraging gradual, supervised reform.[64]

Five weeks later the National Health Conference convened in Washington and gave the National Health Program and its health insurance provisions an enthusiastic reception. The AMA leadership became gravely concerned that the government might use the misguided excitement of the conference delegates as an excuse to push for the passage of the entire program. The health insurance recommendation was seen as the most dangerous part, although the recommendations for care of medical indigents and disability payments also had some objectionable features. Nevertheless, the AMA decided to try to bargain with the Interdepartmental Committee and sent a delegation to Washington in early August for this purpose.[65]

The AMA negotiators offered to support all the other recommendations if the health insurance proposal was dropped from the National Health Program. This offer, if accepted, would have meant that the AMA would have supported the

Interdepartmental Committee's recommendations on public health, maternal and infant care, hospital construction, aid to the indigent and medically indigent, and temporary disability insurance. Support from this quarter would have meant that Congress would have had to give serious consideration to these programs and quite possibly might have passed them. Of course, if the Interdepartmental Committee had accepted the AMA offer, health insurance would have been abandoned entirely. Whether because of Social Security Board pressure, a feeling of confidence instilled by the National Health Conference, or a decision not to compromise before the program was introduced in Congress, the Interdepartmental Committee rejected the offer, and the negotiations were temporarily suspended.[66]

The Board of Trustees of the AMA was not willing to let the Roosevelt administration proceed with this unilateral policy. They called a special session of the House of Delegates for September 16th to re-examine and restate policy on the entire National Health Program.[67] The delegates met and immediately appointed a Special Reference Committee for the Consideration of a National Health Program. The final report of this committee, which was submitted to the House on September 17th, was mildly liberal in tone and definitely more moderate than the earlier statements of either the trustees or the *Journal.* It in large part incorporated the terms offered to the Interdepartmental Committee in August and gave the impression that the AMA was in fundamental agreement with most of the proposals of the National Health Program.

In this report the delegates were urged to endorse the principles and programs of the limited existing public health and maternal and infant hygiene programs, and the extension of hospital facilities where the needs for such extension existed. The House was even urged to accept a limited program of medical care for the indigent (*not* the medically indigent), provided that such programs were administered by the states and gave power to local welfare officials and medical societies. The report also approved of limited hospitalization insurance and endorsed cash indemnity insurance plans under state supervision and with the local medical societies' approval. The AMA would unreservedly endorse temporary disability insurance if family doctors were not required to certify the disability and would condemn "all forms of compulsory health insurance as bureaucratic, inefficient, and potentially harmful to the quality of American medical care." [68]

While these statements appear conciliatory and even liberal at first glance, close scrutiny reveals that they are in fact very similar to positions taken by the AMA in the previous few years. Only in its authors' clear acceptance of temporary disability insurance and in its encouragement of indemnity insurance for the payment of professional fees did this report suggest a new and more liberal emphasis. The endorsements, together with the restatements of earlier policy that make it *appear* to conform to everything but the health insurance recommendations in the National Health Program, were no doubt the result of a decision first to isolate compulsory health insurance and then to eliminate it from serious consideration by the administration.[69]

After a short debate, the House of Delegates adopted the Reference Committee's report and approved proposals to enlarge the Bureau of Medical Economics' program of assisting local medical societies to develop both indigent medical care plans and experiments with the provision of medical service to the community as a whole.[70] The AMA supplemented the delegates' actions by trying to gain the support of other professional and lay organizations for their abbreviated version of the National Health Program. Such endorsements were forthcoming from a deeply divided American Public Health Association in their October 1938 meetings and from the National Farm Bureau Federation and the American Hospital Association. Each group hoped that cooperation with the powerful AMA would help protect or achieve its special interests, which were at stake in the National Health Program.[71]

Perhaps the most important AMA response to the threat of

the unabridged National Health Program was the resumption of negotiations with the federal government. Although the August discussions had come to nothing, by October the AMA and the Interdepartmental Committee were willing to try again. At these meetings both sides presented basically the same positions they had in August. The AMA offered to support the entire National Health Program if and when compulsory health insurance was eliminated; the Interdepartmental and Technical Committees refused; and once again the meeting was adjourned. The Interdepartmental Committee did agree, however, to meet again with the AMA representative in January 1939, after the spokesmen of other interested professional groups had had a chance to converse with the committee.[72]

The January 1939 conversations also accomplished little. After a formal meeting of both sides, the Technical Committee representatives held extensive private discussions with Mr. Woodward of the Bureau of Medical Economics. Nothing came of these talks, and the AMA representatives, along with Parran and Roche, decided to present their differing positions directly to the President.[73]

At the meeting with Roosevelt, the medical leaders once again offered the AMA's help in reaching solutions to the nation's medical care problems but also reaffirmed their opposition to the health insurance proposals of the National Health Program. The Interdepartmental Committee representatives restated their case also, but neither group seemed able to influence the President to alter his stated policy regarding the National Health Program. The approach of war in Europe and the struggle to prepare the American nation for that conflict took more and more of the President's attention, largely at the expense of domestic reform measures such as the National Health Program. Consequently, his special message on health, which was sent to Congress in January, was similar in tone and commitment to his July message to the National Health Conference and went only as far as he had promised Roche and Altmeyer in November.[74]

The medical societies' policy of using negotiations and manipulating public opinion to divide and conquer the reformers was probably responsible for the conservative revisions made in the National Health Program between August 1938 and January 1939.[75] Beneath its facade of unity, however, the organized medical profession was divided over endorsement of the National Health Program and was susceptible to misinterpretation and potential exploitation by the reformers.

Although the majority of doctors understood and agreed with the policies of the AMA and its constituent societies concerning the National Health Program, a minority did withhold its support. Several groups of doctors, both within and without the AMA, held various opinions about what should be done to meet the health needs of the United States, and they publicly presented their views. Dr. Slavit's American League for Public Medicine, a socialist group, wanted the establishment of a national system of tax-supported state medicine in which medical care would be supplied to the population free of charge. Their ideas were politically unrealistic, however, and they never gained more than a handful of members.[76] A much more significant dissenting group was the Committee of Physicians for the Improvement of Medical Care, Inc. This faction of liberal doctors had grown out of the informal meetings of a medical advisory committee, which had been formed in connection with a study of medical opinion undertaken by the American Foundation in the mid-1930's. By November 1937, over 430 doctors had signed its platform calling for increased cooperation between the government and the medical profession in the establishment of a more adequate system of medical care.[77]

Although the members of the Committee of Physicians were dissatisfied with the official AMA policy towards reform, they still retained their memberships and accepted policy in other areas. The committee did not endorse compulsory health insurance, for example, but urged government subsidies to provide medical care to those who would otherwise be unable to obtain it. They endorsed voluntary health insurance and group practice, but only if the plans were subject to the same restrictions imposed by the AMA. In short, the Committee of Physicians did not repudiate any AMA policy or threaten to establish a rival medical organization; it merely requested the AMA to stop its unfair tactics and cooperate more closely with the government in order to retain public confidence and a larger voice in the shaping of future reforms.[78]

Although the Committee of Physicians was at best only a mildly liberal organization, the leadership of the AMA viewed it as a marked and immediate threat. A public quarrel developed between the Committee of Physicians and the AMA because the medical society saw the committee as a divisive force within the profession and as a source of pressure for overhasty liberalization of AMA reform policies. They rightly believed that the committee's public statements weakened the AMA claim that it was the unchallenged spokesman for American medicine, and they feared that the reformers would use the committee's existence to convince the administration that a large number of doctors did not support the more conservative policies of the AMA.[79]

While the health insurance advocates were in reality not as persuasive as the AMA leaders feared, most of them did believe that the bitterness of the controversy between the AMA and the Committee of Physicians was evidence that the profession was becoming deeply divided over the issue of government programs in medical care, and that if such were the case, the AMA could present but feeble opposition to the National Health Program.[80]

The highly inaccurate reading of the significance of the formation of the Committee of Physicians may have contributed to the overoptimistic estimates of the opposition to the National Health Program made by the reformers in the last half of 1938.[81] They expected that once it was made clear to the profession that some form of medical care reform was imminent, the AMA could be prevailed upon to support a federal-state system of compulsory health insurance as the least disruptive type of program. Many experts believe that the system of voluntary cash indemnity insurance which the AMA had endorsed could neither gain public support nor work efficiently, and they expected most doctors to realize this. They believed the medical societies would then change their formal positions and endorse a system of federal compulsory health insurance.[82]

Thus, both the organized medical profession and the pro-insurance reformers believed that their enemy was divided and weak. The medical societies felt that they could split the National Health Program coalition into its component agencies and eliminate those features of the program which were unacceptable. The reformers thought that the medical profession was divided over the recommendations of the National Health Program and would, therefore, be forced to accept compulsory insurance as an alternative to tax-supported state medicine.

Of these two estimates, that of the medical profession was to prove the more accurate for four reasons. First, the President and his advisers did not think that the time was as yet ripe for a compulsory health insurance system, and, therefore, they did not openly support the reformers. Second, the leaders of the lay groups represented at the National Health Conference did not acquaint their constituents with the details of compulsory health insurance as presented by the Technical Committee and, therefore, the public was hardly cognizant of the plan. Third, the mushrooming of voluntary hospitalization plans drew much potential middle-class interest away from the recommended government programs. And fourth, the Interdepartmental Committee coalition was more fundamentally divided than the medical profession over how much support to give to various parts of the National Health Program. The result of these factors was that the advocates of compulsory health insurance were in a much more vulnerable position than the medical societies. Their coalition would collapse more easily under the pressure of open struggle.

In mid-1938 the medical societies began to put such open pressure on the reformers in the form of a massive publicity campaign against the National Health Program. The organized profession, which believed that lay interference in the traditional forms of medical practice could lead only to disaster, began to educate the general public to this view.[83] They found it difficult, however, to communicate their professional feelings to the man in the street, and they therefore emphasized the group of their own beliefs that saw the government as the antithesis of all that was good and true in traditional individualistic America. Compulsory health insurance was opposed "not only because it must inevitably lead to a deterioration in the quality of medical service,"[84] but also because it was "another step towards the breakdown of the American democracy and a trend toward a system fascistic or communistic in character directly opposed to the democratic principle."[85] Experts who favored compulsory health insurance were accused of consciously or unconsciously trying to promulgate such systems through "vast schemes for spending far beyond any needs that can be established."[86]

The leaders of the AMA hoped that this publicity campaign, when combined with their policies of negotiating with and dividing the Interdepartmental Committee and their encouraging of voluntary reform programs in local medical societies, would effectively crush the most odious parts of the National Health Program. They realized that if all three parts of their strategy were successful, compulsory health insurance in the form proposed by the Interdepartmental Committee would be impossible to achieve. As the 1939 session of Congress neared, they intensified and broadened their campaign.

The actions and reactions of the medical societies and the pro-insurance reformers through 1937 and 1938 raised three serious questions concerning the uses and relationships of public opinion, interest groups, and government in government reform movements. First, the growing controversy between reformer and medical society brought up the question of the interrelationships of interest groups and public opinion in the process of legislating social programs. Second, it raised the issue of the legitimate responsibilities and interests of the government in creating or responding to public reform sentiment.

And third, it brought into question the relative importance of individual and professional freedom on the one hand, and the demands and needs of the rest of society on the other.

Each of these questions was based on an underlying disagreement between the reformers and the organized medical profession as to the meaning of liberty and responsibility in an industrialized and urbanized country. The supporters of compulsory health insurance tended to believe in a progressive form of freedom in which organized society guaranteed certain economic and social standards to the citizen in return for the surrender of a portion of his individual freedom. Under compulsory health insurance, for example, the citizen would give up his right to withhold contributions from the health insurance fund in return for a guarantee of adequate medical care. The organized medical profession, on the other hand, clung to the more traditional view that the maximum individual freedom was the best means of guaranteeing economic and social progress. To them the individual right to withhold one's patronage from inferior doctors was the best guarantee of increasingly superior medical care.

Fundamental disagreement on the nature and uses of individual freedom led to different interpretations of the problems of a complex society and to different recommendations on how to solve them. The reformers tended to interpret social welfare problems as the products of an outmoded and inadequate system of political, social, and economic organization which prevented the individual from achieving the most meaningful existence which modern technology and planning could provide. To them the freedom of not being able to afford good medical care was unimportant; the real issue was governmental reform of the medical care system, achieved through an alliance of expert governmental and lay leaders and an educated public and aimed at providing good care for all. The medical profession disagreed. While many of their actions were no doubt based on economic self-interest or emotional fears, most members of the profession probably felt that the problems in medical care were the products of individual failings and weaknesses which could only be corrected through education and voluntary cooperation under the creative leadership of intelligent men. The individual's values and motivation must be preserved in this process, for if they were destroyed through government intervention and compulsion, the only real possibility for improvement would be lost.

Both the reformers and the doctors thus believed that intelligent groups of men should lead the public in solving the problems created by urbanization and industrialization. But their differing ideas of individual freedom and the nature of democratic government logically led them to opposing views of who such leaders should be. The reformers expected the government to be responsive to public opinion and to take an active part in actually shaping it. The government, to these reformers, should be more than a passive broker of diverse public and semiprivate interests; it should be an organic part of society, and as such its employees should give as well as take opinions and advice. The medical profession did not agree with this view. Its members believed that the government primarily should be a passive and impartial referee in the ongoing struggles between private citizens and interest groups. Only after one or another of these groups and its leaders had already gained vast public support need the government consider action, and even then action should be carefully weighed against the standard of individual freedom and responsibility. To do otherwise would substitute government paternalism for the traditional protection of liberties that factionalism and limited government had heretofore guaranteed. The manipulation of public opinion by government officials, they believed, was a most insidious and antidemocratic practice. In time it could only establish a popularly based tyranny which would destroy all possibility for individual excellence and success. While the reformers tended to believe that what they called the welfare of all society was more important than the preservation of all of the liberties and traditions of an individual or group, the medical societies were inclined to believe that these individual liberties were absolute and incontrovertable. To the medical profession the very nature of democracy was endangered by the reformers' desire to trade security and guaranteed services for a small and finite part of the individual's freedom.

The antipathetic viewpoints in large part defined the intellectual positions of the reformers and the organized medical profession throughout this decade. Neither side could, of course, tolerate or accept the ramifications of its opponents' position and, therefore, neither could compromise. The deadlock was to throw the decision to the public and their elected officials.

5

Old Endings and New Beginnings 1939–1943

In late 1938 and early 1939 most health insurance reformers believed that the interest shown by Senator Wagner and the agencies of the coalition, reinforced by the public support which *seemed* so overwhelming at the National Health Conference, would precipitate congressional action on the National Health Program no later than 1941. The medical profession appeared to be internally divided and unable to offer serious opposition, and the reformers seemed united in their support and determined in their commitment. By 1941, however, Congress had not acted on the Wagner Health Bill, the public had given hardly any support to the National Health Program, and the organized medical profession had opposed the legislation in a unified and effective way. The coalition had crumbled into its component parts, with each agency supporting limited legislation in its own field of interest. The weakness of administration support, the political ineptness of the supporters of the National Health Program, and the growing conservative mood of Congress contributed to the outcome, but perhaps the most important and least definable influence of all was the changing national attitude.

After 1938 public and governmental attention was increasingly focused on foreign affairs and preparations for defense. When the long-feared war broke out in Europe, domestic prosperity coincided with rearmament, and Roosevelt, his administration, and the public lost much of their interest in sweeping

New Deal reforms.[1] In the field of health, voluntary insurance plans were mushrooming across the nation and diverting what middle-class interest there might have been in compulsory insurance. The reformers gradually began to focus their attention on less expensive, more limited programs.

Interest in specific medical care reforms died away at the same time as a general and deep-seated change in American attitudes was taking place. The concept of individualistic freedom was gradually being modified by a host of real social forces, and within a few decades, it would be changed enough to enable compulsory health insurance proposals to gain public support and legislative approval.

By the late 1930's and early 1940's the nation had already begun to witness this transformation. Although prosperity had returned, most citizens could not forget the terrors of the depression and therefore clung to New Deal institutions and ideas as protection against the return of chaos and insecurity. The Social Security system, for example, and the newer concept of freedom upon which it was based, thus became an increasingly important part of the national creed.[2] Reforms that went beyond current perceived need and seemed unfamiliar or overly radical were still not wanted, or, in the light of the new prosperity, needed. Nonetheless the philosophical and institutional bases upon which such sweeping reforms could ultimately be built were gradually being assimilated. Thus, barring another profound shift in public belief, the newer ideas would later be there to be drawn upon.

The last major attempt of the health insurance reformers to obtain federal legislation in the 1930's was the Wagner Health Bill of 1939, a direct descendant of the National Health Program of 1938. Although it incorporated the main outlines of the earlier proposal, the bill, in response to political pressures, was weakened and modified in the particular area of compulsory health insurance.[3]

The political pressures which brought about modifications were of several types. An important force came from within the coalition itself and took the form of bureaucratic rivalry. During the last half of 1938 the Children's Bureau and the Public Health Service became increasingly concerned with the risk of tying their favorite programs to the National Health Program. They sensed that the public was not sufficiently interested in compulsory health insurance to override the growing opposition of organized medicine, and they believed that the entire National Health Program would encounter serious congressional opposition unless that part were weakened. Therefore during the closing months of 1938 they prevailed on the third major member of the coalition, the Social Security Board, to moderate its recommendations before including them in the proposed bill.[4] The AMA exerted a less direct form of pressure by mounting a widespread campaign against certain of the National Health Program's unacceptable features and simultaneously strengthening support of voluntary insurance schemes. It thereby helped divide the coalition and gained a potentially important arguing point before Congress. By the time the Wagner Health Bill was introduced, the AMA could maintain that because of the existence of voluntary plans, there was neither the need nor the demand for federal action in the field of health legislation.[5] Another and most complicated form of pressure came out of the unsuccessful conferences which the Interdepartmental Committee held with various medical professional groups during the closing months of 1938. The AMA sent a delegation to meet with representatives of the Interdepartmental Committee on three separate occasions. For its own reasons, the Interdepartmental Committee adopted a policy of listening to but not conferring with the doctors, thereby convincing the AMA that the government was spurning their sincere offers of cooperation and help.

The Interdepartmental Committee also held meetings with the representatives of the voluntary hospitals which produced the same fears and bitterness as those with the doctors. The hospital delegates, with possible coaching from the AMA, stated their concerns about the possible exclusion of their institutions from the proposed legislation. They sought definite assurance that such would not be the case and presented a series of formal policy requests which the committee "gave them to understand" would be respected.[6]

Attempts to use the discussions with the Interdepartmental Committee as a pressure tactic led to serious miscalculations by both the AMA and the reformers. The medical and hospital representatives, for example, later claimed that the Interdepartmental Committee had ignored their suggestions, and, consequently, the series of conferences could have had no influence whatsoever on the final shape of the Wagner bill. Evidence overwhelmingly indicates that the exact opposite was the case, however. Although the Interdepartmental Committee refused to concede anything of significance *during* the negotiations, it did, in fact, adopt most of the AMA and hospital representatives' proposals once the conferences were over. According to Senator Wagner himself, the National Health Bill of 1939 "closely followed the AMA Special Session outline of September 1938."[7]

A policy of accommodation to the AMA position is the only logical explanation for the demands in late 1938 by the Children's Bureau and the Public Health Service that the Social Security Board weaken its health insurance proposals. These agencies must have been deeply influenced by the fears and hostilities which the conferences had exposed, and they did convince the Social Security Board staff to meet their demands in late 1938. By the time the National Health Program was ready for congressional introduction, the sections dealing with health insurance and medical care for the indigent had been lumped together, and programs for aid to the indigent and medically indigent were made far more important than the health insurance program. Once again political pressures and temerity undermined support for compulsory health insurance.[8]

Five weeks after President Roosevelt sent Congress his special message relating to revisions of the Social Security Act and recommending that Congress study the findings of the Interdepartmental Committee, Senator Wagner introduced the National Health Bill of 1939.[9] It represented the final form of the National Health Program as modified by the Interdepartmental Committee and the Technical Committee on Medical Care and was comprised of proposed amendments to the Social Security Act of 1935.

S. 1620, as the Wagner bill was designated, followed the title and section numbers of the existing Social Security Act. Title V of S. 1620 established a federal program to provide actual medical care to infants and mothers through the Children's Bureau and the state governments. It also enlarged or expanded existing educational and remedial programs which the Social Security Act of 1935 had created in the Children's Bureau. Title VI greatly increased the funds available for the Public Health Service programs and for the first time introduced a formula of variable matching funds which acknowledged the wealth differential among the states. Title XII provided for the establishment of a federal program of hospital and medical center construction and maintenance subject to local need and the approval and supervision of the surgeon general of the United States. Title XIII provided funds to the Social Security Board for use in aiding and supervising state governments in their attempts to create federally approved general medical care programs. Although compulsory health insurance was not specifically mentioned, the relevant sections did not exclude this type of program. Title XIV provided funds to the Social Security Board to help the states establish and maintain systems of temporary disability compensation insurance on the model of the existing federal-state unemployment insurance system.[10] The bill also provided for a system of national and state advisory councils for each of its different programs. Thus, there would be 245 separate councils for the public health, maternal and infant, hospital construction, general health, and disability insurance programs on the federal level and on the state level, each of which would consist of experts in the designated fields.[11] Each title also specified that all programs were voluntary, by which the drafters of the bill meant that no state government would be required to establish or participate in a particular program if it chose not to do so. Broad, permissive guidelines for states which did desire to participate were supposed to guarantee that local conditions and problems would be recognized under the law's administration.[12]

All programs included in the Wagner bill were supposed to be aimed primarily at the indigent and medically indigent segments of the population. The systems of variable grants and the language of the bill itself made it clear that the policy of the Interdepartmental Committee was to present a sophisticated New Deal relief measure which could, if the states so desired, be expanded to cover the population at large. Rather than creating a national health program which would start out to meet the needs of the entire population, the Wagner Health Bill of 1939 was consciously aimed at immediate action for the one-third of the nation's "ill-housed, ill-clothed and ill-fed."[13]

After its introduction by Senator Wagner, S. 1620 was referred to the Senate Committee on Education and Labor for public hearings which began in late April 1939. Witnesses who testified during these early hearings were either government experts or lay reformers who gave their full support to S. 1620. Although many of them felt that the bill was weak or badly conceived in its administrative machinery, they endorsed it as introduced. They believed that the Wagner Health Bill, with all its faults, was a concrete program for action which could serve as a rallying point for the farm and labor organizations that wanted extensive federal health programs. The reformers hoped the representatives of these organizations would serve as a counterweight to the expected anti-insurance testimony of the medical societies.

Although many government experts and most lay representatives at the hearings supported S. 1620 without significant reservation, several members of the Interdepartmental Committee coalition openly defected at this time and attacked the bill before the Senate subcommittee. The Public Health Service, which because of bureaucratic rivalry and its special relationship with organized medicine had been the most reluctant member of the coalition, was the most important of these.

As early as 1936 the Public Health Service had viewed the health studies of the Social Security Board's Division of Research and Statistics as an encroachment on its own field of responsibility. PHS members were continually exhorted by their superiors to overcome the Social Security Board challenge and retain full leadership in the fields of medical care studies and planning for indigent medical care. They were also urged to keep abreast of developments in the private sector of medical care so that their agency, rather than the Social Security Board, would become the principal federal department dealing with all aspects of medical care.[14]

Given such attitudes, it is not difficult to understand why the PHS was at best an uneasy member of the National Health Program coalition. Several pro-insurance reformers had hoped that time and the experience of working together would soften the PHS position, but this did not seem to happen. On the contrary, as time went on the service seemed less and less comfortable with the National Health Program and the coalition, and when the hearings on the Wagner Health Bill opened in April 1939, they were ready for a more or less open split.[15] For example, a memo from Surgeon C. E. Rice which embodied the tentative Public Health Service position toward the Wagner Health Bill was presented to the Assistant Surgeon General C. E. Waller for approval on April 14, 1939. It contained the following conclusions:

> 1. I would say that the Service is evidently uncertain as to how much interest or what form of interest it should continue to manifest in the subject of medical care.
>
> 2. From my limited point of view, I would say that *if the Wagner Bill died completely, it might be all to the good* [italics mine]. The following points are based on the assumption that this Bill will not progress beyond hearings.
>
> 3. The Service should continue to manifest interest in this subject and encourage the continuance of a coordinating committee

(the present Technical Committee [of the Interdepartmental Committee] broadened somewhat). This is needed as *there is obviously still much distrust between governmental agencies concerned with this subject* [italics mine].

4. There should be some attempt to form a continuing advisory committee on this subject, advisory to the Coordinating Committee. This advisory committee should have membership from the American Medical Association, labor, etc.

5. Thought might be given to having this Coordinating Committee set up as a statutory body for further study purposes with the advisory group as part of the picture. It might thus receive an appropriation for its use.

6. I would question the advisability of the Service interesting itself to any great extent in the subject of medical relief as carried on by welfare agencies without the full knowledge and cooperation of the Bureau of Public Assistance of the Social Security Board. Possibility of closer cooperation here is worthy of exploration.

7. It would seem more logical for the Service to interest itself in medical practices or medical care patterns that prevail outside the relief group. Cooperative projects between local health and welfare agencies would seem especially fitting for such observations.

8. It would seem especially fitting for the Service to continue to interest itself in some phases of *need* provided; quality of care can be made part of such studies. This can be done with certain diseases which have marked public health interest.[16]

Rice's candid statements were probably found acceptable by the leadership of the Public Health Service, because shortly after they were filed, the service forwarded a distinctly negative report on S. 1620 to the chairman of the Senate subcommittee. The report called for a simpler administrative organization for the proposed programs, greater interdepartmental coordination, a system of required consultation between the surgeon general and the state and federal administrative agencies, and a single Federal Advisory Health Council to serve all of the proposed programs. Most important, it strongly recommended that administrative control of the programs established by Title XIII—namely, those having to do with state medical care programs—be transferred from the Social Security Board to the

Public Health Service. Such a transfer would mean in effect that the Public Health Service, with its traditional aversion to health insurance and its close ties to the medical societies, would decide what types of state programs were to be acceptable to the federal government. To the supporters of compulsory health insurance under S. 1620, this was not a happy possibility.[17]

The main features of the PHS report were verbally explained to the Senate subcommittee by Surgeon General Parran on June 2nd. While Parran conceded the need for federal financial assistance to the states for the establishment of medical care programs, and although he praised the permissive features of the proposed legislation, he did not waver in his criticism of the Wagner Health Bill. The effect of his testimony on the chances for passage was, needless to say, extremely serious. A reluctant President and an increasingly conservative Congress could hardly be expected to support a piece of comprehensive legislation upon which not even the participating administrative agencies could agree.[18] The damage done by the surgeon general's testimony was compounded when other representatives of the coalition agencies attacked S. 1620. The Children's Bureau endorsed the bill, but its parent agency, the Department of Labor, called for the inclusion of a title covering industrial health hazards. The chairman of the Social Security Board, Arthur Altmeyer, personally testified that tighter administration and more detailed terminology was needed.[19]

The administrative features of S. 1620 that drew almost universal criticism were the product of two separate forces. First, they resulted from the bureaucratic rivalry which existed among the coalition members. These agencies wanted to be able to salvage their specific programs if the rest of the bill were scrapped and therefore pushed for separate administrative machinery within each title of the bill. The other was the hesitancy of Senator Wagner to create a centralized administration in his health bill until the executive branch of the federal government had been reorganized. Since a reorganization was expected in 1939, Wagner believed that the subcommittee could modify the bill in executive session after the Reorganization Act had passed.[20]

The effect of the criticisms of the bill's administrative weaknesses by government representatives was disastrous, but when the so-called liberal professional associations joined in, all hope for positive congressional action on S. 1620 seemed to disappear. Representatives of liberal professional groups soon began to testify to the Wagner bill's weaknesses. The American Public Health Association endorsed the broad goals of the bill but also called for more centralized administration and supervision. The Committee of Physicians for the Improvement of Medical Care, Inc., the mildly liberal doctors' group which many reformers believed was representing the true feelings of a large fraction of the medical profession, emphasized the same point and went on to urge that the bill be directed at the needy segment of the population. Kingsley Roberts, the director of the Bureau of Cooperative Medicine, called for a single administrative authority and more emphasis on the development of voluntary cooperative medical care experiments on a national basis.[21]

Although great damage had been done to the chances for congressional passage of S. 1620 by its friends, the *coup de grâce* came from its enemies. Principal among them was the organized medical profession and its various allies and supporters. The representatives of the nation's private hospitals were included in this group. As described above, they had believed that the Interdepartmental Committee had both understood their position *and* written it into the proposed legislation. When the bill was made public, many of them, in alliance with the spokesmen of the religious charities which supported so many of their institutions, felt that they had been misled. They were shocked to discover that the bill did not contain the language they believed was necessary, and they were afraid that the permissiveness of the bill might be misconstrued to justify the construction of federal hospitals which would compete with already existing and adequate private hospital facilities, thus prohibiting indigent patients from using private hospitals to obtain federally sponsored medical care.[22]

Although Senator Wagner explained that this was not the intention of his bill, the representatives of the private hospitals who testified before the subcommittee remained adamantly opposed to the proposed legislation. Some claimed that the bill was so badly written that it could not be amended, a position curiously similar to that of the AMA. Even moderates within the group severely criticized the administrative weaknesses of the bill and urged Congress to adopt more limited and well-defined programs of federal action.[23]

The AMA itself bitterly attacked the Wagner Health Bill both publicly and in the Senate subcommittee hearings. After its representatives met with President Roosevelt in January, the AMA launched a negative publicity campaign. Editorials in the AMA *Journal* condemned the secrecy with which the bill had been drafted and the administrative looseness of its program. The AMA editorials also attacked the anticipated costs, claimed that the need for the bill's enactment had not been proven, and prophesied that the bill, if enacted, would tend to destroy the independence and initiative of local and state governmental agencies. The *Journal* supported the hospital representatives in claiming that the hospital construction title was largely unnecessary, and it cited the AMA's own study of the health needs of the nation to prove that only a handful of Americans were being denied needed medical care under the existing system.[24]

The AMA campaign against the Wagner Health Bill was carried on to the floor of the House of Delegates when it met in May 1939. A special reference committee was established to consider S. 1620 and prepare an extensive and critical report of its provisions. It presented twenty-two distinct arguments against the Wagner bill, ranging from an accusation that the bill did not provide for the food, clothing, and shelter needed by the indigent segment of the population to a statement that the bill would disturb the American concept of democratic government. The report specifically denied that the Wagner bill conformed to the liberal policy resolutions passed by the House of Delegates Special Session of 1938.[25]

In the hope that an alternative measure might prove more acceptable to the AMA, the drafters of the report also proposed a rapid expansion of preventive medicine and medical care for the indigent through a system of local agencies rather than through complex national programs. Needs would be determined and programs administered on a strictly local basis; the federal government would merely supply financial aid in needy areas. Thus, a system in which all states were eligible for federal aid would be unnecessary. The federal cash contribution to this program, which was modeled after existing concepts of disaster relief for stricken areas, could be economically administered by a single federal agency—presumably the Public Health Service. The program would, its sponsors claimed, have the advantage of providing medical care to those who really needed it with the minimum amount of expense to or meddling by the federal government.[26]

The report of the special reference committee was adopted without dissent by the full House of Delegates on May 17th, and the AMA was now ready to present its case to the Senate subcommittee holding hearings on S. 1620. A large number of AMA witnesses soon began to descend on Washington, fulfilling an earlier promise of the chairman of the Board of Trustees, Arthur Booth.[27] The witnesses who appeared before the subcommittee were both clever and clumsy in their policy statements. On the one hand, they clung to the astute tactic of opposing the entire bill rather than particular titles—a tactic which no doubt had been adopted to divide the coalition further by playing upon the fears and bureaucratic rivalries of the participating agencies. On the other hand, individual witnesses fared badly when they ventured theoretical statements concerning the relationship of medical care and the government.

A typical example of clumsiness was the testimony of the trustee, Dr. R. L. Senesich. He first condemned the bill for being too indefinite and for containing provisions which could be used to aid the wealthier states, and then reversed himself by claiming that the bill was too specific in delegating power to the federal government and not leaving enough room to deal with special local problems which might arise. He admitted that federal aid for the indigent was needed but denied that that provided in the Wagner Health Bill would do any good. He claimed that the aid provided by the bill would somehow harm voluntary hospitals, individual practitioners, and the profession in general and lead to a deterioration of all of medical care by regimenting the profession.[28]

Comments to the subcommittee by other AMA witnesses were essentially identical to Dr. Senesich's testimony. With monotonous regularity they claimed that the bill was administratively weak, that the government should concentrate on restoring general prosperity and let medicine take care of itself, that Title XIII required the establishment of a compulsory health system in all of the states, and that government assistance should be limited only to those who absolutely needed it.[29]

The repetitive attacks on S. 1620 were saved from becoming perfunctory only by the impassioned statements of Morris Fishbein, editor of the *Journal of the AMA*. Dr. Fishbein, a nationally known debater whose talents the reformers had previously seen and felt, made the issue of AMA opposition seem alive and important. He saw the Wagner bill as the result of a "relentless, persistent, almost a ruthless drive since 1935" by certain persons within the federal government. Ignoring the nongovernmental support which the National Health Program and the Wagner Health Bill had won, he claimed that this small clique of men had secretly framed the bill without so much as consultation with the doctors who would provide service under its various titles. And yet, he explained, those men had done such a terrible job of drafting the bill that it could not be improved by amendment. Instead, it would have to be abandoned altogether.[30]

After giving his version of the drafting of the bill, Dr. Fishbein moved to a more subtle, and probably more effective, form of attack. He maintained that even if the bill were amended and passed, it could never work effectively. Such detailed and extensive examinations of local conditions would be necessary and such complicated codes of payment, treatment, and practice needed that a virtual army of state and federal bureaucrats would be required to administer the plan. This, of course, would make the program unpopular and costly and would inundate the patient and doctor in a mass of red tape and delay.[31]

The testimony of the doctors before the Senate subcommittee was reinforced by a public anti-insurance campaign waged by the AMA throughout 1939. Its various parts were postulated on the same concepts that had underlain the association's earlier efforts. Ideological, emotional, and economic factors combined to produce an aversion in most doctors to government intervention in medical practice. The familiar arguments for freedom of choice, professional integrity, the doctor-patient relationship, and the sliding scale and fee-for-service were again presented in AMA literature and speeches. The reformers' argument that the Wagner Health Bill would prove to be an economic boon to the vast majority of doctors was answered by a claim that the quality of medical care and not physicians' incomes was the real issue. Since most members either supported the AMA policies or did not openly criticize them, it may be concluded that now as before they represented the feelings of most of the membership.[32]

Even though the AMA's underlying values remained the same as they had been in earlier struggles, the tactics it employed were more sophisticated and probably more effective. The traditional barrage of *Journal* editorials and efforts by the AMA lobbyists were now supplemented by the formation of an organization designed to offset the propaganda being circulated by pro-insurance and anti-AMA groups. The National Physicians' Committee for the Extension of Medical Service, as this group was called, was in theory a "non-profit, nonpolitical organization for maintaining ethical standards and extending medical service to all the people." It was officially dedicated to private medical practice and the education of the public to the achievements of American medicine, but in reality it was unofficially fostered and supported by the AMA as an antireform device.[33]

Several important reasons existed for the creation and support of the allegedly autonomous National Physicians' Committee. First, the AMA in 1939 felt that it might lose tax-free status if it engaged in political activities. The leaders of the committee were doctors who had proven reliable in their policy statements, and a sizable fraction of them either had held or were holding an office in the AMA. They and other medical leaders, therefore, believed that the National Physicians' Committee could safely perform the more obviously political anti-insurance activities and thereby protect the AMA.[34] A second important reason was the unsavory relationship which had arisen between some of the more zealous members of the organized medical profession and Frank Gannett's ultraconservative Committee to Uphold Constitutional Government. Gannett, a man who had an extremely bad press, had formed the Physicians' Committee for Free Enterprise in Medicine and lured several important AMA figures into supporting it. His bitter denunciations of the Wagner Health Bill had proven attractive to these men, but the politically more astute AMA leaders realized that utilization of their own National Physicians' Committee was a far more productive and respectable alternative. Therefore, they urged the profession to support the National Physicians' Committee rather than any other anti-insurance group and began to disengage their friends from the Gannett Committee.[35]

Another AMA tactic which was used for the first time against the Wagner Health Bill was the weekly repetition of a deceptively simple and purposely ambiguous "Platform of the AMA" on the *Journal*'s editorial page (see appendix B). Drafted by the trustees to conform to the 1938 and 1939 resolutions of the House of Delegates, the platform seemed designed to make the AMA and its members appear more progressive regarding government programs of medical care than they actually were.[36]

All these new tactics tended to add to the reformers' confusion regarding the nature of AMA opposition to the Wagner bill. The insurance advocates tried to make the bill as permissive as possible and to shape it as closely as they could to the recommendations of the 1938 special session of the House of Delegates, but the AMA in its 1939 session decided to oppose the entire bill. It had reversed itself on the issue of supporting recommendations I, II, III, and V of the National Health Program of June 1938 after the reformers had made recommendation IV (a national system of medical care) so weak as to be ineffectual. The introduction of new tactics only increased the feeling among the reformers that they had been betrayed.[37]

In trying to analyze the AMA shift in strategy and policy, the reformers tended to fall back on their earlier explanations of the profession's power structure. This faulty view held that the AMA leadership was unrepresentative of the rank-and-file opinion and was using the medical societies to suppress dissent and advance their own ends. By distorting the meaning of the Wagner bill to their own members and creating alliances with other antireform groups, the AMA doctors were allegedly continuing their policy of selfish opposition to all types of government based medical care reforms.[38]

The disappointment of the reformers with the AMA policies drawn up in May 1939 led these individuals to conclude that the AMA leadership was completely insincere in its statements supporting acceptable reform. As proof they stated that the AMA's own Bureau of Legal Medicine had submitted a report on the Wagner bill in March 1939 which "contained no adverse criticisms of the National Health Bill." After the May 1939 session of the House of Delegates however, the reformers claimed that this had all been changed. The junta of reactionary AMA leaders had at that time apparently succeeded in once again moving AMA policy away from moderate reform.[39]

The bitterness of the reformers over the AMA policy shift was increased when it became apparent that the Senate subcommittee was going to take no action on the Wagner Health Bill during the 1939 session. Whether the subcommittee in fact was more influenced by the dissent within the coalition of sponsoring agencies or by the opposition of the AMA and its allies, the reformers blamed the organized medical profession for the pending defeat of the bill.[40]

As the hearings of the subcommittee had dragged on through the late spring, it had become increasingly obvious that the Wagner bill would not be referred to Congress for action. On June 2nd Senator Murray had announced that the subcommittee's report on S. 1620 would be delayed until the second session of the Congress (1940), because more witnesses were to be heard and because the Senators would need more time to study and amend the bill. When the subcommittee adjourned a few weeks later it promised that an interim report would be released shortly, but almost all informed observers knew that the Wagner bill as it stood was dead.[41]

During June and early July the Senate subcommittee prepared its interim report with the help of the Social Security Board's Division of Health Studies. The Senators supporting the Wagner Health Bill decided to postpone any test of strength in the parent committee or on the Senate floor. They claimed that the bill had served its purpose of clearing the air and putting the issues before the public, and this became the formal position of the subcommittee as contained in the interim report. Released in mid-July, the document explained that the subcommittee agreed with the bill's objectives, but also stated that it wanted to consult with representatives of lay and professional organizations at greater length. It reviewed the criticisms of the Wagner Health Bill which had been raised in the hearings, and stated that the subcommittee was considering amendments to clarify or modify certain titles. In its conclusion the report stated that:

> Some misunderstandings seem to have arisen and criticisms have been expressed concerning part of the Bill. Some witnesses have assumed that it would bring about revolutionary or dangerous changes in medical care. We think these fears are unwarranted, but we will welcome further suggestions as to specific amendments which may safeguard the objectives of the Bill. Medical science has

reached a commendable status in this country. The Bill should encourage the further evolutionary development of medical science, teaching and practice.

The Committee has received assurances of many lay and professional groups that they will be prepared to furnish further information and suggestions. We expect to consult further with representatives of these groups.

We have not yet had adequate time to make exhaustive studies of all the problems involved in the legislation proposed by S. 1620. The Committee will continue its study of S. 1620 so that a definitive report on the proposed legislation can be submitted soon after the beginning of the next session of the Congress.[42]

After this interim report was released the supporters of the Wagner bill continued to maintain the public fiction that the bill would be sent to the Senate floor in 1940. Most of them knew, however, that comprehensive health legislation on the model of the Wagner bill would be impossible to achieve in the near future. The National Health Program coalition had begun to crumble at the first signs of outside pressures, and now its various members seemed interested only in saving their own special programs. Indeed the Children's Bureau and the Public Health Service seemed well satisfied when H.R. 6635 quietly passed the Congress in July 1939 and provided them both with many of the funds they had wanted from the Wagner Health Bill. The Reorganization Act of 1939, which brought forth the weak and decentralized Federal Security Administration, did little to reunite these agencies in an effective coalition: the Children's Bureau remained under the protective wing of the Department of Labor, and the Public Health Service and the Social Security Board continued their hidden feud.[43]

Faced with a moribund Wagner Health Bill, the reformers began to consider alternative plans of action to salvage some of their National Health Program proposals. While the clamor for a comprehensive federal health program was continued by uninformed reformers outside the government, such men as Falk and Altmeyer slowly began to shift their attention to other, less comprehensive proposals. Indeed, by late 1939 Falk had abandoned his work on revisions of the bill for the Senate subcommittee and at the instruction of his superiors had begun to prepare a confidential memorandum on "Some Alternatives in the Health Program." In this secret document he openly admitted that the Wagner Health Bill faced great problems in Congress, and while he explained that he still favored its enactment as the best type of program for the country, he also admitted that only programs of a much more limited scope could have a chance of becoming law.[44]

At the same time that the government reformers were modifying their strategy regarding federal health legislation, the President was coming to a decision on the Wagner Health Bill. Roosevelt had never seen the bill as a piece of must legislation, and by December 1939 he was fairly well committed to its abandonment. In that month he held an abortive meeting with Paul de Kruif and some medical moderates in which their proposal for a compromise national health program was discussed and then shelved. Next he called a meeting of the Interdepartmental Committee leadership to discuss new plans for the future. He backed away from discussion of the Wagner Health Bill in a news conference and kept silent about other reform proposals.[45]

By the beginning of 1940 Roosevelt's popularity was at a low point; the President seemed preoccupied with European developments and a third term; the economy was on dead center and the isolationist-interventionist debate was beginning to tear the nation's politics apart. The President's interest in the Wagner bill and the comprehensive National Health Program type of approach had dwindled to nothing. Simultaneously, an increased concentration by his administration on a series of limited federal health bills occurred. The possibility of American involvement in the European war, the continued pressure of the reformers, and the obvious lack of adequate health facilities in many areas of the country helped win some mild support for such noncontroversial, but potentially effective programs.

The most important of the limited bills was concerned with

the federal construction and maintenance of hospitals in poor or rural areas. The proposal had had a long history within the New Deal starting with the construction of hospitals as part of the Public Works Administration (PWA) and WPA programs. The members of the Interdepartmental Committee had first tried to coordinate these early efforts and then had included hospital construction as Recommendation II in their July 1938 version of the National Health Program. The proposal was modified and included in the Wagner bill as Title XII, but when the bill seemed stalled in the subcommittee in mid-1939, interest in an independent federal hospital construction program quickly revived.[46] Harry Hopkins, the administrator of WPA, proposed that a hospital be constructed in every county of the United States using WPA labor. At the same time a more realistic and limited proposal which would provide hospitals for only needy areas gained the support of the Department of the Treasury. Then, in November 1939, the President met with Federal Security Administrator McNutt to discuss the possible substitution of a limited hospital construction program for the nearly defunct Wagner Health Bill.[47]

By mid-December the President had decided to support a limited federal hospital construction program in order to satisfy both the supporters of health legislation and the proponents of public works. In conferences with Roche, Parran, and Altmeyer, Roosevelt proposed that a two-year construction program "in lieu of other public works and health legislation [be introduced] during the next Congress." To be administered by the Public Health Service and cost $50,000,000 per year, the program would use the labor and technical knowledge of the PWA and the WPA to construct moderately sized and inexpensive hospitals in the neediest areas of the nation. These hospitals would be loaned by the federal government to the local communities in which they were built, and their maintenance would then be the *sole responsibility of the locality*. The counties and cities would use them as health centers and could develop "various schemes for medical care." [48]

The last provision, which hinted that the federal government might be willing to let the hospitals be used in conjunction with local systems of compulsory health insurance, divided the Interdepartmental Committee. In a December 19th meeting of the committee, General Parran and the more conservative members proposed that the recommendations be endorsed as they stood. The more liberal members of the Interdepartmental Committee, still smarting from their defeat on the Wagner Health Bill, realized that since the hospitals would be built in the poorest areas, there would be little chance for them to experiment with health insurance unless the federal government supplied maintenance funds. They argued that without such assistance, the poorest and neediest areas would be unable to obtain a federal hospital in the first place, since they could not guarantee to maintain the hospital once it was constructed.[49]

Faced with this deadlock, the Interdepartmental Committee decided to defer action on the President's proposals until its next meeting on January 9, 1940, when the internal conflict seems to have been resolved in favor of the liberal reformers. Both Parran and the Technical Committee on Medical Care agreed that federal maintenance grants were needed at least during the first three years of hospital operation. The building program was also expanded to include the construction of five hundred diagnostic centers in needy metropolitan neighborhoods, and under the revised plan, the Surgeon General, with the advice of a council of experts, was given the power to approve the location and standards of all facilities constructed under the program. Part of his decision on whether or not to approve a proposed hospital would be based on formal manifestations of local and state approval and interest—a policy designed to protect the states from having to participate in an unwanted federal program.[50]

The representatives of the American Medical Association and the American Hospital Association (AHA) who were in Washington to protect their organizations' interests now began to take an active part in the development of the hospital construction proposals. They insisted that all private facilities be used to their maximum before new construction was undertaken by the federal government, and they demanded that new facilities conform to the standards established by the AMA and the American College of Surgeons. When the Interdepartmental Committee met on January 9th, its members apparently believed the AMA and the AHA were not opposed to a system of federal maintenance subsidies, and, therefore, they acted to approve the Technical Committee's hospital construction recommendations. The Interdepartmental Committee, feeling that it had at last achieved a consensus with the AMA, assigned Falk, Eliot, and a Public Health Service appointee to draft a formal committee statement of these proposals for the President. They apparently felt so sure of FDR's approval that they voted to give committee endorsement to this statement *in advance*.[51]

The apparent victory of the liberal supporters of the three-year maintenance grants was dramatically reversed on the following day. Perhaps because of his desire for a noncontroversial bill, and perhaps because of private suggestions from the AMA and AHA, President Roosevelt, at his January 10th conference with the AMA representatives, announced that he would not recommend federal maintenance funds on even the limited three-year basis. Hospitals, he insisted, would be built by the government only where they were the most needed and where they would be maintained by local and state governments.[52] This unexpected statement from the President, made with the apparent approval of the AMA and AHA representatives, confused and upset the draftsmen of the Interdepartmental Committee. Commissioned only the day before to draw up formal proposals which *included* maintenance funds, they had filed these proposals with the President at ten o'clock that morning. Then had come the Presidential statement in effect renouncing their report and leaving them in an embarrassing position.[53]

The following day the whole Interdepartmental Committee was convened to discuss the entire series of events. The pre-approved report of the drafting committee was attacked by Parran as being poorly worded in places, and the rest of the

Interdepartmental Committee agreed that it "needed clarification." They also voted that Interdepartmental Committee leaders should meet directly with the President before clarifying and redrafting their recommendations.[54]

During the conference on January 16th, Roosevelt seemed to end all hope that the administration would support maintenance funds as part of its hospital construction program. The President cut the proposed first-year federal expenditures to $10,000,000 and stood firm against recommendations that federal funds be provided for even a limited maintenance program. Surgeon General Parran, he said, would administer the plan with the help of an advisory council. Group hospitalization and other voluntary contributory schemes should be encouraged. He then directed the Interdepartmental Committee to draft his program in the form of a bill, and he agreed to send a special message to the Congress on the hospital construction proposal.[55]

The Interdepartmental Committee finally had some clear instructions, and its Technical Committee began to draft the President's message and the proposed bill. The message was ready by late January and delivered to Congress on January 30th. The bill was also completed, and Senators Wagner and George agreed to sponsor it in the Senate. On February 1st it was introduced, given number S. 3230, and referred to the Senate Committee on Education and Labor. Representative Lea introduced it in the House, where it received number H.R. 8240 and was referred to the Committee on Interstate and Foreign Commerce.[56] The "Forty Little Hospitals Bill," as S. 3230 was soon nicknamed, was a mild and noncontroversial measure which represented Roosevelt's current ideas on what could feasibly be done by the federal government in the field of medical care. The bill had obtained the prior consent of the AMA and AHA, and consequently aroused little opposition when public hearings were held on it by a subcommittee of the Senate Education and Labor Committee in March and April 1940. Although AMA and hospital witnesses called for a stronger advisory committee and a limit on the Federal Works Agency funds that would be made available for the program, they as well as all other witnesses supported the bill.[57]

Although a consensus was apparent, the bill was extensively amended by the subcommittee. Senator Taft, the chief architect of these changes, proposed that federal funds be given to the states for their use in constructing hospitals and also opposed construction of any federally assisted hospitals in areas where such construction would compete or interfere with existing nongovernmental institutions. He also urged a stronger role for the advisory council, and on April 18th he proposed a formal amendment which would provide federal funds for maintenance and provide for a transfer of title to the states after construction had been completed.[58] Taft's amendments, which very well might have resulted from a compromise between the supporters of a state-oriented, limited program on the one hand, and the liberals who wanted federal maintenance funds on the other, served as the basis for the subcommittee's revisions. The amended bill was then endorsed by the entire Senate committee and referred to the Senate on April 30, 1940. The Senate amended it slightly and then passed it without dissent on May 30th. The House Committee on Interstate and Foreign Commerce did not consider the bill, however, and S. 3230 died with the adjournment of Congress later in the summer.[59]

The failure of the "Forty Little Hospitals Bill" marked the end of effective congressional interest in health legislation prior to American entry into World War II. The crumbling of the National Health Program coalition, the lack of dynamic presidential leadership, and the conservatism of a budget-minded and war-conscious Congress had made positive action on such legislation extremely difficult. Interest by reform groups and individual experts continued, and, in the case of S. 3230, the support of the President and of the AMA and its allies was forthcoming, but the changing mood of the nation made further hope for federal legislation in this area seem unrealistic. The awesome developments in Europe and Asia and the domestic preoccupation with defense they produced stifled almost all hope for quick federal action. Roosevelt's cautious pursuit of a third term did not help matters, and by the autumn of 1940, viable proposals for federal health programs were non-existent.

Although there was no federal program for health put forth in late 1940 and early 1941, several limited nonadministration bills were introduced and were followed in late 1941 and early 1942 by renewed administration proposals for limited programs. The two principal nonadministration health insurance bills were quite different from the health insurance proposals envisioned in the 1938 National Health Program or the system contemplated under the Wagner Health Bill of 1939. They both proposed that federal systems of health insurance be established, but neither of them would have integrated these systems in an overall program of medical care. They were not based on research as extensive as that which had been undertaken by the Interdepartmental Committee and were in reality limited proposals that were designed to meet specific, limited problems.

The politically more realistic of these two bills was introduced in the Senate on March 19, 1940 by Henry Cabot Lodge and given the number S. 3630. The Lodge measure proposed that an annual sum of $15,000,000 from the Old Age and Survivors' Fund of the Social Security Board be used to purchase up to $40 per year's worth of medical care for eligible persons. To become eligible, workers would have to belong to the OAS system and would have to have been unemployed for at least four weeks prior to the onset of the illness. The bill also proposed that the federal government share the costs of selected expensive pieces of medical equipment with the states upon condition that this equipment be made available to the needy free of charge and to the rest of the population at a modest cost. Only certain illnesses and conditions would be covered by the provisions of this section of the bill, and only certain, high-cost drugs would be allowed a federal subsidy.[60] Although the AMA cautiously endorsed the approach of the Lodge bill and recommended only limited amendments, the various government agencies which had heretofore taken an interest in health insurance legislation unanimously disapproved of the proposal. Little more was heard about the Lodge bill; the Senate committee held no hearings on it, and it died with the adjournment of the 76th Congress.[61]

The other major nonadministration health insurance bill proposed during this period was the Model Bill of Abraham Epstein and the American Association for Social Security. Although the Model Bill had been revised and modernized in 1939 to make it more acceptable to contemporary thought on health insurance, the revision process antagonized most of the health insurance reformers within the federal government. Later, when these individuals were supporting the Wagner Health Bill and the "Forty Little Hospitals Bill," Epstein had his extremely controversial bill introduced in Congress. The reformers found that the opponents of health insurance and government medical programs easily confused and panicked powerful individuals by *purposely* and fallaciously identifying the Epstein bill with the reformers' proposals. They heartily condemned Epstein for blindly providing their enemies with this weapon and thoroughly deprecated his bill when they were asked to comment on it. They told the Senate Committee on Education and Labor that the Epstein bill was too detailed and inflexible in its administration and coverage, too expensive to operate efficiently, and too badly drawn up to merit congressional passage.[62]

The brief flurry over the Lodge and Epstein bills in 1939 and 1940 was followed by a period of increasing federal preoccupation with health in relation to national defense. Almost all vestiges of the earlier National Health Program coalition movement disappeared; there was little if anything said about hospital construction or maintenance programs or health insurance, and by January 1941, the Interdepartmental Committee itself had officially become inactive.[63] Simultaneously, voluntary health and hospitalization insurance plans were undergoing phenomenal expansion, and the medical society indemnity insurance plans were continuing to grow and mature. The prosperity which accompanied the multiplication of defense contracts gave an increasing segment of the population the financial means to participate in the prepayment plans. The plans themselves, which had experimentally worked out their kinks in the late 1930's, were now well established and able to accept the new members. By 1942 more than one in every five Americans was participating in some form of voluntary group prepayment health insurance plan.[64]

The medical profession, which had originally been wary of the plans, now cautiously approved of them. It cooperated in their establishment and administration to an increasing extent after 1938, viewing them as a means of robbing the compulsory health insurance reformers of most of their middle-class support. With the defeat of the "Forty Little Hospitals Bill" of 1940, this strategem appeared capped with success. And the AMA, like the reformers they opposed, now turned their attention to defense.

Whether because their statistics showed that the poor were not benefiting from voluntary hospitalization insurance or because they felt that national defense could best be served by having a comprehensive national program of hospitalization, the staff of the Social Security Board's Division of Health Studies began to consider a federal program of hospitalization insurance in late 1941. Linking their recommendations for permanent and temporary disability insurance to a proposal for a per diem cash benefit to be used to purchase medical care during hospitalization, the division staff conceived of their legislative package as an effective way of meeting individual medical disasters. The insured worker, under this plan, would have most of his large medical and hospital bills paid during a serious illness and would also receive cash payments which could be used to support his family.[65]

The proposals were first approved by the Social Security Board, then put into concrete form, and finally, in October 1941, forwarded to the President. The board hoped that the President would start the legislative process by including these proposals in a special message on Social Security amendments he was preparing to send to Congress in January 1942. The President was apparently impressed by the proposals and decided to include them in his more important budget message rather than in his special message on Social Security amendments. He kept his intentions secret, and when he delivered his message on January 5, 1942, he took many doctors and governmental and private reformers by surprise.[66]

The very vagueness of the President's proposals on hospitalization insurance and the fact that very little prior discussion of the possibility of federal legislation had taken place gave most observers the impression that the proposals were a new and unresearched idea. But the Social Security Board had in reality done extensive work on both disability and hospitalization insurance prior to Roosevelt's statement and had built their recommendations to the President on sound statistical evidence.[67]

The President's speech was followed by furious activity at the Social Security Board. Although the nation had entered the war only weeks before and the government and people were anxious and tense, the Social Security Board staff began holding conferences and drafting legislative proposals. After serious consideration, the board decided to recommend only minimal hospitalization coverage and to leave it to "the individual through his own effort to provide for medical care and meet additional costs for hospitalization."[68] Voluntary hospitalization plans would not be threatened, but almost everyone would receive some protection. The board also decided to delay release of any of its proposed drafts until Congress had had a chance to act on President Roosevelt's budget message.

The organized medical profession strongly opposed the federal hospitalization proposals as being the forerunner of an undesirable and unacceptable system of compulsory federal medical care. To them the enactment of this program would spell the doom of the traditional, free medical profession and with it the greatness of American medicine. Why, they asked, should the federal government concern itself with foolish and unnecessary programs during a time of national emergency?[69]

The feeling that a national emergency existed, widely held by Congress and the people at large, caused the unheralded death of the hospitalization proposals. The President's proposals were forgotten almost as soon as they were made, and no bills embodying them were introduced in the wartime Congress. In 1942 the entire nation seemed totally occupied in an all-consuming drive to win the war and had little time for even modest reforms.

By 1943, however, the nation seems to have become more adjusted to life in a total war. Its leaders and many of its citizens began to think about the shape of postwar America, and in this climate a new medical care reform campaign began to take shape. The wartime Emergency Maternal and Infant Care program of the Children's Bureau and the Lanham Hospital Construction Act seemed to show that extensive federal programs in medical care could be economically and efficiently run with a minimum of undesirable red tape. Concern for the world's poor and needy grew in response to the publication of stories revealing the horrors of war, and many liberals began to rally to the banner of Lord Beveridge's "cradle to grave" national social insurance plans. Meanwhile the voluntary health and hospitalization insurance plans continued to grow at a precipitous rate and helped to educate the public to the possibilities and advantages of group prepayment for medical care.[70]

By mid-1943 these forces had combined to produce considerable support for a new proposal, the Wagner-Murray-Dingell bill, which would have established a national system of health insurance similar to the old age insurance of the Social Security Act. It significantly broke with the traditional concept of federal-state cooperative programs and marked the beginning of a new national phase in the struggle for compulsory health insurance in the United States. The reformers, frustrated and defeated in their support for weaker and more permissive legislation, now escalated their attack to the national rather than federal-state level. After 1943 they rarely retreated to the earlier position of the Wagner Health Bill of 1939 or the National

Health Program of 1938; the recommendations they brought forth from the Fair Deal through Medicare were postulated exclusively on the national approach. Symbolically, at least, in the history of government medical care reform, the Wagner-Murray-Dingell bill was as significant a watershed as the coming of the New Deal.[71]

The defeats of the Wagner Health Bill and the "Forty Little Hospitals Bill" taught the advocates of federal health insurance that they could not expect success through support of weak, permissive legislation. Dedicated as they were to their reform as a means of helping the general public, they could not abandon their campaign because of tactical defeats on specific bills. Compulsory health insurance was needed, and if it could not be obtained through a federal-state approach, then it must be procured as a national centralized program.

This change of tactics by the reformers was accompanied by a host of complex developments in post-New Deal America. Widespread wartime prosperity, the phenomenal growth of voluntary insurance programs among the middle classes, and a popular desire to consolidate and strengthen social reform in the postwar years all helped to create an atmosphere amenable to programs of national compulsory health insurance.[72] As a result, compulsory health insurance first emerged as a significant and continuing public issue in the mid-1940's.

The men immediately responsible for this change of tactics in 1943—the reformers who had supported health insurance ever since the late 1920's—played an ambiguous role in these developments. Internally divided by bureaucratic loyalties, pitted against each other by the medical societies and sometimes by the President, and plagued by self-righteousness and the lack of political discipline so often associated with reformers, they were largely relegated to the roles of "idea men." Their vision of a compulsory health insurance system that would provide economic and medical security to the American people remained just a dream until both politicians and lay leaders became interested enough to conduct the political struggle for its enactment. Yet the reformers, unable to act as a united political force in the fashion of the AMA, did have a vital part to play in the history of compulsory health insurance before 1943. They constantly put forth plans based on the assumption that the government had a duty to guarantee adequate medical care to all its citizens, and they thereby helped the public see that medical care was as much a basic human right as unemployment compensation or a decent income in old age. The people would eventually look to the government to make available adequate medical care when voluntary private efforts proved unable to do so.

The development of public acceptance of an ultimate governmental responsibility for adequate medical care did not mean that the battle for compulsory health insurance was won. The distractions of war, political temerity, effective AMA opposition, and growing voluntary health insurance plans all helped delay final enactment. Americans, increasingly dedicated to the idea of individual security as an essential part of individual freedom, would have to wait a generation more for the first federal program of compulsory health insurance.

APPENDIXES
BIBLIOGRAPHY
NOTES
INDEX

APPENDIX A

Chronology

1912	Social Insurance Commission of the AALL created.
1915	Social Insurance Committee of the AMA established.
1916	Publication of AALL Model Bill.
1917	AMA House of Delegates endorses compulsory health insurance.
1920	AMA House of Delegates condemns compulsory health insurance.
1921	Sheppard-Towner Act passed.
1924	Veterans' medical care program revised.
1927	CCMC established.
1929	Sheppard-Towner Act expires.
1929	Baylor University Hospital Plan started—origin of Blue Cross.
1932	Final Reports of CCMC.
Summer, 1933	FERA medical relief program begun.
June, 1934	CES created.
June, 1934	"Ten Principles" of AMA House of Delegates passed.
November, 1934	National Conference on Economic Security.
January, 1935	Final Report of the CES to the President.
February, 1935	Special Session of the AMA House of Delegates condemns health insurance.
March, 1935	Final Report on Medical Care of the CES.
1935	Model Bill of AASS released.
August, 1935	Social Security Act passed by Congress.
Summer, 1935	Beginning of medical programs of WPA.
Autumn, 1935	Interdepartmental Committee to Coordinate Health and Welfare Activities created.
1937	Farm Security Administration takes over and expands medical program of Resettlement Administration.
March, 1937	Technical Committee on Medical Care of Interdepart-

	mental Committee to Coordinate Health and Welfare Activities created.
June, 1937	"Ten Principles of Group Hospitalization" of AMA House of Delegates passed.
November, 1937	Program of Committee of Physicians for the Improvement of Medical Care publicly announced.
February, 1938	National Health Program publicly released.
July, 1938	National Health Conference.
August, 1938	Negotiations between AMA and Interdepartmental Committee.
September, 1938	Special Sessions of AMA House of Delegates on National Health Program.
January, 1939	Senator Wagner introduces S. 1620, the National Health Bill.
Spring, 1939	AMA loses antitrust suit concerning Group Health Association.
Spring, 1939	National Physicians' Committee for the Extension of Medical Service created.
April, 1939	Hearings begin on S. 1620.
May, 1939	AMA House of Delegates condemns S. 1620.
May, 1940	Senate passes S. 3230, the "Forty Little Hospitals Bill."
January, 1942	President Roosevelt calls for federal hospitalization insurance.
1943	First Wagner-Murray-Dingell Bill proposed.

APPENDIX B

Policy Positions

NINE STANDARDS FOR COMPULSORY HEALTH INSURANCE (AALL)

1. Any system must be compulsory in nature and require contributions from the worker, the employer and the public.
2. All wage workers below a fixed income level are to participate; casual and domestic workers are to be included if possible.
3. Voluntary participation is to be permitted for certain groups not included in the compulsory classification.
4. Separation of the funds for temporary (up to 26 weeks) and permanent disability is to be provided for.
5. Local mutual funds are to be used; they are to be managed jointly by the employers and employees and are to be strictly supervised by the government.
6. Permanent disability funds are to be based on a larger administrative area than the local mutual fund.
7. Benefits to members are to include medical care, hospitalization, nursing care and medical supplies. Organization of the distribution of these service benefits is left to the local fund under strict government supervision.
8. Cash benefits are provided to members for temporary or permanent disability.
9. Prevention is to be emphasized so that compulsory health insurance will lead to a health conservation campaign similar to the safety campaign resulting from the passage of Workmen's Compensation.

Abstracted from "Preliminary Standards for Sickness Insurance Recommended by the Committee on Social Insurance of the American Association for Labor Legislation," *ALLR,* 4:595–596 (1914).

Appendix B

SIX ESSENTIALS OF CCMC MAJORITY

1. The plan must safeguard the quality of medical service and preserve the essential personal relationship between doctor and patient.
2. The plan must provide for the future development of preventive and therapeutic services in all kinds and amounts as will meet the needs of substantially all the people and not merely their present effective demands.
3. It must provide services on financial terms which the people can and will meet, without undue hardship, either through individual or collective resources.
4. There should be a full application of existing knowledge to the prevention of disease, so that all medical practice will be permeated with the concept of prevention. The program must include, therefore, not only medical care of the individual and the family, but also a well-organized and adequately supported public health program.
5. The basic plan should include provisions for assisting and guiding patients in the selection of competent practitioners and suitable facilities for medical care.
6. Adequate and assured payment must be provided to the individuals and agencies which furnish the care.

Abstracted from CCMC *Medical Care for the American People* (Chicago: University of Chicago Press, 1932), p. 38.

Appendix B

CCMC MAJORITY RECOMMENDATIONS

1. Medical service should be more largely furnished by groups of physicians and related practitioners, so organized as to maintain high standards of care and to retain the personal relationship between doctor and patient.
2. Methods of preventing disease should be more extensively and more effectively applied, as measures both of service and economy; and should be so financed as to minimize the economic deterrents to their extension.
3. The costs of medical care should be distributed over groups of people and over periods of time, through the use of insurance, taxation or both.
4. The facilities for medical care should be coordinated by appropriate agencies on a community basis, with special attention given to the coordination of rural and urban services.
5. The education of physicians and the members of related professions should be extended and made more relevant to modern conditions.

Abstracted from CCMC *Medical Care for the American People* (Chicago: University of Chicago Press, 1932), pp. 109–134.

Appendix B

CCMC MINORITY RECOMMENDATIONS

1. Government competition in the practice of medicine should be discontinued except for (a) care of the indigent, (b) care of those with diseases best treated in governmental institutions, (c) public health services, (d) medical care for military personnel and those government employees whose occupations prohibit their use of private facilities, (e) care of veterans suffering from *bona fide* service-connected disabilities and diseases, except in the case of tuberculosis and nervous and mental diseases.
2. Expansion of governmental medical care for the indigent should be undertaken with the ultimate objective of relieving the private medical profession of this burden.
3. Community agencies to coordinate medical services are endorsed.
4. United attempts are urged to restore the general practitioner to the central place in medical practice.
5. The corporate practice of medicine, financed through intermediary agencies, is condemned.
6. Careful experiments which are fitted to our present institutions and agencies and which will not interfere with the fundamentals of medical practice are urged.
7. The development by state and county medical societies of plans for supplying medical care are recommended.

Abstracted from CCMC *Medical Care for the American People* (Chicago: University of Chicago Press, 1932), pp. 170–183.

Appendix B

CES HEALTH INSURANCE STATEMENT (THE ELEVEN PRINCIPLES)

1. The fundamental goals of health insurance are: (a) the provision of adequate health and medical services to the insured population and their families; (b) the development of a system whereby people are enabled to budget the costs of wage loss and of medical costs; (c) the assurance of reasonably adequate remuneration to medical practitioners and institutions; (d) the development under professional auspices of new incentives for improvement in the quality of medical services.
2. In the administration of the services the medical professions should be accorded responsibility for the control of professional personnel and procedures and for the maintenance and improvement of the quality of service; practitioners should have broad freedom to engage in insurance practice, to accept or reject patients, and to choose the procedure of remuneration for their services; insured persons should have freedom to choose their physicians and institutions; and the insurance plan shall recognize the continuance of the private practice of medicine and of the allied professions.
3. Health insurance should exclude commercial or other intermediary agents between the insured population and the professional agencies which serve them.
4. The insurance benefits must be considered in two broad classes: (a) Cash payments in partial replacement of wage-loss due to sickness and for maternity cases, and (b) health and medical services.
5. The administration of cash payments should be designed along the same general lines as for unemployment insurance and, so far as may be practical, should be linked with the administration of unemployment benefits.
6. The administration of health and medical services should be designed on a State-wide basis, under a Federal law of a permissive character. The administrative provisions should be adapted to agricultural and sparsely settled areas as well as to industrial sections, through the use of alternative procedures in raising the funds and furnishing the services.
7. The costs of cash payments to serve in partial replacement of wage loss are estimated as from 1 to 1¼ percent of payroll.
8. The costs of health and medical services under health insurance, for the employed population with family earnings up to $3,000 a year, is not primarily a problem of finding new funds, but of budgeting

CES, *The Report of the Committee on Economic Security to the President* (Washington, D.C.: GPO, 1935), pp. 42–43.

present expenditures so that each family or worker carries an average risk rather than an uncertain risk. The population to be covered is accustomed to expend, on the average, about 4½ percent of its income for medical care.

9. Existing health and medical services provided by public funds for certain diseases or for entire populations should be correlated with the services required under the contributory plan of health insurance.
10. Health and medical services for persons without income, now mainly provided by public funds, could be absorbed into a contributory insurance system through the payment of relief or other public agencies of adjusted contributions for these classes.
11. The role of the Federal Government is conceived to be principally (a) to establish minimum standards for health insurance practice and (b) to provide subsidies, grants, or other financial aids or incentives to States which undertake the development of health insurance systems which meet the Federal standards.

Appendix B

AMA TEN PRINCIPLES

1. All features of medical service in any method of medical practice should be under the control of the medical profession. No other body or individual is legally or educationally equipped to exercise such control.
2. No third party must be permitted to come between the patient and his physician in any medical relation. All responsibility for the character of medical service must be borne by the profession.
3. Patients must have absolute freedom to choose a legally qualified Doctor of Medicine who will serve them from among all those qualified to practice and who are willing to give service.
4. The method of giving the service must retain a permanent, confidential relation between the patient and the "family physician." This relation must be the fundamental and dominating feature of any system.
5. All medical phases of all institutions involved in the medical service should be under professional control, it being understood that hospital service and medical service should be considered separately. These institutions are but expansions of the equipment of the physician. He is the only one whom the laws of all nations recognize as competent to use them in the delivery of service. The medical profession alone can determine the adequacy and character of such institutions. Their value depends on their operation according to medical standards.
6. However the cost of medical service may be distributed, the immediate cost should be borne by the patient, if able to pay, at the time the service is rendered.
7. Medical service must have no connection with any cash benefits.
8. Any form of medical service should include within its scope all qualified physicians in the locality covered by its operation who wish to give service under the conditions established.
9. Systems for the relief of low income classes should be limited strictly to those below the "comfort level" standard of income.
10. There should be no restrictions by nonmedical groups on treatment or prescribing unless formulated and enforced by the medical profession.

JAMA, 102:2199–2201 (1934).

Appendix B

THE NATIONAL HEALTH PROGRAM RECOMMENDATIONS

I. The Committee recommends the expansion of existing cooperative programs under Title VI (Public Health Work) and Title V (Maternal and Infant Hygiene) of the Social Security Act.

II. The Committee recommends a ten-year program for the expansion of the Nation's hospital facilities by the provision of 360,000 beds . . . and by the construction of 5,000 health and diagnostic centers in areas whose populations lack access to hospitals. These new hospital units would require financial assistance during the first three years of operation.

III. The Committee recommends that the Federal Government, through grants-in-aid to the States, implement the provision of public medical care to two broad groups of the population: (1) to those for whom local, State, or Federal Governments, jointly or singly, have already accepted some responsibility through the public provisions of the Social Security Act, through the work relief programs, or through provisions of general relief; (2) to those who, though able to obtain food, shelter and clothing from their own resources, are unable to procure medical care.

IV. The Committee recommends *consideration* [italics mine] of a comprehensive program designed to increase and improve medical services for the entire population. Such a program would be directed toward closing the gaps in a health program of national scope left in the provisions of Recommendations I and III. To finance the program two sources of funds could be drawn upon: (a) general taxation or special tax assessments, and (b) specific insurance contributions from the potential beneficiaries of an insurance system. The Committee recommends *consideration* [italics mine] of both methods, recognizing that they may be used separately or in combination.

V. Temporary disability insurance can *perhaps* be established along lines analogous to unemployment insurance; permanent disability (invalidity) insurance *may* be developed through the system of old-age insurance [italics mine].

Abstracted from "A Summary, A National Health Program: Report of the Technical Committee on Medical Care," *Proceedings of National Health Conference*, pp. 29–32.

Appendix B

AMA TEN PRINCIPLES FOR GROUP HOSPITALIZATION

1. All plans must conform to law and be nonprofit and a majority of all plans' directors must be representatives of the local medical societies or hospital organizations.
2. All reputable hospitals in the local area must be included in the plan.
3. The organized medical profession must have a voice in the organization and administration of the plans.
4. The plans must exclude all medical services from coverage.
5. Fiscal affairs must be handled on an insurance accounting basis, with appropriate supervision from State agencies.
6. There must be an upper limit for participation in the plan.
7. There must be no commercial salesmanship or misleading advertising in regard to enrolling new members.
8. There must be no division of funds on the basis of recruiting new members.
9. The plans must not be used to relieve the financial distress of participating hospitals and must be oriented solely towards the welfare of the patient.
10. The plans must not be seen as a panacea for the economic problems of hospitals or hospitalization: only a small percentage of medical costs are covered. Hospitals should experiment with other plans for relieving medical problems.

JAMA, 108:2219 (1937).

Appendix B

AMA POLICY STATEMENT ON NATIONAL HEALTH PROGRAM

1. The A.M.A. endorses the principles and programs for public health and maternal and infant hygiene with the understanding that such programs will include as little actual medical care as possible.
2. The A.M.A. endorses the program for extension of hospital facilities where the needs exist and endorses the use of all acceptable voluntary hospitals in any hospitalization program.
3. The A.M.A. desires the establishment of a well-coordinated program for general economic betterment of the American people tied to a program of health education and public health. Since private philanthropy is no longer able to carry much of the burden of medical care of the indigent, government support is welcome provided:
   a. public welfare administrative proceedings are simplified;
   b. medical care for the indigent is arranged for by the local welfare official with the local medical profession;
   c. programs are administered on a state by state basis with wide latitude for local conditions.
4. The A.M.A. approves hospitalization service insurance providing all such plans do not incorporate medical services or medical care. The A.M.A. encourages local medical societies to develop plans in accordance with local needs; endorses cash indemnity insurance for the payment of professional bills incurred during a prolonged or emergency illness providing such plans have the approval of the medical society concerned and are under state government supervision; and condemns all forms of compulsory health insurance as bureaucratic, inefficient and potentially harmful to the quality of American medical care.
5. The A.M.A. unreservedly endorses temporary disability insurance providing cash payments during unemployment caused by illness provided that the family doctor is not called upon to certify such illness.
6. The House of Delegates of the A.M.A. appoints a committee of seven under the chairmanship of President Abell to confer with the appropriate representatives of the Federal government concerning the National Health Program.

JAMA, 111:1191–1217 (1938).

Appendix B

PLATFORM OF THE AMA

The American Medical Association advocates:

1. The establishment of an agency of the Federal government under which shall be coordinated and administered all medical and health functions of the Federal government exclusive of those of the Army and Navy.
2. The allotment of such funds as the Congress may make available to any state in actual need, for the prevention of disease, the promotion of health and the care of the sick on proof of such need.
3. The principle that the care of the public health and the provision of medical service to the sick is primarily a local responsibility.
4. The development of a mechanism for meeting the needs of expansion of preventive medical services with local determination of needs and local control of administration.
5. The extension of medical care for the indigent and the medically indigent with local determination of needs and local control of administration.
6. In the extension of medical services to all the people, the utmost utilization of qualified medical and hospital facilities already established.
7. The continued development of the private practice of medicine, subject to such changes as may be necessary to maintain the quality of medical services and to increase their availability.
8. Expansion of public health and medical services consistent with the American system of democracy.

JAMA, 113:2060 (1939).

BIBLIOGRAPHY

Interviews with the following persons provided information essential to this study: Arthur J. Altmeyer, Washington, D.C., July 1965; Nelson Cruickshank, Washington, D.C., July 1965; Michael M. Davis, Chevy Chase, Md., April 1965; Martha M. Eliot, Cambridge, Mass., September 1965; I. S. Falk, New Haven, Conn., June 1965; Morris Fishbein, New York, N.Y., June 1965; Gordon Fortney, Washington, D.C., July 1965; Louis B. Reed, Washington, D.C., July 1965; and C. Rufus Rorem, New York, N.Y., April 1965. Also helpful were telephone conversations with Joseph Huthmacher, Washington, D.C., July 1965; and with C. Rufus Rorem, New York, N.Y., April 1965. I received valuable information from letters written to me by Wilbur J. Cohen, April 22, 1965 and December 1, 1965; Frances Perkins, March 3, 1965; Josephine Roche, March 12, 1965; C. Rufus Rorem, March 5, 1965, May 6, 1965, May 20, 1965; and Nathan Sinai, March 11, 1965. It was my privilege also to consult the personal papers of Arthur J. Altmeyer, John D. Dingell Sr., Morris Fishbein, and C. Rufus Rorem.

In addition, heavy reliance has been placed upon the following records on deposit in the National Archives in Washington, D.C.; Children's Bureau, 1913–1943, Record Group (R.G.) 102; Committee on Economic Security, 1934–1935, R.G. 47; Department of Health, Education, and Welfare and its predecessors, 1935–1943, R.G. 235; Department of Labor, 1935–1943, R.G. 147; Farm Security Administration and its predecessors, 1934–1943, R.G. 96; Federal Security Administration, 1939–1943, R.G. 47; Public Health Service, 1910–1943, R.G. 90; Social Security Board, 1935–1943, R.G. 47; and Works Progress Administration and its predecessors, 1933–1943, R.G. 69. I have also used the records of the Interdepartmental Committee to Coordinate Health and Welfare Activities, 1936–1940, in the Franklin D. Roosevelt Library, Hyde Park, New York.

Abbott, Edith. *Public Assistance: American Principles and Policies, with Select Documents.* 5 vols. Chicago: The University of Chicago Press, 1940.

Allen, Frederick. *Only Yesterday: An Informal History of the Nineteen Twenties.* New York: Harper & Brothers, 1931.

Altmeyer, Arthur J. "Progress Toward Health Security," *The American Labor Legislation Review,* 29:5–11 (1939).

American Academy of Political and Social Science. *The Medical Profession and the Public: Currents and Counter-Currents.* Philadelphia: The Academy, 1934.

American Association for Social Security. *Social Security in the United States.* New York: The Association, 1934–1940. (Annual volumes.)

American Association of Medical Social Workers. *Medical Care for Relief Clients.* New York: The Association, 1935.

Anderson, Odin. "Compulsory Medical Care Insurance, 1910–1950," *Annals of the American Academy of Political and Social Science,* 273:106–113 (1951).

Andrews, John B., ed. "A Brief for Health Insurance," *American Labor Legislation Review,* 6:155–236 (1916).

———, ed. "General Discussion," *American Labor Legislation Review,* 7:51 (1917).

———, ed. "Health Insurance Bill as Developed from Tentative Drafts," *American Labor Legislation Review,* 9:209–240 (1919).

——— "No Time to Falter," *American Labor Legislation Review,* 29:147–148 (1939).

———, ed. "Preliminary Standards for Sickness Insurance Recommended by the Committee on Social Insurance of the American Association for Labor Legislation," *American Labor Legislation Review,* 4:595–596 (1914).

———, ed. "Recent American Opinion on Health Insurance," *American Labor Legislation Review,* 6:351–371 (1916).

———, ed. "Second National Conference of Health Insurance Commissioners," *American Labor Legislation Review,* 8:133–135 (1918).

Bealle, Morris A. *Medical Mussolini.* Washington, D.C.: Columbia Publishing Company, 1939.

Bernstein, Irving. *The Lean Years: A History of the American Worker, 1920–1933.* Boston: Houghton Mifflin Company, 1960.

Bierring, Walter L. "The Family Doctor and the Changing Order," *Journal of the American Medical Association,* 102:1995–1998 (1934).

Block, Maxine, ed. "Thurman W. Arnold," *Current Biography,* pp. 26–28 (1940).

Bremner, Robert H. *From the Depths: The Discovery of Poverty in the United States.* New York: New York University Press, 1956.

Brown, Josephine C. *Public Relief, 1929–1939.* New York: Henry Holt and Co., 1940.

Bruno, Frank J. *Trends in Social Work, 1874–1956: A History Based on the Proceedings of the National Conference of Social Work.* New York: Columbia University Press, 1957.

Burns, A. E. and E. A. Williams. *Federal Work, Security, and Relief Programs.* Washington, D.C.: WPA, 1941.

Bibliography

Burns, James M. *Roosevelt: The Lion and the Fox.* New York: Harcourt, Brace & World, 1956.

Burrow, James G. *A.M.A.: Voice of American Medicine.* Baltimore: The Johns Hopkins Press, 1963.

Cabot, Hugh. "The Case of the Progressive Physician." In *Social Security in the United States, 1939,* pp. 181–185. New York: The American Association for Social Security, 1939.

——— *The Doctor's Bill.* New York: Columbia University Press, 1935.

——— *The Patient's Dilemma: The Quest for Medical Security in America.* New York: Reynal and Hitchcock, 1940.

Chamberlain, Joseph P. "The Practicability of Compulsory Sickness Insurance in America," *American Labor Legislation Review,* 4:49-72 (1914).

Chambers, Clarke A. *Seedtime for Reform: American Social Service and Social Action, 1918–1933.* Minneapolis: University of Minnesota Press, 1963.

Collins, Selwyn D. *Studies of Sickness and Health of 9,000 Families Based on Nation-wide Periodic Canvasses, 1928–1931.* Washington, D.C.: GPO, 1933.

Committee of Physicians. "Attitude and Intent of Committee of Physicians in Presenting Principles and Proposals in the Provision of Medical Care," *Journal of the American Medical Association,* 110:141B–142B (1938).

Committee of Physicians for the Improvement of Medical Care, Inc. "Statement of Members," *New England Journal of Medicine,* 217:887–890 (1937).

Committee on the Cost of Medical Care. *The Five Year Program of the Committee on the Cost of Medical Care.* Washington, D.C.: The Committee, 1928.

Committee on the Costs of Medical Care. *Medical Care for the American People: The Final Report.* Chicago: The University of Chicago Press, 1932.

Committee on Economic Security. *Report to the President.* Washington, D.C.: GPO, 1935.

Corothers, Doris. *Chronology of the Federal Emergency Relief Administration, May 12, 1933 to December 31, 1935.* Washington, D.C.: GPO, 1937.

Croly, Herbert. *The Promise of American Life.* New York: Capricorn Books, 1964.

Davis, Michael M. "Change Comes to the Doctor." In *The Medical Profession and the Public: Currents and Counter-Currents,* pp. 63–74. Philadelphia: The American Academy of Political and Social Science, 1934.

——— "Doctors' Bills and People's Millions," *Journal of the American Medical Association,* 94:1014–1017 (1930).

——— *Eight Years' Work in Medical Economics.* Chicago: The Julius Rosenwald Fund, 1937.

Davis, Michael M. "Organization of Medical Service," *American Labor Legislation Review,* 6:16–20 (1916).
——— "Organized Action in Medical Care," *Survey Graphic,* 22:207–209, 229–231 (1933).
——— *Paying Your Sickness Bills.* Chicago: The University of Chicago Press, 1931.
——— *Public Medical Services: A Survey of Tax-Supported Medical Care in the United States.* Chicago: The University of Chicago Press, 1937.
——— "Sickness Insurance and Medical Care," *The Milbank Memorial Fund Quarterly,* 12:287–305 (1934).
———, and C. Rufus Rorem. *The Crisis in Hospital Finance and Other Studies in Hospital Economics.* Chicago: The University of Chicago Press, 1932.
de Kruif, Paul. *Health Is Wealth.* New York: Harcourt, Brace and Co. 1940.
Dodd, Paul A. and E. F. Penrose. *Economic Aspects of Medical Services with Special Reference to Conditions in California.* Washington, D.C.: Graphic Arts Press, 1939.
Douglas, Paul. *Social Security in the United States: An Analysis and Appraisal of the Federal Social Security Act.* 2d ed. New York: McGraw-Hill Book Company, 1939.
Emerson, Haven. "Signs of the Times in Public Health," *Journal of the American Medical Association,* 112:737–739 (1939).
——— "The Social Cost of Sickness," *American Labor Legislation Review,* 6:11–15 (1916).
Epstein, Abraham, *Insecurity: A Challenge to America,* 2d rev. ed. New York: Random House, 1938.
Falk, I. S. "An Introduction to National Problems in Medical Care," *Law and Contemporary Problems,* 6:497–506 (1939).
——— "Cash and Medical Benefits in Health Insurance," *American Labor Legislation Review,* 26:73–77 (1936).
——— "Formulating an American Plan of Health Insurance," *American Labor Legislation Review,* 24:87–94 (1934).
——— "Fundamental Facts on the Costs of Medical Care," *Milbank Memorial Fund Quarterly,* 11:130–150 (1933).
——— "The Present and Future Organization of Medicine," *Milbank Memorial Fund Quarterly,* 12:115–125 (1934).
——— "Roads Ahead in Health Security," *Survey Graphic,* 27:382–383 (1939).
——— *Security against Sickness: A Study of Health Insurance.* Garden City, N.Y.: Doubleday, Doran and Co., 1936.
———, C. Rufus Rorem, and Martha D. Ring. *The Costs of Medical Care.* Chicago: The University of Chicago Press, 1933.
Farley, James A. *Behind the Ballots: The Personal History of a Politician.* New York: Harcourt, Brace and Co., 1938.
Fishbein, Morris, "The Doctor and the State." In *The Medical Profession and the Public: Currents and Counter-Currents,* pp. 88–101. Phila-

delphia: The American Academy of Political and Social Science, 1934.

——— "The Future of Medical Practice." Address before the Duke University School of Medicine, Oct. 13, 1938.

——— *A History of the American Medical Association, 1847–1947, with the Biographies of the Presidents of the Association by Walter L. Bierring, and with Histories of Publications, Councils, Bureaus, and Other Official Bodies* (by various authors). Philadelphia: W. B. Saunders Co., 1947.

——— "Maintain the Doctor-Patient Relation," *The Rotarian,* 54:15, 58–59 (September 1939).

——— "Medicine and the National Policy." Address before the New York County Medical Society, Jan. 24, 1938.

———"Medicine in the Changing Social Order." Address before the Service Clubs of Binghamton, N.Y., April 4, 1940.

———"Our Changing Times." Address before the West Virginia Medical Society, Wheeling, W. Va., May 8, 1935.

——— "Social Aspects of Medical Care." Address before the Annual Banquet of the Chicago Hospital Council, Jan. 25, 1939.

Fisher, Irving. "The Need for Health Insurance," *American Labor Legislation Review,* 7:9–23 (1917).

Foster, William T. "Doctors, Patients, and the Community." In *The Medical Profession and the Public: Currents and Counter-Currents,* pp. 102–112. Philadelphia: The American Academy of Political and Social Science, 1934.

Frost, Clyde D. and Elizabeth R. Day. *How Do Physicians and Patients Like the Middle Rate Plan for Hospital Care?* Chicago: The Julius Rosenwald Fund, 1932.

Garceau, Oliver. *The Political Life of the American Medical Association.* Cambridge: Harvard University Press, 1941.

Glenn, John M., Lilian Brandt, and F. Emerson Andrews. *Russell Sage Foundation, 1907–1946,* 2 vols. New York: Russell Sage Foundation, 1947.

Goldmann, Franz. *Prepayment Plans for Medical Care.* New York: Joint Committee of the Twentieth Century Fund and the Good Will Fund, and the Medical Administration Service Inc., 1941.

——— *Public Medical Care: Principles and Problems.* New York: Columbia University Press, 1945.

——— *Voluntary Medical Care Insurance in the United States.* New York: Columbia University Press, 1948.

Goldwater, S. S. "The Specialist: What Shall We Do with Him?" *Journal of the American Medical Association,* 88:1961–1963 (1927).

Hard, William. "Is Health Insurance Paternalism?" *American Labor Legislation Review,* 6:123–126 (1916).

Harris, Louis I. "The Doctor Looks at Health Insurance." In *Social Security in the United States, 1935,* pp. 44–56. New York: The American Association for Social Security, 1935.

Harris, M. L. "The General Practitioner in the Medical Scheme," *Journal of the American Medical Association,* 91:1683–1686 (1928).
Hays, Samuel P. *The Response to Industrialism.* Chicago: The University of Chicago Press, 1957.
Health Insurance Commission of the State of Illinois. *Report of the Health Insurance Commission of the State of Illinois.* Springfield, Ill.: Illinois Journal Co., 1919.
Heer, Clarence. "A Study of the Formulae for Grants-In-Aid in the Wagner Bill," *Law and Contemporary Problems,* 6:666–678 (1939).
Hillquit, Morris. *History of Socialism in the United States.* New York: Funk & Wagnalls, 1903.
Hirsh, Joseph. "The National Health Bill, Past, Present, and Future," *American Labor Legislation Review,* 29:111–113 (1939).
Hobbs, Margaret A. "Tendencies in Health Insurance Legislation," *American Labor Legislation Review,* 6:138–141 (1916).
Howard, D. S. *The WPA and Federal Relief Policy.* New York: Russell Sage Foundation, 1943.
Ickes, Harold L. *The Secret Diary of Harold L. Ickes.* New York: Simon and Schuster, 1954.
Interdepartmental Committee to Coordinate Health and Welfare Activities. *The Need for a National Health Program: Report of the Technical Committee on Medical Care.* Washington, D.C.: GPO, 1939.
——— *Proceedings of the National Health Conference, July 18, 19, 20, 1938,* Washington, D.C.: GPO, 1938.
——— *Toward a Better National Health.* Washington, D.C.: GPO, 1939.
Josephson, Emanuel M. *Merchants in Medicine.* New York: Chedney Press, 1941.
Kalet, Anna. "Voluntary Health Insurance in New York City," *American Labor Legislation Review,* 6:142–154 (1916).
Kingsbury, John A. *Health in Handcuffs: The National Health Crisis and What Can Be Done.* New York: Modern Age Books, 1939.
——— "Health Insurance Menaced by Medical Politics," *American Labor Legislation Review,* 26:30–34 (1936).
——— *Health Security for the Nation.* New York: League for Industrial Democracy, 1938.
——— "Mutualizing Medical Costs," *Survey Graphic,* 23:285–286 (1934).
Lape, Esther E., ed. *American Medicine: Expert Testimony out of Court.* 2 vols. New York: American Foundation, 1937.
Lapp, John A. "The Findings of Official Health Insurance Commissions," *American Labor Legislation Review,* 10:27–40 (1940).
Leland, R. G. "Prepayment Plans for Hospital Care," *Journal of the American Medical Association,* 100:870–873 (1933).
———, and A. M. Simons. "Do We Need Compulsory Public Health Insurance? No." *Annals of the American Academy of Political and Social Science,* 170:121–127 (November 1933).
Lindsay, Samuel M. "Next Steps in Social Insurance in the United States," *American Labor Legislation Review,* 9:107–114 (1919).

Lubell, Samuel. *The Future of American Politics.* 3d ed. New York: Harper & Row, Publishers, 1965.
Lubove, Roy. *The Struggle for Social Security, 1900–1935.* Cambridge: Harvard University Press, 1968.
Lynd, Robert S., and Helen M. Lynd. *Middletown: A Study in Contemporary American Culture.* New York: Harcourt, Brace and Co., 1929.
MacKenzie, Frederick. "Health Insurance or State Medicine: An Issue for the Doctors," *American Labor Legislation Review,* 12:128–130 (1922).
Magnuson, Paul B. "Medical Care for Veterans," *Annals of the American Academy of Political and Social Science,* 273:76–83 (1951).
Maslow, Harold: "The Background of the Wagner National Health Bill," *Law and Contemporary Problems,* 6:606–618 (1939).
Means, James H. *Doctors, People, and Government.* Boston: Little, Brown and Company, 1953.
Merton, Robert. *Social Theory and Social Structure.* Glencoe, Ill.: The Free Press, 1957.
Mowry, George. *The Era of Theodore Roosevelt and the Birth of Modern America, 1900–1912.* New York: Harper & Row, Publishers, 1962.
National Archives Microfilms Publications. *Workingmen's Social, Accident, and Sickness Insurance.* Code number I 465. (Microfilm of a collection of historical documents.)
National Legislative Reference Committee of the Progressive Party. *Progressive Congressional Program.* New York: Progressive National Service, 1914.
New York State Legislature, Temporary Legislative Commission to Formulate a Long Range Health Program. *Preliminary Report . . . May 15, 1939.* Albany: J. B. Lyon Co., 1939.
Newsholme, Sir Arthur. *Medicine and the State.* Baltimore: The Williams & Wilkins Co., 1932.
Norby, Maurice. "Hospital Service Plans," *Law and Contemporary Problems,* 6:545–558 (1939).
Parran, Thomas. "Health Services of Tomorrow," In *The Medical Profession and the Public: Currents and Counter-Currents.* Philadelphia: The American Academy of Political and Social Science, 1934.
Parsons, Talcott. *The Social System.* Glencoe, Ill.: The Free Press, 1951.
Pink, Louis H. *The Story of Blue Cross.* Public Affairs Pamphlet Series, no. 101. New York: Public Affairs Committee, 1945.
Reed, Louis B. *Health Insurance: The Next Step in Social Security.* New York: Harper & Brothers, 1937.
Richardson, J. T. "The Origin and Development of Group Hospitalization in the United States," *The University of Missouri Studies,* vol. 20, no. 3 (1945).
Riis, Jacob. *How the Other Half Lives: Studies among the Tenements of New York.* New York: Scribner, 1890.
Roche, Josephine. "Address on the Work and Plans of the Interdepartmental Committee to Coordinate Health and Welfare Activities," *Journal of the American Medical Association,* 111:52–54 (1938).

Roche, Josephine. "The Worker's Stake in a National Health Program," *American Labor Legislation Review,* 28:125–130 (1938).

Roemer, Milton I. "Rural Programs of Medical Care," *Annals of the American Academy of Political and Social Science,* 273:160–168 (1951).

Romasco, Albert. *The Poverty of Abundance: Hoover, the Nation and the Depression.* New York: Oxford University Press, 1965.

Roosevelt, Elliott, ed. *F.D.R.: His Personal Letters.* 4 vols. New York: Duell, Sloan & Pearce, 1947–1950.

Rorem, C. Rufus. "Approved List of Hospital Insurance Plans." Reprint (undated) of an article in *Hospitals,* found by author in Mr. Rorem's files.

——— *Blue Cross Hospital Service Plans: Description and Appraisal of a Nation-Wide Program for the Distribution of Adequate Hospital Care on a Non-Profit, Non-Political Basis.* 2d ed. Chicago: American Hospital Association, 1940.

——— "Enabling Legislation for Non-Profit Hospital Service Plans," *Law and Contemporary Problems,* 6:528–544 (1939).

——— *Group Budgeting for Hospital Care: How to Organize a Plan of Group Hospitalization.* 2d. rev. ed. Chicago: American Hospital Association, 1936.

——— "Health Problems from the Layman's Point of View." Address before the Minnesota State Medical Association, May 4, 1937.

——— *Hospital Care Insurance: An Historical and Critical Analysis of the Periodic Payment Plan for the Purchase of Hospital Care (Group Hospitalization).* Chicago: American Hospital Association, 1937.

——— *The Middle Rate Plan for Hospital Patients: The First Year's Experience of the Baker Memorial of the Massachusetts General Hospital.* Chicago: The Julius Rosenwald Fund, 1931.

——— *Non-Profit Hospital Service Plans.* Chicago: American Hospital Association, 1940.

——— "Private Group Clinics," *Survey Graphic,* 63:410–411 (1930).

——— "Recent Developments in Hospital Service Plans." Reprint (undated) of an article in *Hospitals,* found by author in Mr. Rorem's files.

——— "Voluntary Hospital Care Insurance." Reprint (undated) of an article in *State Government,* found by author in Mr. Rorem's files.

——— "What About Dependents? *The Modern Hospital,* 48:53–55 (1937).

Rorty, James. *American Medicine Mobilizes.* New York: W. W. Norton & Company, 1939.

Ross, Mary "California Weighs Health Insurance," *Survey Graphic,* 24: 213–217, 268–269 (1935).

——— "Health Inventory, 1934," *Survey Graphic,* 23:15–17, 38–40 (1934).

——— "Sickness Bills by Installment," *Survey Graphic,* 24:109–111 (1935).

Rubinow, Isaac M. "Compulsory Health Insurance in the United States," *American Labor Legislation Review,* 8:85–107 (1918).

——— "Health Insurance through Local Mutual Funds," *American Labor Legislation Review,* 7:69–78 (1917).

——— *The Quest for Security*. New York: Henry Holt and Co., 1934.
——— "Sickness Insurance," *American Labor Legislation Review*, 3:162–171 (1913).
———*Social Insurance*. New York: Henry Holt and Co., 1913.
Seager, Henry R. "Plan for a Health Insurance Act," *American Labor Legislation Review*, 6:21–25 (1916).
Shadid, Michael M. *A Doctor for the People: The Autobiography of the Founder of America's First Co-operative Hospital*. New York: Vanguard Press, 1939.
Simons, A. M. and Nathan Sinai. *The Way of Health Insurance*. Chicago: The University of Chicago Press, 1932.
Sinai, Nathan, Odin Anderson, and Melvin L. Dollar. *Health Insurance in the United States*. New York: The Commonwealth Fund, 1946.
Somers, Herman, and Anne Somers. *Doctors, Patients, and Health Insurance*, abridged ed. New York: Doubleday & Company, 1961.
Sumner, William Graham, *What Social Classes Owe to Each Other*. Caldwell, Idaho: The Caxton Printers, 1961.
Swackhamer, Gladys V. *Choice and Change of Doctors: A Study of the Consumer of Medical Services*. New York: The Committee on Research in Medical Economics, 1939.
Swope, Chester. "Federal Hospital Program." In *Congressional Record*, 86:8136–8138 (1940).
Sydenstricker, Edgar. "Medical Practice and Public Needs." In *The Medical Profession and the Public: Currents and Counter-Currents*, pp. 21–30. Philadelphia: The American Academy of Political and Social Science, 1934.
——— "Sickness and the New Poor," *Survey Graphic*, 23:160–162 (1934).
Tugwell, Rexford G. *The Democratic Roosevelt: A Biography of Franklin D. Roosevelt*. Garden City, N.Y.: Doubleday & Company, 1957.
U.S., Bureau of Census. *Historical Statistics of the United States, Colonial Times to 1957*. Washington, D.C.: GPO, 1960.
U.S., Congress, House, Committee on Labor. *Hearings . . . for the Establishment of a National Insurance Fund and for the Mitigation of the Evil of Unemployment*. 64th Cong., 1st sess., April 6, 11, 1916.
U.S., Congress, Senate. *Congressional Record*. 76th–78th Congs., January 1939–January 1943.
U.S., Congress, Senate, Committee on Education and Labor. *Hearings . . . on S. 1620*. 76th Cong., 1st sess., April 27, May 4, 5, 11, 25, 26, June 1, 2, 29, July 13, 1939.
U.S., Congress, Senate, Committee on Education and Labor. *Hearings . . . on S. 3230*. 76th Cong., 2nd sess., March 18, 19, 1940.
Wagner, Robert F. "Federal Hospital Construction Program." In *Congressional Record*, 86:1359–1360 (1940).
——— "The National Health Bill," *American Labor Legislation Review*, 29:13–44 (1939).
——— "Protection and Care of Public Health." In *Congressional Record*, 84:1976–1982 (1939).

Warnshuis, Frederick. "Michigan Makes Ready," *Survey Graphic,* 23:639–640 (1934).
Warren, B. S., and Edgar Sydenstricker. *Health Insurance: Its Relation to the Public Health.* Washington, D.C.: GPO, 1916.
Wecter, Dixon. *The Age of the Great Depression, 1929–1941.* New York: The Macmillan Company, 1948.
Weybright, Victor. "When Life Comes First . . ." *Survey Graphic,* 28: 734–737 (1939).
Wilbur, Ray L. *The First Three Years' Work of the Committee on the Costs of Medical Care and Its Plans for the Future.* Washington, D.C.: The Committee on the Costs of Medical Care, 1930.
Williams, T. Harry, Richard N. Current, and Frank Freidel. *History of the United States,* 2 vols. New York: Alfred A. Knopf, 1960.
Willoughby, W. F. "The Philosophy of Labor Legislation," *American Labor Legislation Review,* 4:37–46 (1914).
——— "The Problem of Social Insurance: An Analysis," *American Labor Legislation Review,* 3:153–161 (1913).
Winslow, Charles E. A. *Health Care for Americans.* Public Affairs Pamphlet no. 104. New York: Public Affairs Committee, 1945.
Witte, Edwin E. *The Development of the Social Security Act.* Madison: University of Wisconsin Press, 1962.
——— "Health Security Progress," *American Labor Legislation Review,* 30:5–7 (1940).

NOTES

INTRODUCTION

1. U.S., Bureau of Census. *Historical Statistics of the United States, Colonial Times to 1957* (Washington, D.C.: GPO, 1960), pp. 37, 178, 677.

2. Robert H. Bremner. *From the Depths: The Discovery of Poverty in the United States* (New York: New York University Press, 1956).

3. Clarke A. Chambers. *Seedtime for Reform: American Social Service and Social Action, 1918–1933* (Minneapolis: University of Minnesota Press, 1963).

1. BACKGROUND DEVELOPMENTS, 1900–1932

1. U.S., Bureau of Census, *Historical Statistics of the United States, Colonial Times to 1957* (Washington, D.C.: GPO, 1960).

2. Clarke A. Chambers, *Seedtime for Reform: American Social Service and Social Action, 1918–1933* (Minneapolis: University of Minnesota Press, 1963).

3. Many citizens believed that if reforms were not instituted, the future of American society might become something like that described by Jack London in *The Iron Heel.* See Samuel P. Hays, *The Response to Industrialism.* (Chicago: The University of Chicago Press, 1957), pp. 37–43.

4. Isaac M. Rubinow, *The Quest for Security* (New York: Henry Holt and Co., 1934), p. 511.

5. Chambers, *Seedtime for Reform;* Robert S. and Helen M. Lynd, *Middletown: A Study in Contemporary American Culture* (New York: Harcourt, Brace and Co., 1929), pp. 468–469; William Graham Sumner, *What Social Classes Owe to Each Other* (Caldwell, Idaho: The Caxton Printers, 1961).

6. Lynd and Lynd, *Middletown,* pp. 468–469.

7. This attitude still retains some popularity and is a major theme in the public debate over public welfare.

8. T. Harry Williams, Richard N. Current, and Frank Freidel, *History of the United States* (New York: Alfred A. Knopf, 1960), II, 299–301.

9. This theme is developed in Jacob Riis, *How the Other Half Lives: Studies among the Tenements of New York* (New York: Scribner, 1890).

10. Michael M. Davis, interview, April 1965. List of AALL members may be found in *American Labor Legislation Review (ALLR)* 2:156–157 (1912).

11. The AALL had a typical pressure group structure: almost all power was concentrated in the hands of the executive committee and executive director, and the illustrious personages on the letterhead did little more than lend their names.

12. Davis interview; Frank J. Bruno, *Trends in Social Work, 1874–1956: A History Based on the Proceedings of the National Conference of Social Work* (New York: Columbia University Press, 1957), pp. 221–223; National Legislative Reference Committee of the Progressive Party, *Progressive Congressional Program* (New York, Progressive National Service, 1914), pp. 43–47.

13. Davis interview; I. S. Falk, interview, June 1965.

14. Bruno, *Trends,* pp. 258–262; W. F. Willoughby, "The Problem of Social Insurance: An Analysis," *ALLR,* 3:153–161 (1913).

15. John B. Andrews, ed., "A Brief for Health Insurance," *ALLR,* 3:153–161, 189, 228, 231 (1913).

16. Ibid., pp. 211, 230, 232.

17. The committee was created in December 1912 and was chaired by Professor Edward T. Devine. Some of its members were Frederick L. Hoffman, an insurance statistician, Isaac M. Rubinow, a statistician for the U.S. Department of Labor, and John B. Andrews, the Secretary of the AALL. *ALLR,* 5:32–35 (1915); Joseph P. Chamberlain, "The Practicability of Compulsory Sickness Insurance in America," *ALLR,* 4:49–72 (1914); Isaac M. Rubinow, "Compulsory Health Insurance in the United States," *ALLR,* 8:93 (1918).

18. The Model Bill is found in *ALLR,* 6:239–268 (1916).

19. Ibid.

20. John B. Andrews, "Secretary's Report, 1915," *ALLR,* 6:103–111 (1916).

21. Haven Emerson, "The Social Cost of Sickness," *ALLR,* 6:11–15 (1916); Michael M. Davis, "Organization of Medical Service," *ALLR,* 6:16–20 (1916); Henry R. Seager, "Plan for a Health Insurance Act," *ALLR,* 6:21–25 (1916); Miles M. Dawson, quoted in Andrews, "A Brief for Health Insurance," p. 199.

22. Anna Kalet, "Voluntary Health Insurance in New York City," *ALLR,* 6:142–154 (1916).

23. James M. Burrow, *A.M.A.: Voice of American Medicine* (Baltimore: The Johns Hopkins Press, 1963), pp. 150–151. The ten states which had health insurance commissions were California, New Jersey, New York, Ohio, Connecticut, Illinois, Massachusetts, Pennsylvania, Wisconsin, and New Hampshire. John B. Andrews, ed., "Second National Conference of Health Insurance Commissioners," *ALLR,* 8:133–135 (1918).

24. Burrow, *A.M.A.;* Morris Fishbein, *A History of the American Medical Association, 1847–1947* (Philadelphia: W. B. Saunders Co., 1947), pp. 1–287.

25. Burrow, *A.M.A.,* pp. 105–106, 132–141.

26. "Report," *ALLR,* 3:125 (1913); Fishbein, *History,* pp. 278–281.

27. Fishbein, *History,* p. 298. Specific characteristics that the authors

of the Social Insurance Committee Report felt were necessary in any compulsory plan included: (1) free choice of physician by the patient; (2) remuneration proportional to amount of services rendered; (3) separation of official medical supervision from the daily care of the sick; (4) adequate professional representation on the appropriate administrative agencies.

28. Morris Fishbein, interview, June 1965.

29. "Recent American Opinion on Health Insurance," *ALLR,* 6:351 (1916); Andrews, "A Brief for Health Insurance," pp. 162–163, 227.

30. Andrews, "A Brief for Health Insurance," pp. 155–236.

31. Isaac M. Rubinow, "Health Insurance through Local Mutual Funds," *ALLR,* 7:69–78 (1917).

32. U.S., Congress, House, Committee on Labor, *Hearings . . . for the Establishment of a National Insurance Fund and for the Mitigation of the Evil of Unemployment.* 64th Cong., 1st sess., April 6, 11, 1916, pp. 120–121.

33. Ibid.

34. Health Insurance Commission of the State of Illinois, *Report* (Springfield, Ill.; Illinois Journal Co., 1919), pp. 162–173; Nelson Cruickshank, interview, July 1965.

35. S. P. Bush, in John B. Andrews, ed., "General Discussion," *ALLR,* 7:60–61 (1917).

36. William G. Curtis, chairman of the Educational Committee of the Insurance Economics Society of America, to Surgeon General Rupert Blue, May 29, 1917, Public Health Service, Record Group (R.G.) 90, National Archives, Washington, D.C.; Falk interview; Davis interview.

37. Curtis to Blue, May 29, 1917; Falk interview.

38. Falk interview.

39. Emery R. Hayhurst, G. D. Selby, George V. Sheridan, Francis D. Tyson, and Walter S. Foster, in Andrews "General Discussion," pp. 51, 55, 56, 57, 96–98; Irving Fisher, "The Need for Health Insurance," *ALLR,* 7:9–23 (1917); Mary Ross, "California Weighs Health Insurance," *Survey Graphic,* 24:268–269 (1935).

40. Falk interview.

41. Frederick Allen, *Only Yesterday: An Informal History of the Nineteen Twenties* (New York: Harper & Brothers, 1931).

42. Samuel M. Lindsay, "Next Steps in Social Insurance in the United States," *ALLR,* 9:107–114 (1919).

43. "Health Insurance Bill as Developed from 'Tentative Drafts,'" *ALLR,* 9:209–210 (1919); John A. Lapp, "The Findings of Official Health Insurance Commissions," *ALLR,* 10:27–40 (1940). The commissions of Wisconsin, Connecticut, and Pennsylvania saw no demand or need for compulsory health insurance; the Illinois commission was openly opposed; and the commissions of New York, California, and Ohio merely endorsed their earlier approval of compulsory health insurance.

44. Burrow, *A.M.A.,* pp. 146–149; Fishbein, *History,* p. 304.

45. Fishbein, *History,* pp. 146–149; Fishbein interview.

46. Fishbein, *History,* pp. 320–321.

47. *ALLR,* vol. 13 (1923).

48. Allen, *Only Yesterday.*

49. Ibid.; Irving Bernstein, *The Lean Years: A History of the American Worker, 1920–1933* (Boston: Houghton Mifflin Company, 1960).

50. Albert Romasco, *The Poverty of Abundance: Hoover, the Nation, and the Depression* (New York: Oxford University Press, 1965), pp.18–19.

51. Ibid.; Lynd and Lynd, *Middletown,* pp. 468–469.

52. *Journal of the American Medical Association (JAMA).*

53. I. S. Falk, C. Rufus Rorem, and Martha D. Ring, *The Costs of Medical Care* (Chicago: The University of Chicago Press, 1933), pp. 196–197.

54. Michael M. Davis, "Doctors' Bills and People's Millions," *JAMA,* 94:1014–1017 (1930); Falk et al., *Costs of Medical Care,* p. 97; S. S. Goldwater, "The Specialist: What Shall We Do with Him?" *JAMA,* 88:1961–1963 (1927).

55. Abraham Flexner's famous *Medical Education in the United States and Canada* exposed the poor quality of most of the nation's medical schools and aroused a storm of public criticism of them. For specific statistics, see U.S., Bureau of Census, *Historical Statistics,* p. 34.

56. An example of this feeling is found in Hugh Cabot's *The Patient's Dilemma: The Quest for Medical Security in America* (New York: Reynal and Hitchcock, 1940), pp. 18–19: "[T]he light-hearted view that the busy family doctor with a little black bag can diagnose and treat 85 percent of disease is somewhere in error . . . In view of the knowledge [required of doctors] . . . it may occur to our mythical average man that some reorientation in the status of the general practitioner is over-due."

57. In this and following chapters the term *reformers* is used to describe that more or less definable group of interested individuals who supported reform of medical care from leadership positions. Although this group was not entirely static on every issue, a body of perhaps fifteen to twenty individuals was working for reform on the national, state and local levels from the days of the AALL on, and its members were in constant contact with each other.

58. Construction of nongovernmental hospitals also mushroomed faster than population growth, although distribution of these facilities tended to exclude the rural and poorer regions of the nation. Falk et al., *Costs of Medical Care,* pp. 361–365.

59. Paul B. Magnuson, "Medical Care for Veterans," *Annals of the American Academy of Political and Social Science,* 273:76–83 (1951); Burrow, *A.M.A.,* pp. 158–160; Martha M. Eliot, interview, September 1965.

60. C. Rufus Rorem, *The Middle Rate Plan for Hospital Patients: The First Year's Experience of the Baker Memorial of the Massachusetts General Hospital* (Chicago: The Julius Rosenwald Fund, 1931), pp. 7–36; Michael M. Davis, *Eight Years' Work in Medical Economics* (Chicago: The Julius Rosenwald Fund, 1937).

61. A. M. Simons and Nathan Sinai, *The Way of Health Insurance* (Chicago: The University of Chicago Press, 1932); Falk interview; Committee on the Cost of Medical Care, *The Five Year Program of the Committee on the Cost of Medical Care* (Washington, D.C.: CCMC, 1928), p. 10. The committee changed its name to the Committee on the *Costs*

of Medical Care after various members of the medical profession objected to what they believed was an unfair implication in the original title; Davis interview.

62. Committee on the Costs of Medical Care, *Medical Care for the American People: The Final Report* (Chicago: The University of Chicago Press, 1932), pp. 109–134.

63. Ibid., pp. 152–183.

64. "The Committee on the Costs of Medical Care," editorial, *JAMA,* 99:1950–1952 (1932).

65. John A. Kingsbury, *Health in Handcuffs: The National Health Crisis and What Can Be Done* (New York: Modern Age Books, 1939), pp. 40–41.

66. Falk interview; James Rorty, *American Medicine Mobilizes* (New York: W. W. Norton & Company, 1939), p. 200.

67. "Proceedings of the Atlantic City Session," *JAMA,* 84:1633–1667 (1925); "Report of Officers," *JAMA,* 90:1459–1460 (1928).

68. C. Rufus Rorem, interview, April 1965.

69. A study of the medical profession that includes much data on the self image of the doctor is Esther E. Lape, ed., *American Medicine: Expert Testimony out of Court,* 2 vols. (New York: American Foundation, 1937).

70. See, for example, M. L. Harris, "The General Practitioner in the Medical Scheme," *JAMA,* 91:1683–1686 (1926); Fishbein interview.

71. "Proceedings of the New Orleans Session," *JAMA,* 74:1256, 1319 (1920); Burrow, *A.M.A.,* pp. 153–157; Rorem interview. The codification of ethical medical behavior had begun early in the decade. AMA policy that formerly attacked state medicine, socialized medicine, and compulsory health insurance was now redefined so as to make participation in programs of this type unethical. Such internal professional trends as group practice, pay clinics, and specialization were also condemned, so that by the end of the decade, the average member of the AMA was left with little or no ethical choice concerning the style of his medical practice. If he decided to ignore the medical societies and participate in a questionable type of practice, the local, state, and national medical societies were willing and able to discipline him. By using concerted pressure they could remove his hospital privileges, frighten away his malpractice insurance company, and spread the word to the public that he was unethical and probably untrustworthy. Only a small number of the nation's doctors were willing to take these risks in order to support the new cooperative experiments in medical care.

72. Fishbein, *History,* pp. 336–337. In *JAMA*: "Proceedings of the St. Louis Session," 78:1613–1644, 1709–1718 (1922); "Current Comment," 79:138–139 (1922); "Hygeia: A Journal of Individual and Community Health," 79:132 (1922); "Proceedings of the San Francisco Session," 81:28–42, 116–136 (1923); "Association News," 82:1448 (1924); "Proceedings of the Chicago Session," 82:1938–1973, 2033–2051 (1924); "Proceedings of the Atlantic City Session," 84:1633–1667, 1735–1747 (1925); "Proceedings of the Detroit Session," 95:41–52 (1930); "Reports of Officers," 96:1479–1504 (1931). The Board of Trustees of the AMA was given control of several

important AMA publications: *The Bulletin* of the AMA, which was changed from a house organ to a general administration gazette and sent to the 56,000 AMA Fellows, and *Hygeia,* which was designed to educate and inform the lay public. Administrative modernization and reorganization also helped concentrate power in the Board of Trustees. Periodic meetings between the legislative committees of the various state medical associations and the trustee-controlled Bureau of Legal Medicine and Legislation were instituted in 1922. Two years later the position of field secretary was placed under the board in an attempt to further strengthen the links between state and national societies. The Council on Public Health and Education, a semiautonomous agency which had been the center of pro-insurance sentiment during the AALL campaign, was replaced by two bureaus under trustee control: the Bureau of Medical Economics and the Bureau on Health and Public Instruction. To assure adequate political representation of the AMA in Washington, an Advisory Committee on Legislative Activities was established, and a full-time lobbyist retained. In *JAMA:* "Association News," 83:1005–1006 (1924); R. G. Leland, "The Costs of Medical Education," 96:682–690 (1931); "Reports of Officers," 96:1479–1504 (1931).

73. Kingsbury was an emotional but very well-spoken reform leader. A more detailed discussion of his experience in the reform struggle will be given below.

74. Both Theodore Roosevelt in his Bull Moose stage and Herbert Croly in his *Promise of American Life* (New York: Capricorn Books, 1964) advanced these ideas.

75. The faith in education and rationality which many progressives shared is discussed in Hays, *Response to Industrialism,* pp. 74–75.

76. This concept of freedom was shared by Woodrow Wilson and Louis Brandeis.

77. See above, note 69.

78. Rorty, *American Medicine Mobilizes;* Kingsbury, *Health in Handcuffs.* Doctors as a group were one of the wealthiest professions in America. But prosperity was unevenly spread within the profession, and many individual doctors had low incomes. An interesting portrayal of the different stereotypes of doctors is found in Sinclair Lewis' *Arrowsmith.*

79. Falk interview.

2. WASHINGTON: THE FIRST BATTLE, 1933–1935

1. U.S., Bureau of Census, *Historical Statistics of the United States, Colonial Times to 1957* (Washington, D.C.: GPO, 1960).

2. Dixon Wecter, *The Age of the Great Depression, 1929–1941* (New York: The Macmillan Company, 1948), pp. 13–15, 41–43.

3. James M. Burns, *Roosevelt: The Lion and the Fox* (New York: Harcourt, Brace & World, 1956), pp. 161–182.

4. Ibid., pp. 209–226.

5. Edwin E. Witte, *The Development of the Social Security Act* (Madison: University of Wisconsin Press, 1962), pp. 3–5; I. S. Falk, interview, June 1965.

6. Witte, *Development of the Social Security Act,* pp. 6–8, 201–202.
7. Ibid., pp. 8–12.
8. Ibid., pp. 12–13, 27–41. Because of failing health, Dr. Sydenstricker asked that his assistant at the Milbank Fund, Dr. Falk, be retained by the CES as a staff member for the Technical Committee on Medical Care. His request was accepted, and Dr. Falk soon came to carry the major burden of the Technical Committee's work. Falk interview.
9. Witte, *Development of the Social Security Act,* pp. 18–20.
10. Ibid., pp. 173–175. Witte, Report on Progress of Work, September 1934, Director's File, Committee on Economic Security, Record Group (R.G.) 47, National Archives, Washington, D.C.; Edgar Sydenstricker and I. S. Falk, Outline, Sept. 12–15, 1934, Early Drafts File, CES, R.G. 47; Witte to Frances Perkins, Sept. 21, 1934, Secretary's File Department of Labor, R.G. 147, National Archives, Washington, D.C.
11. Witte, *Development of the Social Security Act,* pp. 174–175; Public Opinion File, CES, R.G. 47; Sydenstricker and Falk, Outline, CES, R.G. 47.
12. Witte, *Development of the Social Security Act,* p. 177; Medical Advisory Committee File, CES, R.G. 47. Although the major medical associations were not asked to make nominations to the advisory committee, it was deemed advisable to include the presidents of the AMA, the American College of Surgeons, and the American College of Physicians, as well as eminent doctors who represented various geographical regions of the country and who had not committed themselves on health insurance. Public Opinion File, CES, R.G. 47.
13. Throughout early November, Witte wrote urgent notes to Sydenstricker revealing this concern and recommending that the advisory committees be modified to meet the demands of the recalcitrant doctors. For example, he urged that Michael Davis and Thomas Parran, two well-known and controversial pro-insurance reformers, be removed from the advisory committees on hospitals and public health, respectively, thus removing two of Sydenstricker's most effective potential allies in those fields. Sydenstricker refused and assured Witte that the anti-CES campaign was not official AMA policy and would soon let up. He explained that the advisory committees were fairly chosen to give adequate representation to the anti-insurance forces, and that therefore balancing the committees by dropping Davis and Parran was unnecessary. Witte, although still greatly worried, agreed to let the committees' memberships stand. Witte to Sydenstricker, Oct. 23 and 29, 1934, and Sydenstricker to Witte, Oct. 24 and 25, 1934, in Director's File, CES, R.G. 47.
14. Witte to Perkins (undated), Director's File, CES, R.G. 47.
15. Witte, *Development of the Social Security Act,* pp. 41–47.
16. Ibid., pp. 178–179.
17. Minutes of the National Conference on Economic Security, pp. 207–218, National Conference File, CES, R.G. 47; Falk interview.
18. Minutes of the National Conference on Economic Security.
19. See p. 46.
20. Witte's draft of Perkins' speech, Nov. 12, 1934, Perkins File, and

Address of Miss Frances Perkins before the National Conference on Economic Security, Nov. 14, 1934, Speeches File, CES, R.G. 47; Falk interview.

21. Witte to Perkins, Nov. 14, 1934, Perkins File, CES, R.G. 47; Witte, *Development of the Social Security Act,* p. 178.

22. In the presence of AMA President Bierring and of Dr. Leland and Mr. Simons of the AMA Bureau of Medical Economics, Dr. Bruce revealed that Dr. Luce had been boycotted by the leaders of the Michigan State Medical Society after he had submitted his favorable report on health insurance, and that a representative of the AMA national headquarters had "given him to understand that he might get back into good standing by reversing his position" at the National Conference on Economic Security. Luce had apparently accepted this offer, which explains his unexpected statement at the round table discussion. Witte, *Development of the Social Security Act,* pp. 178–179, n. 93; Falk interview.

23. Witte, *Development of the Social Security Act,* pp. 178–179, n. 92; Falk interview.

24. Witte, *Development of the Social Security Act,* pp. 179–180.

25. Ibid., p. 181; Falk interview.

26. CES, R.G. 47: Report by the Executive Director of the Progress of the Work of the CES, Nov. 27, 1934, Miscellaneous Reports File; Minutes of the Hospital Advisory Committee, Nov. 20, 1934, Hospital Advisory Committee File; Witte to Perkins, Nov. 30, 1934, Perkins File.

27. The timing of these events is important. Since the CES report was due in early January and the Economic Security Bill would be introduced in Congress in the early days of 1935, a health insurance report being submitted for approval of the CES in March would have to be sent to Congress as an amendment to the original CES bill.

28. Committee on Economic Security, *The Report of the Committee on Economic Security to the President* (Washington, D.C.: GPO, 1935), pp. 42–43.

29. Director's File, CES, R.G. 47: Witte to Walter L. Bierring, Dec. 11, 1934; Witte to R. G. Leland, Dec. 11, 1934; Olin West to Witte, Dec. 18, 1934; Bierring to Witte, Dec. 19, 1934; Witte to West, Dec. 21, 1934; West to Witte, Dec. 26, 1934.

30. CES, R.G. 47: Witte to Paul Kellogg, Jan. 3, 1935, Correspondence File; Witte to Sydenstricker, January 1935 (?), Director's File. See also Witte, *Development of the Social Security Act,* p. 182.

31. Falk interview; Arthur J. Altmeyer, interview, July 1965; Morris Fishbien, interview, June 1965.

32. Sydenstricker to Witte, Jan. 10, 1935, Director's File, CES, R.G. 47.

33. Ibid.

34. Witte, *Development of the Social Security Act,* p. 182.

35. Indeed, Leland and Simons emphasized that they had not endorsed the Interim Report and that they still opposed compulsory health insurance. Witte, *Development of the Social Security Act,* pp. 185–186; Leland to Witte, Jan. 5, 1935, Director's File, CES, R.G. 47.

36. Witte, *Development of the Social Security Act,* pp. 185–186.

37. Ibid.; Sydenstricker to Cushing, Feb. 11, 1935, Director's File, CES, R.G. 47.

38. Bierring to Witte, Feb. 4, 1935, and Cushing to Witte, Feb. 4, 1935, in Director's File, CES, R.G. 47.

39. Witte to Bierring, Feb. 8, 1935, and Witte to Cushing, Feb. 8, 1935, in Director's File, CES, R.G. 47.

40. Sydenstricker to Witte, Feb. 11, 1935, and Sydenstricker to Cushing, Feb. 11, 1935, in Director's File, CES, R.G. 47.

41. Sydenstricker's rebuttal of Cushing did not stop with these letters. Since Witte had forwarded Cushing's letter to the President and to the CES, Sydenstricker felt that his own letter to Cushing would be insufficient to offset the potential adverse effects of Cushing's letter on high administration officials. He therefore appeared in person before the CES during its meeting on Feb. 15, 1935 and recounted his version of what had happened in the advisory committee meetings. He spoke rather harshly to Dr. Witte, blaming him for not defending his subordinates with adequate vigor. Witte answered that he did not agree with Sydenstricker and that he thought the comments contained in Cushing's letter had not warranted a harsher response. Sydenstricker to Witte, Feb. 11, 1935, and Witte to Sydenstricker, Feb. 19, 1935, in Director's File, CES, R.G. 47.

42. Sydenstricker to Witte, Feb. 21, 1935, Director's File, CES, R.G. 47.

43. Ibid.

44. Minutes of the Joint Meeting of the Executive Committee of the Technical Board and the Public Health Committee, March 5, 1935, Minutes File, CES, R.G. 47.

45. Preliminary Draft of the Committee on Economic Security Report to the President on Risks to Economic Security Arising out of Ill Health, March 7, 1935, Reports to President File, CES, R.G. 47.

46. The total cost to the federal government of both health insurance and disability programs was estimated at $10,000,000 for the first year of operation and $60,000,000 for each year thereafter. The states were expected to contribute approximately six times these amounts, although premiums payable by the insured were to make up the bulk of the program's income. The insurance plans were to be tied in with existing programs of public health, hospital construction, and preventive medicine, and, once the appropriate studies had been made and legislation passed, with programs of permanent disability insurance and medical care for the uninsured. Preliminary Draft of the CES Report to the President on Risks. This document was revised slightly and became the Final Report on Health Insurance of the CES.

47. Witte, *Development of the Social Security Act,* pp. 187–189. Witte implies that Perkins now was in favor of including health insurance in the Economic Security Bill. There is no other evidence for this view, although if such was the case, one might be led to believe that Witte did indeed determine much more of the CES policy than is generally accepted.

48. Witte, *Development of the Social Security Act,* pp. 187–189.

49. Ibid.; Altmeyer interview.

50. Although the letter(s) of transmittal and the Health Insurance Report were never released to the public, it is difficult to understand why such mildly worded documents should have been treated so cautiously. The letter states that the health insurance proposals were "especially cautious; they call for no drastic or hurried Federal action" and are "in effect merely proposing that the Federal government shall undertake to give small financial aid to those states which develop systems of health insurance designed with due regard to necessary safe-guards." The second version of the letter asked that introduction of legislation be delayed pending further research by the newly created Social Security Board and recommended that the report serve as a basis for "discussion to the end that such differences of opinion as now exist may be resolved and eventuate in constructive legislation." Altmeyer interview; Witte, *Development of the Social Security Act,* pp. 205–207.

51. John B. Andrews to Witte, June 10, 1935, Andrews File, and Witte to Paul Kellogg, Feb. 28, 1935, Staff Correspondence File, in CES, R.G. 47.

52. Sydenstricker to Witte, May 14, 1935, Director's File, CES, R.G. 47.

53. Despite strong administration and public pressure, congressional conservatives and radicals had united in delaying action on the bill. It had taken a special effort by Perkins and Roosevelt to get the bill through the House and out of the Senate Finance Committee, and by May the bill was still awaiting floor debate in the Senate. When it was finally passed in modified form on June 19, it was referred to a conference committee where it remained for six weeks. A comprehensive compromise was finally reached which passed both houses of Congress on August 9 and received the President's signature on August 14. Witte, *Development of the Social Security Act,* pp. 75–108.

54. Altmeyer interview.

55. Witte, *Development of the Social Security Act,* pp. 188–189; Falk interview.

56. "Proceedings of the Cleveland Session," *JAMA,* 102:2109–2119, 2191–2207 (1934); Fishbein interview.

57. Fishbein interview.

58. "Proceedings of the Cleveland Session," *JAMA,* 102:2109–2119, 2191–2207 (1934).

59. Fishbein interview.

60. Although there is little specific evidence to support this view, the tone of Sydenstricker's correspondence in late 1934 indicates that he supported this interpretation of the AMA's actions. For example, as late as September 1934, Sydenstricker stated that the passage of the "Ten Principles" indicated that "a large and substantial fraction of medical practitioners will endorse a sound insurance program." Sydenstricker and Falk, Outline, CES, R.G. 47.

61. "The Administration Studies Social Insurance," editorial, *JAMA,* 103:609–610 (1934). See p. 46.

62. See above, note 60.

63. *JAMA,* vols. 103–104 (1934–1935); Public Opinion File, CES, R.G. 47.

64. Several local and state societies were also rebelling against official

AMA policy during these months. The AMA was eager to regain the confidence of these groups, and its anxiety may have been a cause of the AMA's "good behavior" towards the CES, as well as an underlying motive for the passage by the House of Delegates of the "Ten Principles."

65. "Progress of Plans for Economic Security," editorial, *JAMA,* 104: 318–320 (1935).

66. "Association News," *JAMA,* 104:405 (1935).

67. Witte, *Development of the Social Security Act,* pp. 182–184. See above, note 64.

68. Abstracted from "Proceedings of the Special Session," *JAMA,* 104: 747–753 (1935).

69. *JAMA,* vols. 104–105 (1935); "Reports of Officers," *JAMA,* 104: 1607–1613 (1935); "Proceedings of the Atlantic City Session," *JAMA,* 104: 2355–2372 (1935).

70. "Proceedings of the Atlantic City Session," pp. 2355–2372.

3. VOICES FROM THE HINTERLAND, 1932–1943

1. Michael M. Davis, "Change Comes to the Doctor," in the American Academy of Political and Social Science, *The Medical Profession and the Public: Currents and Counter-Currents* (Philadelphia: AAPSS, 1934), pp. 72–73; Michael M. Davis, *Eight Years' Work in Medical Economics* (Chicago: The Julius Rosenwald Fund, 1937).

2. One exception was an unauthorized boycott of the Borden's Milk Company by some members of the AMA, an action which was designed to strike at the endowment of the Milbank Fund and which led to the dismissal of Director John Kingsbury and the abandonment of the fund's interest in health insurance. I. S. Falk, interview, June 1965; Morris Fishbein, interview, June 1965; James Rorty, *American Medicine Mobilizes* (New York: W. W. Norton & Company, 1939), pp. 112–130.

3. Davis, "Change Comes to the Doctor," pp. 72–73.

4. Falk interview.

5. Ibid.

6. The Survey Associates was founded in 1911 by Helen S. Pratt, Henry R. Seager, and Agnes Brown Leach. Its early supporters included Jane Addams and Florence Kelly, and its Cooperating Membership consisted of such individuals as Josephine Roche and Michael M. Davis.

7. Paul Kellogg, "Our Twenty Years of Survey Associates," *Survey Graphic* vol. 22, no. 5 (May 1933), pp. 1–4; also *Survey Mid-Monthly;* Edwin S. Witte, *The Development of the Social Security Act* (Madison: University of Wisconsin Press, 1962), pp. 52, 55–58, 61–62.

8. C. Rufus Rorem, interview, April 1965.

9. *Old Age Security Herald* (later renamed *Social Security*).

10. Ibid.

11. Louis B. Reed, interview, July 1965; Michael M. Davis, interview, April 1965. Abraham Epstein was an extroverted person who tended to take opposition to his own ideas as a personal criticism and who found it extremely difficult to concede that opinions other than his own could be correct. Emotional and zealous in his approach to his work, he tended

to be hypercritical of those in positions which he felt he was better qualified to fill. These personality factors, when considered with the extremely personal nature of the AASS administrative organization, help explain the rather peculiar course taken by the Association toward health insurance in the 1930's (Davis interview). An interesting example of the friction Epstein created is found in the Chairman's File, Office of the Commissioner, Social Security Administration, Department of Health, Education and Welfare, Record Group (R.G.) 235, National Archives, Washington, D.C. After Epstein had written an article in *Harper's* criticizing the Social Security Act, Witte apparently became quite angry and sent a stinging critique of the article entitled "Consistency Thou Art a Jewel" (undated) to Altmeyer.

12. It went against the developing theory that the entire population needed coverage and that local areas and population groups needed extensive autonomy within any compulsory system. Falk interview; "Health Insurance Standards Set up at Conference of Experts," *Social Security,* vol. 8, no. 6 (June–July 1934), p. 3; "Conference on Health Bill," *Social Security,* vol. 8, no. 8 (October 1934), p. 8

13. When the Interdepartmental Committee to Coordinate Health and Welfare Activities began working on health insurance recommendations in 1937, they found that the Epstein bill was a source of rather constant embarrassment and confusion in their dealings with legislators and doctors. Arthur J. Altmeyer, interview, July 1965; Falk interview; General Correspondence File, Division of Research and Statistics, 1935–1943, Social Security Board, R.G. 47, National Archives, Washington, D.C.; Proceedings File, Records of the Interdepartmental Committee to Coordinate Health and Welfare Activities, 1936–1940, Franklin D. Roosevelt Library, Hyde Park, New York.

14. Reed interview.

15. See chapter 2.

16. Witte to Isadore Lubin, Sept. 19, 1934, Director's File, Records of the Committee on Economic Security, R.G. 47; Falk interview.

17. Mary Ross, "California Weighs Health Insurance," *Survey Graphic,* vol. 24, no. 5 (May 1935), pp. 213–217, 268–269.

18. Rorty, *American Medicine Mobilizes,* pp. 211–212.

19. Harold Maslow to I. S. Falk, Aug. 4, 1937, General Correspondence File, Division of Research and Statistics, 1935–1943, Social Security Board, R.G. 47.

20. Chairman's File, Office of the Commissioner, Social Security Administration, HEW, R.G. 235; Miscellaneous Documents File, Division of Research and Statistics, 1935–1943, Social Security Board, R.G. 47.

21. Ibid.; *Social Security,* vol. 12, no. 2 (February 1938), p. 6; memo from Reed to Falk, Jan. 28, 1938, General Correspondence File, Division of Research and Statistics, 1935–1943, Social Security Board, R.G. 47.

22. New York State Legislature, "Preliminary Report of the New York State Temporary Legislative Commission to Formulate a Long-Range State Health Program," (Albany: J. B. Lyon Co., 1939); *Social Security,* vol. 13, no. 6 (June 1939), p. 5; Rorem interview.

23. Edith Abbot, *Public Assistance: American Principles and Policies, with Select Documents* (Chicago: The University of Chicago Press, 1940), pp. 349–385.

24. John A. Kingsbury, *Health in Handcuffs: The National Health Crisis and What Can Be Done* (New York: Modern Age Books, 1939), p. 1; I. S. Falk, "Roads Ahead in Health Security," *Survey Graphic,* vol. 27, no. 7 (July 1938), pp. 382–383.

25. Michael M. Davis, "Organized Action in Medical Care," *Survey Graphic,* vol. 22, no. 4 (April 1933), pp. 207–209, 229–231.

26. Falk interview; Altmeyer interview; Michael M. Davis, *Public Medical Services: A Survey of Tax-supported Medical Care in the United States* (Chicago: The University of Chicago Press, 1937), pp. 19–28; Doris Corothers, *Chronology of the Federal Emergency Relief Administration, May 12, 1933, to December 31, 1935* (Washington, D.C.: GPO, 1937), pp. 5–18; memo from H. J. Davis to Harry Hopkins, Aug. 25, 1935, Medical Care File, Records of the Federal Emergency Relief Administration, R.G. 69, National Archives, Washington, D.C.

27. Corothers, *Chronology of the FERA,* pp. 17–18.

28. Ibid.

29. This is evident from the large amount of correspondence regarding the problems of the FERA medical program in the FERA files.

30. FERA, R.G. 69: Hopkins-Parran correspondence during April and May 1934, Medical Care File; Dr. William C. Woodward to Aubrey Williams, June 20, 1934, Medical Care File; Dr. C. A. Lanon to C. E. Waller, Jan. 4, 1935, Old Subject File; correspondence under heading "Medical Care, States," Old Subject File.

31. In late 1934 the situation had grown so serious that the FERA medical director, Dr. C. E. Waller, met with Dr. West and Mr. Leland of the AMA to try to "tone up" the national program and correct some of the problems which were wasting money and effort in various states. Corothers, *Chronology of FERA,* p. 55; C. E. Waller to Olin West, Nov. 9, 1934, Old Subject File, FERA, R.G. 69.

32. Memo from Josephine Roche to Harry Hopkins, June 27, 1935, Old Subject File, FERA, R.G. 69. Such groups would be veterans, Indians, federal prisoners, etc.

33. Josephine C. Brown, *Public Relief, 1929–1939* (New York: Henry Holt and Co., 1940), pp. 257–258; Rorem interview; Davis, "Change Comes to the Doctor," pp. 69–70.

34. Davis, *Eight Years' Work,* pp. 33–37; "Medical Care, Hospitalization," Miscellaneous Documents section, Old Subject File, FERA, R.G. 69; J. C. Brown, *Public Relief,* pp. 258–259.

35. J. C. Brown, *Public Relief,* pp. 380–382.

36. Roche memo, June 27, 1935, Old Subject File, FERA, R.G. 69; Administrative Correspondence File, Civil Works Administration, R.G. 69.

37. Falk interview; Alex Nordholm to Falk, May 4, 1935, Director's File, Committee on Economic Security, R.G. 47, National Archives, Washington, D.C. Falk to Nordholm, May 22, 1935, Director's File, CES, R.G. 47. Letters by Ellen Woodward, Assistant WPA Administrator, in response to

inquiries from citizens on how the WPA worked, Correspondence File, Works Progress Administration, R.G. 69.

38. Anthony J. Borowski, "Report on WPA Public Health Projects," January 1940, Public Health File, WPA, R.G. 69.

39. Rorem interview.

40. Falk interview; Reed interview; James G. Burrow, *A.M.A.: Voice of American Medicine* (Baltimore: The Johns Hopkins Press, 1963), pp. 210–212; Davis, *Public Medical Services,* pp. 92–93; R. C. Williams to Eliot, Sept. 21, 1936, Medical Care File, Farm Security Administration, R.G. 96, National Archives, Washington, D.C.; Present Status of Medical Care Program of the Resettlement Administration of the Department of Agriculture, memo from R. C. Williams to Roche, April 5, 1937, Medical Care File, FSA, R.G. 96.

41. Medical Care Manual (n.d.), Medical Care File, FSA, R.G. 96.

42. Limiting itself to an advisory and financial role, the Resettlement Administration (and later the FSA) was extremely careful to avoid offending the local medical societies and published specific instructions advising its personnel on how to deal with these professional groups. Medical Care Manual and memo from Williams to Roche, April 5, 1937, in Medical Care File, FSA, R.G. 96.

43. Milton I. Roemer, "Rural Programs of Medical Care," *Annals of the American Academy of Political and Social Science,* 273:160–168 (1951).

44. Ibid.; Rorem interview.

45. Rorty, *American Medicine Mobilizes,* pp. 143–146, 280; Kingsbury, *Health in Handcuffs.*

46. Rorty, *American Medicine Mobilizes,* p. 288; Committee on the Costs of Medical Care, *Medical Care for the American People: The Final Report* (Chicago: The University of Chicago Press, 1932).

47. Michael M. Shadid, *A Doctor for the People:The Autobiography of the Founder of America's First Co-operative Hospital* (New York: Vanguard Press, 1939).

48. Rorty, *American Medicine Mobilizes,* p. 280.

49. Ibid., pp. 286–287; Falk interview.

50. Herman Somers and Anne Somers, *Doctors, Patients, and Health Insurance,* abridged ed. (New York: Doubleday & Company, 1961), pp. 305, 210–211.

51. See chapter 4.

52. Mary Ross, "Sickness Bills by Installment," *Survey Graphic,* vol. 24, no. 3 (March 1935), pp. 109–111.

53. Somers and Somers, *Doctors, Patients, and Health Insurance,* pp. 282–284.

54. Ibid.; Rorem interview.

55. Somers and Somers, *Doctors, Patients, and Health Insurance,* pp. 284–303; Rorem interview.

56. Rorem interview; Burrow, *A.M.A.,* pp. 228–229; Davis, *Eight Years' Work,* pp. 24–25.

57. Falk interview; Rorem interview; Davis, *Eight Years' Work,* pp. 24–29.

58. C. Rufus Rorem, *Blue Cross Hospital Service Plans: Description and*

Appraisal of a Nation-Wide Program for the Distribution of Adequate Hospital Care on a Non-Profit, Non-Political Basis, 2d ed. (Chicago: American Hospital Association, 1940), pp. 7–9; J. T. Richardson, "The Origin and Development of Group Hospitalization in the Uniited States," *The University of Missouri Studies,* vol. 20, no. 3 (1945) pp. 12–18.

59. Rorem, *Blue Cross.*

60. Richardson, "Origin and Development," pp. 22–23; Rorem interview.

61. Rorem interview; Richardson, "Origin and Development," pp. 18–19, 29–33.

62. Richardson, "Origin and Development," pp. 36–42; C. Rufus Rorem, "Enabling Legislation for Non-Profit Hospital Service Plans," *Law and Contemporary Problems,* 6:528–544, passim (1939); C. Rufus Rorem, *Non-Profit Hospital Service Plans* (Chicago: American Hospital Association, 1940), p. 2.

63. Rorem interview.

64. Various attempts were made by some of the national leaders. For examples, see C. Rufus Rorem: "What About Dependents?" *The Modern Hospital,* 48:53–55; "Approved List of Hospital Care Insurance Plans" and "Recent Developments in Hospital Service Plans," reprints (undated) of articles in *Hospitals,* found by the author in Mr. Rorem's files; *Blue Cross,* pp. 44–45.

65. See chapter 2; C. Rufus Rorem, "Voluntary Hospital Care Insurance," reprint (undated) of an article in *State Government,* found by the author in Mr. Rorem's files.

66. Rorem interview; Falk interview; Davis interview.

67. Oliver Garceau, *The Political Life of the American Medical Association* (Cambridge: Harvard University Press, 1941), pp. 90–96.

68. Ibid., pp. 18–19, 30–49, 61–67; Fishbein interview.

69. Garceau, *Political Life,* pp. 68–90; Fishbein interview; *Journal of the American Medical Association (JAMA).*

70. Garceau, *Political Life,* pp. 68–90.

71. *JAMA;* see chapter 1.

72. See chapter 1.

73. *JAMA,* vols. 94–113 (1930–1939).

74. Morris Fishbein, *A History of the American Medical Association, 1847–1947* (Philadelphia: W. B. Saunders Co., 1947), pp. 406–408.

75. Garceau, *Political Life,* pp. 103–111; Rorem interview.

76. Such local experimentation took place in areas covered by the various titles of the Social Security Act of 1935. Unemployment insurance was started by Wisconsin in the early 1930's and old age pensions existed in many private corporations and in a score of states by 1934.

4. WASHINGTON: THE BATTLE RENEWED, 1936–1939

1. Martha M. Eliot, interview, September 1965.

2. Arthur J. Altmeyer, interview, July 1965.

3. I. S. Falk, interview, June 1965; document entitled The Interdepartmental Committee on Health and Welfare Activities, April 14, 1936, Documents of the Interdepartmental Committee to Coordinate Health and

Welfare Activities, Franklin D. Roosevelt Library, Hyde Park, New York (hereafter cited as Interdep. Comm., Hyde Park).

4. Altmeyer interview; Minutes of the Meeting of the Interdepartmental Committee, March 4, 1937, Interdep. Comm., Hyde Park.

5. Minutes of Technical Committee on Medical Care, April 8, 1937, Interdep. Comm., Hyde Park.

6. Minutes of the Technical Committee on Medical Care, May 5, June 22, 1937; Minutes of Conference of Interdepartmental and Technical Committees, Sept. 28, 1937; Summary of Work of the Technical Committee on Medical Care, Dec. 17, 1937, Interdep. Comm., Hyde Park.

7. For the text of the principles, see Minutes of Technical Committee on Medical Care, Oct. 15, 1937, Interdep. Comm., Hyde Park.

8. Eliot interview; Minutes of Technical Committee on Medical Care, Oct. 29, 1937, Interdep. Comm., Hyde Park. During October 1937, Surgeon General Parran and Deputy WPA Administrator Aubrey Williams were added to the Interdepartmental Committee membership.

9. Summary of the Work of the Technical Committee on Medical Care, Dec. 17, 1937.

10. See chapter 2; Falk interview; Minutes of Technical Committee on Medical Care, Nov. 15 and 20, 1937, Interdep. Comm., Hyde Park.

11. Minutes of Technical Committee on Medical Care, Nov. 15 and 20, 1937.

12. Minutes of Technical Committee on Medical Care, Nov. 29, 1937, Interdep. Comm., Hyde Park.

13. Although the system of priorities and the decision to define medical indigency in a liberal manner seriously weakened the health insurance proposals of the Technical Committee, they were not as damaging to that reform as Witte's 1934 decision to place health insurance in the long time, comprehensive category had been. Federal compulsory health insurance was still part of the National Health Program and was open for public and congressional consideration as such. It was weakened and made the least essential part of the National Health Program, but it still was included. Minutes of the Technical Committee on Medical Care, Nov. 29, 1937; Summary of the work of the Technical Committee on Medical Care, Dec. 17, 1937; Falk interview. See also chapter 2.

14. Summary of the Work of the Technical Committee on Medical Care, Dec. 17, 1937.

15. Memo from Parran to President Roosevelt, Dec. 23, 1937, Interdep. Comm., Hyde Park; Falk interview.

16. Falk interview; Although the idea of a separate program for the needy had been presented as early as mid-1937, it only gained strength when members of the Interdepartmental Committee began to support it in the late months of that year. Minutes of the Interdepartmental Committee, Feb. 10, 1938, Interdep. Comm., Hyde Park.

17. Altmeyer interview; Altmeyer to Rudolph Forster, March 8, 1938, Chairman's File, Social Security Board, Department of Health, Education, and Welfare, Record Group (R.G.) 47, National Archives, Washington, D.C.

18. Interdepartmental Committee to Coordinate Health and Welfare

Activities, *Proceedings of the National Health Conference, July 18, 19, 20, 1938* (Washington, D.C.: GPO, 1938), pp. 27–28 and passim (hereafter cited as *Proceedings*).

19. Ibid.

20. Ibid.

21. Abstracted from "A Summary, A National Health Program: Report of the Technical Committee on Medical Care," *Proceedings*, pp. 29–32.

22. Ibid.

23. Ibid., pp. 31–32.

24. Louis Reed, interview, July 1965.

25. *Proceedings*, pp. 55–61.

26. Ibid.

27. Ibid., pp. 65–107.

28. Altmeyer interview.

29. *Proceedings*, pp. 101–103.

30. Ibid., pp. 110–111, 113–114, 114–115.

31. Ibid., pp. 115–118.

32. Ibid., pp. 129–131, 134–136, 140–142.

33. Ibid., pp. 149–152; Falk interview.

34. *Proceedings*, pp. 152–157; Falk interview.

35. Altmeyer interview. Most of the governmental supporters of health insurance felt very encouraged by the developments at the National Health Conference. Louis Reed recollects that at a party given by Margaret Klem in July 1938 at which Sinai, Mountin, Perrott, Falk, and others were present, a straw poll on the guests' expectations regarding enactment of the National Health Program was taken. Fifty percent of those present thought such enactment would occur in 1939; the rest predicted that it would be within the next four years. Reed interview.

36. Altmeyer interview.

37. Ibid.

38. John Peters, "Confidential Report on the Conference on Health Insurance of the Republican Platform Committee of August 3, 1938," Director's File, Social Security Board, HEW, R.G. 47; Progress Reports, August to November 1938, Division of Health Studies File, Social Security Board, HEW, R.G. 47; Miscellaneous Documents File of Bureau of Research and Statistics, Social Security Board, HEW, R.G. 47.

39. The approved programs now included a formula for the distribution of matching funds, standards for service and employment of personnel, and cost estimates totalling $275,000,000 per year to the federal government in the last year of a gradually expanding five-year program. The proposals were primarily extensions or corollaries of existing Public Health Service or Children's Bureau programs and represented the major interests of these two senior agencies. Memo from the Interdepartmental Committee to President Roosevelt, Dec. 12, 1938, Interdep. Comm., Hyde Park.

40. The intensity of the medical society protests will be described later in this chapter. There seems to be little doubt that these protests had some effect on the Interdepartmental Committee's decision to tone down the

National Health Program. Various drafts of proposed amendments to the Social Security Act which were prepared during these months are preserved in the Franklin D. Roosevelt Library at Hyde Park, often with Falk's comments written in the margins. A typical letter from an administration employee which was critical of the Social Security drafts is that of Fred K. Hoechler to Martha Eliot, Nov. 9, 1938, Interdep. Comm., Hyde Park.

41. Altmeyer interview; Progress Reports from August to December 1938, Division of Health Studies, Social Security Board, HEW, R.G. 47.

42. Altmeyer interview.

43. Memo from Falk to Roche, Dec. 20, 1938, Division of Health Studies, Social Security Board, HEW, R.G. 47.

44. Social Security Board, Report on Recommended Changes in the Social Security Act, Dec. 30, 1938, Interdep. Comm., Hyde Park.

45. John A. Kingsbury, *Health in Handcuffs: The National Health Crisis and What Can be Done* (New York: Modern Age Books, 1939), pp. 76–78.

46. There seems to have been more optimism among reformers outside the government than among those inside. This does *not* mean that men such as Falk and Reed felt that health insurance was doomed; indeed quite the opposite. These men, and most others in the government, expected a significant amount of public support for the National Health Program to develop by 1939, which would put pressure on Congress.

47. As late as January 1939, most pro-insurance reformers in the government still privately hoped that the National Health Program would get positive action from Congress. Most of them agreed on the desirability of reforms such as health and disability insurance and hoped to see these systems erected sooner or later in the United States. The following pages discuss the divisions which split the reformers in spite of their fundamental agreements.

48. Reed interview; Altmeyer interview.

49. Eliot interview.

50. Reed interview.

51. Falk interview; Altmeyer interview.

52. Michael M. Davis, interview, April 1965; Rorem interview.

53. Rorem interview.

54. Ibid.

55. Memo from Falk to Altmeyer, Oct. 20, 1938, Director's File, Social Security Board, HEW, R.G. 47; General Files, Public Health Service, R.G. 90, National Archives, Washington, D.C.

56. James G. Burrow, *A.M.A.: Voice of American Medicine* (Baltimore, The Johns Hopkins Press, 1963), pp. 201–207; *Journal of the American Medical Association (JAMA)*, 1935–1937.

57. *JAMA*, 1935–1937.

58. Ibid.; Rorem interview.

59. This demand by ordinary doctors helped produce many local medical society plans designed to provide service to the needy. Service bureaus, as they were often called, were designed primarily to distribute the load

of needy patients more equitably among the medical society's members. Although some of them received financial support from local welfare departments, the plans were for the most part reorganizations, centralizations, and rationalizations of traditional charity work along lines that conformed to the policies and ethical code of the organized medical profession. Burrow, *A.M.A.*, pp. 209–210.

60. "Extension of Medical Service to the Indigent," resolution introduced in the AMA House of Delegates by the AMA trustees, *JAMA*, 108:2219 (1937).

61. *JAMA*, passim; resolution entitled "Ten Principles for Group Hospitalization," introduced in the House of Delegates and passed June 8, 1937, *JAMA*, 108:2219 (1937).

62. Most reformers confused this shift with an imagined retreat by the AMA on the issue of compulsory health insurance. One who did not make this mistake was C. Rufus Rorem, who at this time was working with the AMA to develop private group hospitalization plans.

63. Editorial, *JAMA*, 110:652–654 (1938); *JAMA* vol. 110.

64. "Proceedings of the House of Delegates," *JAMA*, 111:51–59 (1938).

65. Altmeyer interview.

66. Ibid.

67. Burrow, *A.M.A.*, pp. 215–218; editorials, *JAMA*, 111:426–429, 936 (1938).

68. "Minutes of the Special Session of the House of Delegates, Sept. 16–17, 1938," *JAMA* 111:1191–1217 (1938).

69. Burrow, *A.M.A.*, pp. 217–221.

70. "Minutes of the Special Session," pp. 1191–1217.

71. Rorem interview; editorial, *JAMA*, 111:1775 (1938).

72. "Organization Section," *JAMA*, 111:1570–1572, 1941 (1938). For a more detailed description of the Interdepartmental Committee's negotiations with these various groups, see chapter 5.

73. "Organization Section," *JAMA*, 112:437 (1939).

74. Ibid. See also pp. 116–117.

75. See above, note 39, and below, note 80. See also series of Progress Reports of Division of Health Studies, Social Security Board, HEW, R.G. 47.

76. See p. 113.

77. Kingsbury, *Health in Handcuffs*, pp. 72–73; James Rorty, *American Medicine Mobilizes* (New York: W. W. Norton & Company, 1939), pp. 217–223.

78. Committee of Physicians, "Attitude and Intent of Committee of Physicians, in Presenting Principles and Proposals in the Provision of Medical Care," *JAMA*, 110:141B–142B (1938).

79. Ibid.; Fishbein interview; "The American Foundation Proposals for Medical Care," *JAMA*, 109:1280–1281 (1937); "Principles and Proposals of the Committee of Physicians," *JAMA*, 109:1816–1817 (1937); Morris Fishbein, "Social Aspects of Medical Care," address before the Annual Banquet of the Chicago Hospital Council, Jan. 25, 1939, and "Medicine and the National Policy," address before the New York County Medical

Society, Jan. 24, 1938, in Fishbein document collection. Dr. Fishbein was by far the most fluent defender of the AMA position during these years. Since he constantly received votes of confidence from the trustees and the House of Delegates of the AMA, I have assumed that most of his statements and beliefs are a fair representation of the opinion of the organized profession.

80. An example of this type of thinking is found in Rorty, *American Medicine Mobilizes,* p. 217. Dr. Falk also expressed these sentiments during his interview with the author.

81. This may be one of the reasons the Interdepartmental Committee refused to consider the offer of the AMA when it was presented in July and October of 1938 and again in January 1939.

82. See above, note 79.

83. These sentiments run throughout Fishbein's statements and *JAMA.* The medical societies' opposition to government intervention in medical care is more completely discussed in chapter 2.

84. Fishbein, "Social Aspects of Medical Care."

85. Ibid.

86. Morris Fishbein, "Our Changing Times," address before the West Virginia State Medical Association, May 8, 1935, in Fishbein document collection.

5. OLD ENDINGS AND NEW BEGINNINGS, 1939–1943

1. James M. Burns, *Roosevelt: The Lion and the Fox* (New York: Harcourt, Brace & World, 1956), pp. 324–326, 383–384.

2. Samuel Lubell, *The Future of American Politics,* 3d ed. (New York: Harper & Row, Publishers, 1965), pp. 45–48.

3. See chapter 4.

4. Martha M. Eliot, interview, September 1965; see chapter 4.

5. See chapter 4.

6. U.S., Congress, Senate, Committee on Education and Labor, *Hearings . . . on S. 1620,* 76th Cong., 1st sess., April 27, May 4, 5, 11, 25, 26, June 1, 2, 29, July 13, 1939 (Washington, D.C.: GPO, 1939), testimony of William F. Monoaban, Claude W. Munger, and Rev. A. M. Schwitalla, pp. 602–621, 631–647, 651–656, 643–647.

7. Ibid., pp. 151–179, 593–602; comment by Senator Ellender, p. 327.

8. See chapter 4.

9. The President's special message was sent on January 23, 1939. Arthur J. Altmeyer, interview, July 1965; *Hearings on S. 1620.*

10. The text of S. 1620 may be found in *Hearings on S. 1620,* pp. 1–16.

11. Ibid.

12. Ibid.; Robert F. Wagner, "The National Health Bill," *American Labor Legislation Review (ALLR),* 29:13–44 (1939).

13. Ibid.; See note 7.

14. George St. J. Perrott to Thompson (n.d.), Records of the Interdepartmental Committee to Coordinate Health and Welfare Activities, Franklin D. Roosevelt Library, Hyde Park, New York (hereafter cited as Interdep. Comm., Hyde Park).

15. Falk interview.

16. Memo from Surgeon C. E. Rice to Asst. Surgeon C. E. Waller, April 14, 1939, Interdep. Comm., Hyde Park.

17. Treasury Department Report on S. 1620, May 18, 1939, Records of the Public Health Service, Record Group (R.G.) 90, National Archives, Washington, D.C.; Thomas Parran to Senate subcommittee, June 2, 1939, *Hearings on S. 1620,* pp. 657–678.

18. Parran to Senate subcommittee, June 2, 1939.

19. Report of Labor Department on S. 1620, May 2, 1939, Department of Labor, Record Group (R.G.) 174, National Archives, Washington, D.C.; Arthur J. Altmeyer to Senate subcommittee, June 2, 1939, *Hearings on S. 1620,* pp. 701–703.

20. I. S. Falk, interview, June 1965.

21. *Hearings on S. 1620,* pp. 130–139, 180–194, 871–876.

22. See above, note 6.

23. See above, note 6.

24. This negative reasoning did not persuade many of the reformers; they claimed that the relevant issue was the availability of adequate care, not the frequency with which it was denied. *Journal of the American Medical Association (JAMA),* vol. 112 (1939); Falk interview.

25. "Minutes of the House of Delegates," June 3, 1939, *JAMA* 112: 2295–2297 (1939).

26. Ibid.; Dr. Arthur Booth to Senate subcommittee, *Hearings on S. 1620,* pp. 151–179.

27. Ibid., passim.

28. Ibid., pp. 368–390.

29. Ibid., pp. 320–426, passim.

30. Ibid., pp. 426–502.

31. Ibid.

32. *JAMA,* vol. 112 (1939).

33. "Organization Section," *JAMA,* 114:665 (1940); C. Rufus Rorem, interview, April 1965.

34. Ibid.

35. John A. Kingsbury, *Health in Handcuffs: The National Health Crisis and What Can Be Done* (New York: Modern Age Books, 1939), pp. 177–182; letter from Gannett Committee to Kingsley Roberts is typical of the committee's literature, Correspondence File, Bureau of Research and Statistics, Records of the Social Security Board, R.G. 47, National Archives, Washington, D.C.

36. See Appendix.

37. Altmeyer interview; Rorem interview; Kingsbury, *Health in Handcuffs.*

38. Kingsbury, *Health in Handcuffs.*

39. Memo from Ruth Stocking to I. S. Falk, March 15, 1939, Director's Fire, Bureau of Research and Statistics, Social Security Board, R.G. 47.

40. Kingsbury, *Health in Handcuffs.*

41. Progress Reports of the Division of Health Studies, March to July 1939, Health Studies File, Bureau of Research and Statistics, Social Security Board, R.G. 47; Senator Murray, *Hearings on S. 1620,* p. 678.

42. Progress Report of the Division of Health Studies, July 1939, Health

Studies File, Bureau of Research and Statistics, Social Security Board, R.G. 47; Falk interview; "Preliminary Report of Subcommittee on S. 1620," *JAMA,* 113:685–687 (1939).

43. H.R. 6635 was a basically noncontroversial bill which passed Congress with little or no fanfare.

44. Confidential memo from Falk to F. V. Coe entitled "Some Alternatives in the Health Program," Director's File, Bureau of Research and Statistics, Social Security Board, R.G. 47.

45. Morris Fishbein, interview, June 1965; Paul de Kruif, *Health is Wealth* (New York: Harcourt, Brace and Co., 1940), pp. 96–116; Michael M. Davis, interview, April 1965; Altmeyer interview; Falk interview; J. M. Burns, *Roosevelt,* pp. 366–370, 415–418; James G. Burrow, *A.M.A.: Voice of American Medicine* (Baltimore: The Johns Hopkins Press, 1963), pp. 225–226.

46. Altmeyer interview.

47. Altmeyer interview; Treasury Department report on S. 3631, March 29, 1938, Public Health Service, R.G. 90, National Archives, Washington, D.C.; Minutes of Interdepartmental Committee, Dec. 19, 1939, Interdep. Comm., Hyde Park; Victor Weybright, "When Life Comes First . . ." *Survey Graphic* 28:734–737 (1939).

48. A Federal Hospital Program, memo (unsigned) of Dec. 19, 1939, Interdep. Comm., Hyde Park.

49. Minutes of Interdepartmental Committee, Dec. 19, 1939, Interdep. Comm., Hyde Park.

50. Minutes of Interdepartmental Committee, Jan. 9, 1940, Interdep. Comm., Hyde Park; Interdepartmental Committee, "The Program for Construction of Hospitals in Areas Where They Are Most Needed; A Report to the President from the Interdepartmental Committee to Coordinate Health and Welfare Activities" (undated, but most assuredly the report filed on Jan. 10), Interdep. Comm., Hyde Park.

51. Minutes of Interdepartmental Committee, Jan. 9, 1940, Interdep. Comm., Hyde Park.

52. Burrow, *A.M.A.,* pp. 226–227; Morris Fishbein, *A History of the American Medical Association, 1847–1947* (Philadelphia: W. B. Saunders Co., 1947), pp. 454–455.

53. Minutes of Interdepartmental Committee and Technical Committee on Medical Care, Jan. 11, 1940, Interdep. Comm., Hyde Park.

54. Ibid.

55. Notes on Interview of Interdepartmental Committee with President Franklin D. Roosevelt (unsigned), Jan. 16, 1940, Interdep. Comm., Hyde Park.

56. Franklin D. Roosevelt, "Public Health Service Message from the President," Jan. 30, 1940, PHS, R.G. 90; memo from Dr. Draper to Mary Switzer, Jan. 30, 1940, PHS, R.G. 90; Progress Report of Division of Health Studies (undated but most assuredly for January 1940), Health Studies File, Bureau of Research and Statistics, Social Security Board, R.G. 47.

57. John B. Andrews in *ALLR,* 30:53–54 (1940); Progress Report of

Division of Health Studies, May 1940, Health Studies File, Bureau of Research and Statistics, Social Security Board, R.G. 47.

58. "Current Comment," in *JAMA,* 114:1670 (1940).

59. Ibid.; Altmeyer interview.

60. Remarks by Senator Lodge in introducing S. 3630, U.S., Congress, Senate, *Congressional Record,* 76th Cong., 3d sess., 1940, pp. 3045–3048.

61. Editorial, *JAMA,* 114:1271 (1940); Federal Security Agency report to Senate committee on S. 3630, May 23, 1940, PHS, R.G. 90; Department of Labor report to Senate committee on S. 3630 (undated), Department of Labor, R.G. 174.

62. Falk interview; Rorem interview; Federal Security Agency report to Senate committee on S. 3660, May 6, 1940, FSA Reports File, Records of the Department of Health, Education, and Welfare, R.G. 235, National Archives, Washington, D.C.

63. The government reformers did continue their research on various health, disability, and compensation plans, but did not shape it into specific legislative proposals or discuss it in public. Letter (unsigned) to Roche, Aug. 8, 1940 and letter (unsigned) to Dr. S. J. Seerling, Jan. 14, 1941, Interdep. Comm., Hyde Park.

64. U.S., Bureau of Census, *Historical Statistics of the United States, Colonial Times to 1957* (Washington, D.C.: GPO, 1960), p. 677.

65. Altmeyer interview; Progress Reports of Division of Health Studies, June to December 1941, Health Studies File, Bureau of Research and Statistics, Social Security Board, R.G. 47.

66. Altmeyer interview; Rorem interview.

67. See note 65.

68. Progress Reports of Division of Health Studies, January to March 1942, Health Studies File, Bureau of Research and Statistics, Social Security Board, R.G. 47.

69. Burrow, *A.M.A.,* pp. 291–292; *JAMA,* passim; Fishbein interview.

70. U.S., Bureau of Census, *Historical Statistics,* p. 677.

71. Reed interview; Falk interview; Altmeyer interview.

72. Lubell, *Future of American Politics,* p. 71.

INDEX

Index